Iran under the Safavids

To my wife Kathleen

IRAN UNDER THE SAFAVIDS

ROGER SAVORY

Professor, Department of Middle East and Islamic Studies
Trinity College, University of Toronto

CAMBRIDGE UNIVERSITY PRESS

Cambridge
London New York New Rochelle
Melbourne Sydney

CAMBRIDGE UNIVERSITY PRESS
Cambridge, New York, Melbourne, Madrid, Cape Town, Singapore, São Paulo

Cambridge University Press
The Edinburgh Building, Cambridge CB2 8RU, UK

Published in the United States of America by Cambridge University Press, New York

www.cambridge.org
Information on this title: www.cambridge.org/9780521224833

First published 1980
This digitally printed version 2007

A catalogue record for this publication is available from the British Library

Library of Congress Cataloguing in Publication data

Savory, Roger.

Iran under the Safavids.

Includes bibliographical references and index.

1. Iran – History – 16th–18th centuries.
2. Safavids. I. Title.
DS292.S26 955′.03 78-73817

ISBN 978-0-521-22483-3 hardback
ISBN 978-0-521-04251-2 paperback

Contents

Illustrations

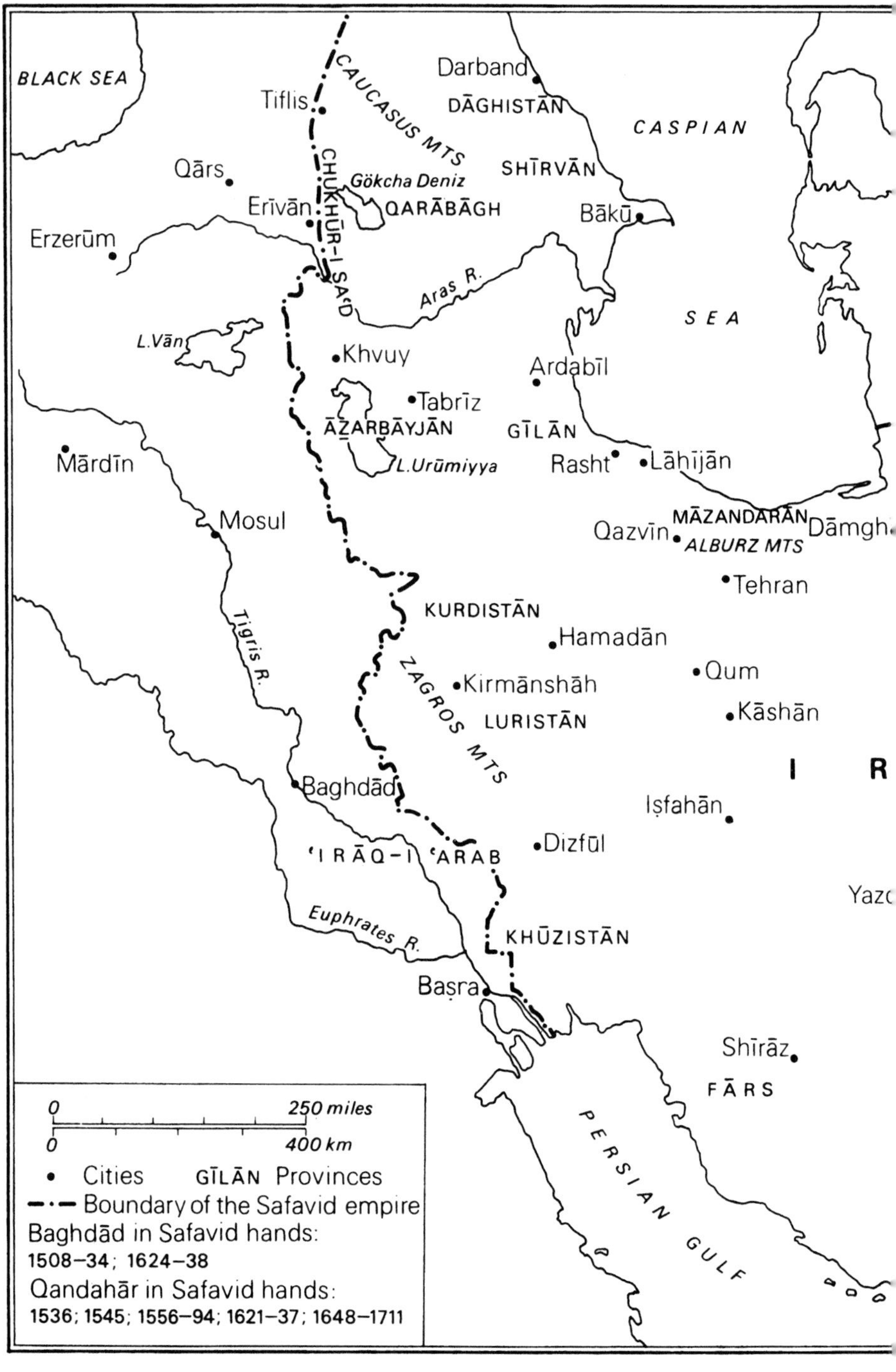
BLACK SEA
Tiflis
CAUCASUS MTS
Darband
DĀGHISTĀN
CASPIAN
SEA
Qārs
CHUKHŪR-I SA'D
Gökcha Deniz
SHĪRVĀN
Erīvān
QARĀBĀGH
Bākū
Erzerūm
Aras R.
L.Vān
Khvuy
Ardabīl
Tabrīz
ĀZARBĀYJĀN
GĪLĀN
Mārdīn
L.Urūmiyya
Rasht
Lāhījān
Mosul
MĀZANDARĀN
Qazvīn
ALBURZ MTS
Dāmgh
Tehran
KURDISTĀN
Tigris R.
Hamadān
ZAGROS MTS
Kirmānshāh
Qum
LURISTĀN
Kāshān
I R
Baghdād
Iṣfahān
'IRĀQ-I 'ARAB
Dizfūl
Yazd
Euphrates R.
KHŪZISTĀN
Baṣra
Shīrāz
FĀRS
PERSIAN GULF
0 250 miles
0 400 km
• Cities GĪLĀN Provinces
Boundary of the Safavid empire
Baghdād in Safavid hands:
1508–34; 1624–38
Qandahār in Safavid hands:
1536; 1545; 1556–94; 1621–37; 1648–1711

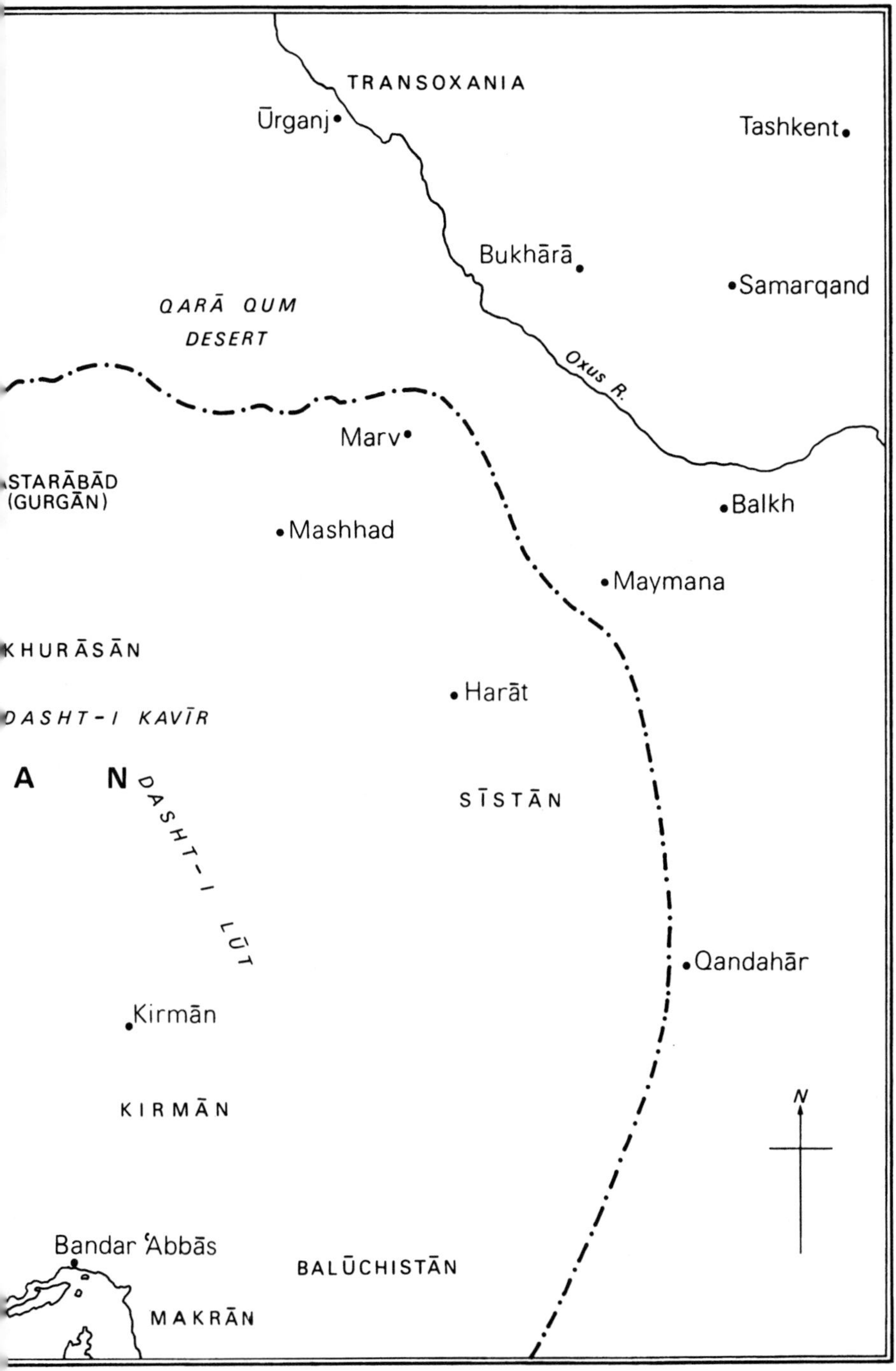

The Safavid empire in the sixteenth and seventeenth centuries

Acknowledgements

I acknowledge with thanks receipt of a grant from the Canada Council which enabled me to go to Iran in 1974 to carry out field research for this book. I would like also to record my debt of gratitude to Shojaeddin Shafa for the way in which he facilitated my work in Iran.

My special thanks are due to my wife, who did much of the work of selecting and obtaining prints of the illustrations; to my daughter-in-law Teresa, who drew the plan for the map; to my colleague Lisa V. Golombek, who selected a number of items from the Royal Ontario Museum collection for inclusion among the illustrations; to my colleague Glyn M. Meredith-Owens; and to Renata Holod, Judith Lerner, The Revd D. G. Montanari, Michael Rogers, Yvette Sauvan, Norah Titley, Betty Tyers, Anthony Welch, Stuart Cary Welch and Donald Wilber, for their efforts to track down portraits of elusive shahs and other illustrations. In addition, I wish to thank Anthony Welch for sending me a copy of his excellent work, *Shāh 'Abbas and the Arts of Isfahan*, and R. W. Ferrier and Bert Fragner for making some of their unpublished work available to me; unfortunately Dr Fragner's material arrived too late to be incorporated in my chapter on the Safavid economy.

Finally, my sincere thanks are due to Robert Seal, who first encouraged me to write this book; to the staff of Cambridge University Press, especially Andrew Brown for his unfailing help and valuable advice at all stages of the book's production; and to Roloff Beny, for graciously allowing me to use his outstanding photograph of the Chihil Sutūn fresco for the book jacket.

The title of Chapter 1 was suggested by a phrase in Vladimir Minorsky's translation of *Tadhkirat al-Mulūk*.

Trinity College
University of Toronto

R.S.

I

The Lords of Ardabīl

The town of Ardabīl, situated in eastern Āẕarbāyjān in north-western Iran, lies at an altitude of some 1,524 metres on a plateau surrounded by mountains; the highest of these, Mt Savalān (4,810 metres), an extinct volcano from which snow rarely departs completely, even in summer, rears its massive bulk 20 miles west of the town.

For a short time during the tenth century, Ardabīl had been the chief city of the province of Āẕarbāyjān, but it had soon been superseded by the city of Tabrīz, 130 miles to the west. Tabrīz rapidly established itself as an important station on one of the world's great trade routes from the Far East and Central Asia, and as the hub of a network of highroads leading to Mesopotamia and the Mediterranean ports, to Anatolia and Constantinople, and north through the Caucasus to the Ukraine, the Crimea and eastern Europe. The supremacy of Tabrīz was assured when Ardabīl was sacked and left in ruins by the Mongols in 1220, while Tabrīz escaped a similar fate the following year by payment of a large indemnity to its conquerors. At the beginning of the fourteenth century, Ardabīl was no more than a small provincial town, lying slightly off the beaten track, as it still does today.

At first sight, therefore, Ardabīl seemed an unlikely choice as the nerve-centre of a revolutionary movement. Yet its relative remoteness and unimportance constituted advantages for the leaders of this movement, who wanted as little as possible to attract the curiosity and almost certain hostility of the authorities at Tabrīz. At the back of Ardabīl, too, lay the impenetrable mountains, forests and swamps of Gīlān, and the proximity of this refuge was to save the movement from extinction at the end of the fifteenth century.

Such considerations, however, were presumably far from the

mind of the first member of the Safavid family of whom we have historical knowledge, a certain Fīrūzshāh "of the golden hat" (*zarrīnkulāh*), whom we find established as a wealthy landowner in the Ardabīl region sometime during the eleventh century. The origins of the Safavid family are still enveloped in obscurity. Hinz has talked about an alleged migration of Fīrūzshāh to Āẕarbāyjān from the Yemen, and has taken this to be an indication of the Arab origin of the family. Ayalon has claimed that the Safavids were Turks. Kasravī, after a careful examination of the evidence, came to the conclusion that the Safavids were indigenous inhabitants of Iran, and of pure Aryan (i.e., Iranian) stock; yet they spoke Āẕarī, the form of Turkish which was the native language of Āẕarbāyjān. The only point at issue for Kasravī was whether the Safavid family had been for long resident in Āẕarbāyjān, or had migrated from Kurdistān. More recently, Togan re-examined the evidence, and suggested that the ancestors of the Safavids may have accompanied the Kurdish Ravadid prince Mamlān b. Vahsūdān when the latter conquered the regions of Ardabīl, Arrān, Muqān and Dār-Būm in 1025.

Why is there such confusion about the origins of this important dynasty, which reasserted Iranian identity and established an independent Iranian state after eight and a half centuries of rule by foreign dynasties? The reason is that the Safavids, having been brought to power by the dynamic force of a certain ideology, deliberately set out to obliterate any evidence of their own origins which would weaken the thrust of this ideology and call in question the premises on which it was based. In order to understand how and why the Safavids falsified the evidence of their origins, one must first be clear about the nature of the Safavid *da'va* (propaganda, or ideological appeal), and about the bases on which the power of the Safavid shahs rested.

The power of the Safavid shahs had three distinct bases: first, the theory of the divine right of the Persian kings, based on the possession by the king of the "kingly glory" (*hvarnah; khvarenah; farr*). This ancient, pre-Islamic theory was reinvested with all its former splendour and reappeared in the Islamic garb of the concept of the ruler as the "Shadow of God upon earth" (*ẓill allāh fi'l-arżi*); second, the claim of the Safavid shahs to be the representatives on earth of the Mahdī, the 12th and last Imām of the Ithnā 'Asharī Shī'īs, who went into occultation in A.D. 873/4 and whose return to earth will herald the Day of Judgement; third, the position of the Safavid shahs as the *murshid-i kāmil* or perfect spiritual director, of the Ṣūfī Order known as the Ṣafaviyya.

Before these points are discussed in detail, reference should be made to what may be called the "official" version of the early history of the Safavid family. The earliest extant genealogy of the Safavid house (*dūdmān*) is that contained in the *Ṣafvat al-Ṣafā* of Ibn Bazzāz, written about 1357/8, less than twenty-five years after the death of Shaykh Ṣafī al-Dīn Abu'l-Fatḥ Isḥāq Ardabīlī (1252–1334), who founded the Ṣafaviyya Order and set the Safavid house on the path to future greatness. The *Ṣafvat al-Ṣafā* is primarily hagiography, and must therefore be used with caution, but is of vital importance both because of its early date and because its account, as subsequently amended, became the "official" version followed by all later histories up to and including the genealogical work entitled *Silsilat al-Nasab-i Ṣafaviyya*; the latter was a late Safavid work written during the reign of Shāh Sulaymān (1666–94) by a descendant of Shaykh Ṣafī al-Dīn's spiritual director Shaykh Zāhid-i Gīlānī.

The purpose of the "official" Safavid genealogy was to establish the descent of the Safavid house from the 7th Shī'ī Imām, Mūsā al-Kāẓim, and through him to 'Alī himself, the 1st Shī'ī Imām; but even in the "official" Safavid genealogy, there are inconsistencies and variations in the number of links in the genealogical chain. There is little dispute about the five links in immediate descent from the Imām Mūsā al-Kāẓim, and only minor inconsistencies in the chain between Fīrūzshāh Zarrīnkulāh and Shaykh Ṣafī al-Dīn. It is the middle portion of the genealogy, consisting of eight links in the "official version", on which the greatest doubt has been cast; of these eight persons, four are unspecified Muḥammads.

Following the "official" version of early Safavid history, it appears that Fīrūzshāh was appointed Governor of the province of Ardabīl and its dependencies by a son of Ibrāhīm b. Adham; this son is described as "King of Iran". Ibrāhīm b. Adham was an eighth-century ascetic whose life has been much embellished by legend. There is no historical basis for the belief that he was a prince of Balkh who renounced worldly pomp in favour of a life of abstinence. We are further told that Fīrūzshāh converted to Islam the inhabitants of Āẕarbāyjān and Muqān, who were infidels (*kāfir*). Both of these statements are patently false. Ibrāhīm b. Adham died in A.D. 777, so no son of his could possibly have been alive in the eleventh century, and the inhabitants of Muqān and Arrān had embraced Islam during the seventh and eighth centuries. Fīrūzshāh was a man of wealth and authority, and owned much property and livestock; indeed, his animals were so numerous that he selected for his residence a place called Rāngīn, on the edge of the forests of Gīlān, where the pasturage was excellent. Fīrūzshāh became noted for the nobility of his character, the excellence of his manners, the felicity of his conversation and the generosity of his behaviour. He was said to be a *sayyid* (descendant of the Prophet), and, as a result of his abundant piety and zealous religious observance, the people of the region became his disciples (*murīd*). After his death, his son 'Ivaż moved to Isfaranjān, a village in the Ardabīl district. On the other hand, a "non-establishment" source states that Fīrūzshāh was the first member of the Safavid house to come to Ardabīl; this statement is not necessarily incompatible with the "official" account, for "Ardabīl" may mean "the Ardabīl district".

The son of 'Ivaż, Muḥammad Ḥāfiẓ, disappeared at the age of seven, and the customary rites of mourning were performed for him. After seven years had elapsed, Muḥammad suddenly reappeared, wearing a jujube (reddish-brown) coloured robe, and with a white turban wound around the ordinary hat of the period. Round his neck was hung a copy of the Qur'ān. In answer to questions about his absence, he replied that he had been carried off by *jinn*, who had taught him the Qur'ān and instructed him in the obligatory sciences, such as the precepts and laws of God. From then onwards, Muḥammad Ḥāfiẓ lived a life of perfect piety and scrupulous religious observance. Two new, predictive elements have been introduced into the "official" account at this point: the supernatural element (the abduction by *jinn*); and the repetition of the socio-religiously significant number "7".

Muḥammad's son, Ṣalāḥ al-Dīn Rashīd, lived an uneventful life as a small landowner (*dihqān*) and agriculturalist at the village of Kalkhvurān near Ardabīl. According to the *Silsilat al-Nasab*, Ṣalāḥ al-Dīn's son, Quṭb al-Dīn Abu'l-Bāqī Aḥmad, was living at Kalkhvurān at the time of the Georgian invasion of Iran and capture of Ardabīl in 1203/4. During the sack of Ardabīl, Quṭb al-Dīn took refuge with his infant son Amīn al-Dīn Jibrā'īl[1] in a cellar, with one of his followers on guard above. The guard, attacked by a marauding Georgian, succeeded in overcoming him, but the sound of the struggle brought further Georgians to the spot. Before they arrived, the guard pulled a large grain-bin over the entrance to the cellar. The Georgians killed the guard and left. The cellar was too cramped for the number of people, mainly women and children, concealed in it, and Quṭb al-Dīn was forced to seek another hiding-place. Before he found one, he was caught by the Georgians, and left for dead with a severe wound in his neck. He was later recovered from a pile of corpses of other victims by a band of ruffians out for loot, and taken back to the cellar to be nursed by his relatives. Quṭb al-Dīn was still alive in 1252/3, when Shaykh Ṣafī al-Dīn was born. Shaykh Ṣafī al-Dīn, recounting the story of these events in later days, used to say that, when Quṭb al-Dīn lifted him up on his shoulder, he could put four fingers into the gash left by the sword wound.

Amīn al-Dīn Jibrā'īl, like his forefathers, combined the successful practice of agriculture with the holy life. He did not mix at all with the common people, but was always silent and at his devotions. He chose as his spiritual director Mawlānā Imām al-Rabbānī Khvāja Kamāl al-Dīn 'Arabshāh. He married Dawlatī, the daughter of 'Umar Bārūqī, who bore him Shaykh Ṣafī al-Dīn in 1252/3; six years later, Amīn al-Dīn Jibrā'īl died.

With the birth of Shaykh Ṣafī al-Dīn, the history of the Safavid family enters a new and decisive phase. According to the traditional hagiographical accounts, signs of future greatness were stamped upon his brow from infancy. He did not mix with other boys, but spent his time in prayer and fasting until God removed the veil from his heart. He experienced visions, seeing angels in the form of birds which in turn assumed human shape and conversed with him. Sometimes the *awtād* and *abdāl*[2] would approach him and comfort him with the assurance that he would reach the state of gnosis and become the focus for the hopes of the world.

When he was about twenty years of age, Shaykh Ṣafī al-Dīn sought a spiritual director among the recluses of Ardabīl, but none could meet his needs. A certain Shaykh Najīb al-Dīn Buzghūsh at Shīrāz was recommended to him, and Ṣafī al-Dīn journeyed to that city only to find that Shaykh Najīb al-Dīn had died before his arrival. Ṣafī al-Dīn remained at Shīrāz for some time. Many dervishes gathered round him and conversed with him, and he continued to ask advice from the local shaykhs regarding a possible spiritual director. Eventually, he was advised that no one in the world could analyse his mystical state and interpret his visions except Shaykh Zāhid-i Gīlānī. After a protracted search, during which he experienced visions in which Shaykh Zāhid was present, and after suffering illness and hardship, Ṣafī al-Dīn succeeded in finding the latter at a village on the shores of the Caspian Sea. He reached Shaykh Zāhid's residence during Ramażān and, although it was Shaykh Zāhid's custom not to receive visitors during the month of fast, Ṣafī al-Dīn was at once summoned into his presence. Unlike other spiritual directors whom he had visited, Shaykh Zāhid did not turn away his face, but gazed steadily upon him, and Ṣafī al-Dīn knew that he had reached the goal of his aspirations. At once, he made the formal act termed *tawba*, that is, repentance of his sins and renunciation of the worldly life. Ṣafī al-Dīn remained in Shaykh Zāhid's private quarters until the end of Ramażān. He was granted yet another audience with the Shaykh during Ramażān, because Ṣafī al-Dīn was in doubt as to whether his mystical states and visions were inspired by God or by Satan. Shaykh Zāhid resolved his doubts and answered his questions, and affirmed his exalted spiritual status; there was but one veil between Ṣafī al-Dīn and God, he declared, and that veil had now been removed.

When Ṣafī al-Dīn reached Gīlān in 1276/7, he was twenty-five years of age, and Shaykh Zāhid was sixty. He followed Shaykh Zāhid's spiritual guidance for twenty-five years, until the death of the latter in 1301. As Shaykh Zāhid grew older, he became more and more dependent on Ṣafī al-Dīn who, when the Shaykh's eyesight failed him, used to sit at his side, describe visitors to him and conduct interviews for him. At some point during this period, the close bonds between the two men were further cemented by a reciprocal marriage alliance: Ṣafī al-Dīn married Shaykh Zāhid's daughter, Bībī Fāṭima, and gave his own daughter in marriage to Shaykh Zāhid's son, Ḥājjī Shams al-Dīn Muḥammad. Ṣafī al-Dīn had three sons by Bībī Fāṭima: Muḥyī al-Dīn, who died in 1323/4, Ṣadr al-Milla va'l-Dīn Mūsā and Abū Sa'īd.

---

1. The dervish Naṣr ibn Sukharā'ī

Some of Shaykh Zāhid's disciples grew jealous of Ṣafī al-Dīn's favoured position and of his influence with the Shaykh, who expressed his affection and esteem for Ṣafī al-Dīn in the most forthright terms: "Ṣafī's hand," he said, "is my hand; whoever is a convert of his is mine also; whoever is a convert of mine but not of his, is wanted neither by me nor by him. I am Ṣafī and Ṣafī is I." The Ardabīlīs present flung themselves into a joyful dance[3] at these words, and shouted ecstatically. Zāhid nodded and said, "You are indeed right to rejoice, because today is your day."[4]

Equally unequivocal was Shaykh Zāhid's designation of Ṣafī al-Dīn to succeed him as head of the Zāhidiyya Order. When Shaykh Zāhid saw that Ṣafī al-Dīn was competent to give spiritual guidance, he granted him a prayer-mat and authority to teach. Ṣafī al-Dīn protested his inadequacy for the task; his only goal, he said, was the threshold of Zāhid. Zāhid replied:

> Ṣafī, God has shown you to the people, and His command is that you obey His call. . . I have broken the polo-stick of all your adversaries, and cast the ball before you. Strike it where you will; the field is yours. I have been able to live the life of a recluse, but you cannot. Wherever you are bidden, you must go, to make converts and give instruction. It is God who has given you this task.[5]

Although this passage may have been written with the advantage of hindsight, nevertheless it is a fact that, with the assumption by Shaykh Ṣafī of the leadership of the Zāhidiyya Order, henceforth named the Ṣafaviyya Order after him, there commenced the period of active proselytism which transformed what had been a Ṣūfī Order of purely local significance into a religious movement whose influence was felt throughout Iran, Syria and Asia Minor.

Shaykh Ṣafī al-Dīn's succession was resented by some members of Shaykh Zāhid's family. One of Ṣafī's principal opponents was Jamāl al-Dīn 'Alī, Shaykh Zāhid's son by his first wife, who had assumed that he would succeed his father. Designation by the incumbent shaykh, and not a father–son relationship, was the important criterion in determining the succession, and so the supporters of Shaykh Ṣafī were on firm ground. Ironically, after Ṣafī became leader of the Order, the father–son relationship not only assumed paramount importance in deciding who the next leader should be, but was tacitly assumed to be the only possible basis for selecting him. Ṣafī al-Dīn's determination to keep the leadership of the Ṣafaviyya Order in his family makes it clear that, from an early stage, he intended to use the Order as a stepping-stone to political power.

Every year, Shaykh Ṣafī visited the tomb of his spiritual director, Shaykh Zāhid, and took costly gifts for his children and the attendants of the shrine. Ḥājjī Shams al-Dīn Muḥammad, Zāhid's son and Ṣafī's son-in-law, was the object of Ṣafī's especial favour. At the time of his marriage to Ṣafī's daughter, Ṣafī had made over to him estates and other property, and year by year he increased his gifts to Ḥājjī Shams al-Dīn and paid off any debts incurred by him. Shaykh Ṣafī rejected a suggestion by his wife that he make over two-thirds of his estates to his son-in-law, but he did agree to pass on to the latter income accruing from his own property. However, Shaykh Ṣafī's beneficence did not extend to the descendants of Jamāl al-Dīn 'Alī, who had challenged him for the leadership of the Zāhidiyya Order. Shaykh Ṣafī appears to have been party to the usurpation by his son-in-law of the revenue from certain *vaqfs* (lands held in mortmain) which rightfully belonged to Jamāl al-Dīn's son, Badr al-Dīn, because a decree of the Mongol Īlkhān Abū Sa'īd dated 1320 ordered the restoration of this revenue to Badr al-Dīn. On the other hand, Shaykh Ṣafī was ready to do battle with the Mongol authorities in defence of Ḥājjī Shams al-Dīn's descendants if their rights were infringed, as for instance when a Mongol *amīr* attempted to convert some of their private estates (*milk*) into tribal pasture (*yurt*), or when boundary disputes arose.

Toward the end of his life, Shaykh Ṣafī made a will in favour of his second son, Ṣadr al-Dīn Mūsā, appointing him his successor and vicegerent, charging him with the administration of the votive offerings, effects and private estates belonging to the Order and making him responsible for the continuance, as far as was possible, of the practice of providing sustenance for the poor at God's gate. Shaykh Ṣafī al-Dīn died on 12 September 1334. Ṣadr al-Dīn Mūsā had been born in 1304/5, and was therefore thirty years old when he succeeded his father as leader of the Ṣafaviyya Order. Since his elder brother had predeceased Shaykh Ṣafī al-Dīn, and his three younger brothers died soon after their father, and left no issue, Shaykh Ṣadr al-Dīn acquired any *vaqf* property and lands which they possessed, and so became not only the spiritual heir but the sole material heir of Shaykh Ṣafī al-Dīn.

Shaykh Ṣadr al-Dīn's long term of office (1334–91) was marked by an important development: the sacred enclosure of the Safavid family at Ardabīl was begun and completed in ten years under his direction. The tomb of Shaykh Ṣafī al-Dīn is antedated by the *ḥaram-khāna*, which was built between 1324 and 1334,[6] but many of the ancillary buildings, including rooms for private meditation, the *dār al-ḥuffāẓ*, or room housing the Qur'ān-reciters, the *chīnī-khāna*, or room later used to house Shāh 'Abbās I's gift of porcelain to the shrine, but whose original function is unknown, were added by Ṣadr al-Dīn Mūsā; after the establishment of the Safavid dynasty, further buildings were added by Shāh Ismā'īl I and Shāh Ṭahmāsp, and Shāh 'Abbās I embellished and restored many parts of the shrine. At the same time, Shaykh Ṣadr al-Dīn continued his father's efforts to spread the Safavid religious propaganda, and many of the Ilkhanid *amīrs* and Mongol nobility became disciples of the Shaykhs of Ardabīl. Already during the lifetime of Shaykh Ṣafī al-Dīn, Rashīd al-Dīn, the great *vazīr* of the Īlkhāns Ghāzān Khān and Öljeitū, had demonstrated great veneration for the Safavid Shaykh, and among the Mongol *amīrs* who counted themselves as his disciples was the powerful Amīr Chūbān. Several sources record versions of a conversation which is alleged to have taken place between Shaykh Ṣafī al-Dīn and Amīr Chūbān. Asked by the Amīr whether the king's soldiers or his own disciples were the more numerous, the Shaykh is said to have replied that his disciples were twice as numerous; another version of his reply alleges that in Iran alone for every soldier there were a hundred Ṣūfīs. To this the Amīr is said to have replied:

> You speak truly, for I have travelled from the Oxus to the frontiers of Egypt, and from the shores of Hurmūz to Bāb al-Abvāb [Darband], which are the furthest limits of this kingdom, and I have seen the disciples of the Shaykh embellished and adorned with the ornaments and garb of the Shaykh, and they have spread the sound of the *ẓikr*[7] to those parts.[8]

Regular contact was maintained between Ardabīl and these Safavid proselytes, and the basic organisation of the Ṣafaviyya Order was established by Shaykh Ṣafī al-Dīn. The Safavid propaganda network already extended to eastern Anatolia and Syria, and many recruits were made among the pastoral Turcoman tribes inhabiting those regions. Members of these tribes later constituted the élite of the Safavid fighting forces, and it is significant that, during the early years of the fourteenth century, the Ṣafaviyya Order was establishing itself in regions in which it subsequently caused the greatest anxiety to the Ottoman sulṭāns. The traffic between these regions and Ardabīl was on a large scale; we are told that, in the space of three months, the number of novices and devotees who visited Shaykh Ṣafī al-Dīn via the Marāgha and Tabrīz road alone was 13,000 and the number coming from other parts was on a comparable scale.

The succession of Shaykh Ṣadr al-Dīn to the leadership of the Order coincided with the break-up of the Ilkhanid empire in Iran and Mesopotamia. In the absence of a strong central government, families of powerful *amīrs* such as the Chubanids and Jala'irids carved out principalities for themselves. In the Armenian highlands round Lake Vān, the strength of the federation of Turcoman tribes known as the Qarā Quyūnlū (those of the Black Sheep) was on the increase; initially dependents of the Jala'irids, in 1390 they seized from their overlords control of the province of Āẕarbāyjān. In other parts of Iran, such as Harāt and Sabzavār in Khurāsān, and in the provinces of Fārs and Kirmān, local Iranian dynasties established themselves.

The political turbulence of the times naturally had an adverse effect on the position of the Safavid shaykhs at Ardabīl. The town of Ardabīl itself changed hands on several occasions. Malik Ashraf was clearly not one of the Chubanid *amīrs* who venerated the leader of the Safavid Order, for "by fair and specious words" he lured Shaykh Ṣadr al-Dīn to Tabrīz and threw him into prison. Although Malik Ashraf is known to have had a distaste for theologians and religious leaders in general, it is tempting to see in his action against the Safavid leader some recognition of the growing political significance of the Safavid movement. On the other hand, many shaykhs, doctors of religion and men of learning voluntarily went into exile to escape from Malik Ashraf's oppressive rule. When Shaykh Ṣadr al-Dīn had been in prison for three months, Malik Ashraf experienced a terrifying dream as a result of which he released the Shaykh with profuse apologies. Some time later, Malik Ashraf regretted having released the Shaykh, and sent some men to Ardabīl to re-arrest him. Shaykh Ṣadr al-Dīn, forewarned by his spiritual insight of the ruler's intention, abandoned the seat of his spiritual authority and fled to Gīlān. The fact that Malik Ashraf thought it necessary to attempt to re-arrest the Safavid leader indicates, I think, that there was some political motive underlying his hostility toward Shaykh Ṣadr al-Dīn.

Many members of the religious classes who left Āẕarbāyjān at this period fled north through the Caucasus and sought refuge with Jānī Beg Maḥmūd, ruler of the Blue Horde of western Qipchāq (1340–57) and a descendant of Chingiz Khān. The laments of these refugees about their ill-treatment at the hands of Malik Ashraf provided Jānī Beg with a convenient excuse for invading Āẕarbāyjān. He captured Malik Ashraf near Tabrīz and put him to death. Jānī Beg received Shaykh Ṣadr al-Dīn in royal fashion at his camp at Awjān near Tabrīz. According to the traditional Safavid account, Jānī Beg gave the Shaykh a private audience, in the course of which he said that he had heard that the Shaykh had been in exile for a long time, and that the condition of the Safavid dervishes living in the ancestral sanctuary at Ardabīl had deteriorated. He advised the Shaykh to return to Ardabīl and minister to the poor. He instructed the Shaykh to draw up an inventory of all the lands, workshops and estates belonging to himself and his followers so that he (Jānī Beg) might allot them to the Shaykh as a *suyūrghāl*,[9] protected by a maledictory clause, so that the profit accruing from this property might be assigned to the Safavid Order. Unfortunately, the necessary inventories could not be completed before Jānī Beg left Iran, and the decrees assigning this property and revenue were never issued by the Khān.

Even if these decrees had been issued, it is doubtful whether the Safavid shaykhs would have enjoyed the uninterrupted beneficial possession of these revenues, because the Ardabīl area continued to be fought over by rival rulers during the last quarter of the fourteenth century. About 1372, the Jala'irid *amīr* Aḥmad b. Uvays held Ardabīl as a *suyūrghāl* from his father. He seems to have accorded his protection to the Safavid shaykhs, because a decree dated 1372 forbids governors and other officials in areas under his jurisdiction to "make any demands or write drafts on places which are in the hands of the disciples [of Shaykh Ṣadr al-Dīn]".[10] Apparently the property of the Safavid Order had enjoyed immunity from taxation for some time, because the decree referred to "certain ancient tax exemptions enjoyed by the estates and *awqāf* [lands held in mortmain] belonging to the Safavid shrine".

In 1390, the Qarā Quyūnlū *amīrs* wrested Āẕarbāyjān from the Jala'irids, and Ardabīl was allotted as a *suyūrghāl* to the *amīrs* of the Jāgīrlū tribe of Turcomans, who quartered their cavalry, retainers and servants for the summer in the pastures of the Ardabīl area. In 1413, a dispute between the Jāgīrlū khān and his overlord, the Qarā Quyūnlū ruler, led to the former's plundering Safavid property at Ardabīl and imprisoning a member of the Safavid family. Given the political turmoil of the time, however, it would seem that Shaykh Ṣadr al-Dīn was reasonably successful in protecting from usurpation the property belonging to the Ardabīl shrine and the lands in the province of Ardabīl and surrounding districts which belonged to the Safavid family, and in rendering immune from the *ad hoc* exactions of local officials and military commanders the income deriving from this property.

Shaykh Ṣadr al-Dīn died in 1391/2 and, like his father, was buried in the Ardabīl sanctuary. Before his death he had nominated his son Khvāja 'Alī as his successor and vicegerent, and had entrusted to him the "prayer-mat of spiritual guidance", and had charged him with the care of God's servants. Khvāja 'Alī was head of the Order from 1391/2 to his death on 15 May 1427. Under the leadership of Khvāja 'Alī, the esoteric doctrine of the Safavid Order first assumed an unequivocally Shi'ite character, but one must take particular care not to give the pietistic legends and additions of later Safavid ideologists the authority of historical fact. Both Sayyid Aḥmad Kasravī[11] and Horst[12] have rejected as fabrications the legend of Khvāja 'Alī's three meetings with the great conqueror Tīmūr, who ravaged Western Asia in a series of campaigns between 1381 and 1404. The last of these meetings occurred in 1404, shortly before Tīmūr's death, when the latter passed through Ardabīl on his way back to Central Asia after his celebrated victory over the Ottoman Sulṭān Bāyazīd I at the battle of Ankara (27 July 1402).

According to the traditional Safavid account, Tīmūr summoned Khvāja 'Alī and gave him a poisoned cup to drink. A number of dervishes present began rhythmically to chant the *ẕikr* "There is no god but God." As their fervour increased, Khvāja 'Alī went into a trance, and rose to join the dance. The heat produced by the physical exercise sweated the poison out of his body. Tīmūr was so overcome with wonder that he seized the hem of Khvāja 'Alī's robe, and became his disciple and convinced follower. The *Tārīkh-i 'Ālam-ārā-yi 'Abbāsī* makes no mention of a poisoned cup, but states that Tīmūr became Khvāja 'Alī's disciple after a display of the Shaykh's powers of telepathy. Tīmūr handed over to Khvāja 'Alī the prisoners taken in his campaign against the Ottomans. Khvāja 'Alī set the men free and settled them near the holy shrine of Ganja bi-Kūl. Their descendants became known as the Ṣūfiyān-i Rūmlū.[13] The anonymous history of Shāh Ismā'īl[14] contains a fuller version: "The Shaykh [Khvāja 'Alī] begged for the liberation of the prisoners of Rūm[15], and Tīmūr freed them all and appointed them to the service of the family of Ardabīl. He also issued an order to the rulers and governors of Rūm to the effect that the men whom he had freed 'and who are Ṣūfīs of the Safavid family', wherever they be, should not be oppressed or prevented from visiting their *murshid* (spiritual director); they must be exempted from payment of peasant dues as well as from government taxes. Out of his own lawful money Tīmūr bought fields and villages in the neighbourhood of Ardabīl and allotted them as a *vaqf* (benefaction) to the resting-place of Shaykh Ṣafī, which he recognised as constituting asylum. He also made over to the Safavid family the land taxes of the district. To those of the prisoners who expressed the desire to return to Rūm, permission was granted to do so. Khvāja 'Alī appointed his representatives to all the tribes and said: 'Let your comings and goings be not infrequent, for the advent of the righteous Duodeciman religion is nigh and you must be ready to sacrifice your lives.'" The lands purchased by Tīmūr were not in the Ardabīl district alone, but comprised villages and hamlets in regions as far away as Iṣfahān and Hamadān. According to the *Silsilat al-Nasab*, Tīmūr is said to have constituted these lands into a *vaqf* to the male issue of Khvāja 'Alī, but since the lands thus donated had not come into the possession of the Safavid family in their entirety before Tīmūr's death the following year in 1405, the benefaction became non-operative, and at the time of the compilation of the *Silsilat al-Nasab* (*ca* 1660), none of the lands in question was in the possession of the descendants of Khvāja 'Alī. As a further embellishment to this account, the instrument relating to this benefaction is said to have fallen into the hands of the troops of Shāh 'Abbās I near Balkh in 1602/3. 'Abbās I refused to take cognisance of the acquisition of these lands by the Safavid family. He said it had been a royal transaction; perhaps the title-deeds had been drawn up, but the landowners in question had not received payment; otherwise, he reasoned, at least a portion of the property would still be in the hands of the beneficiary. The view that the story of the benefaction by Tīmūr either to Khvāja 'Alī and his descendants or to the shirine of Shaykh Ṣafī al-Dīn itself is a fabrication is supported by the great Safavid historian Iskandar Beg Munshī. With his usual honesty, he writes: "Although I have not found this tradition in the historical chronicles, or in any other accounts of the circumstances of the Safavid family, either in prose or poetry, nevertheless it is widely rumoured and disseminated by a succession of verbal reports, and so I have written it down." He goes on to say, however, "the actual *vaqf* document, written in an antique hand, and embellished with the Mongol seal and with the personal seal of Amīr Tīmūr, fell into Safavid hands during a campaign in the region of Balkh, while Safavid forces were laying siege to Andikhūd, and was brought to the notice of Shāh 'Abbās I".[16]

We are told that Tīmūr's son Shāhrukh also held Khvāja 'Alī in respect. In 1420, in the course of his campaign in north-western Iran against the Qarā Quyūnlū, Shāhrukh entered Ardabīl and visited the tomb of Shaykh Ṣafī al-Dīn, and sought to obtain spiritual blessings from the presence of Khvāja 'Alī. Shāhrukh was in the habit of demonstrating his sympathy with popular religious sentiment by showing veneration for the holy men and visiting the tombs of the celebrated shaykhs of the regions through which he passed, but his visit to Khvāja 'Alī is particularly interesting in view of the by then manifestly Shī'ī tendencies of the Safavid Order. It appears that the political benefits of such an action outweighed in the mind of the Sunnī ruler any religious antipathy he may have felt, and this view is supported by the fact that on several occasions Shāhrukh visited the shrine of the 8th Shī'ī Imām at Mashhad.

About the year 1427, Khvāja 'Alī decided to make the pilgrimage to Mecca, and set out, leaving his third son, Ibrāhīm, at Ardabīl as spiritual director and supervisor of the Safavid mausoleum. Ibrāhīm could not bear the separation from his father, and followed him to Mecca, where they performed the rites of the pilgrimage together. From Mecca, they went to Jerusalem, where Khvāja 'Alī died and was buried by Ibrāhīm. Ibrāhīm then returned to Ardabīl to assume the duties of his father's vicegerent and successor, which he performed until his own death in 1447. Little is known about the development of the Safavid Order during this period. What is clear, is that Ibrāhīm maintained and strengthened the network of adherents who were actively engaged in spreading Safavid propaganda in Anatolia and elsewhere. At the head of this organisation was an officer called the *khalīfat al-khulafā*; this office has been felicitously termed by Minorsky the "special secretariat for Ṣūfī affairs". Through the *khalīfat al-khulafā* and his subordinates, called *pīra*, the leaders of the Safavid Order and, later, the Safavid shahs, controlled and maintained close contact with their Ṣūfī disciples both within and without the borders of Iran. The presence of large numbers of Safavid supporters in eastern Anatolia ultimately came to be recognised by the Ottomans as a serious threat to their authority in that area. The *khalīfat al-khulafā* was regarded as the deputy and lieutenant of the *murshid-i kāmil* himself, that is, the perfect spiritual director, or leader of the Safavid Order. All Ṣūfīs of the Order obeyed the orders of the *khalīfat al-khulafā* as they would the orders of their leader himself. It was the duty of Ṣūfīs of the Safavid Order to visit the Safavid shrine at Ardabīl and be spiritually enriched by an audience with their Shaykh. We are told that by the time of Shaykh Ibrāhīm the throng of disciples crowding round the Safavid sanctuary had become so great that not all of them could be admitted into the presence of the Shaykh. Ibrāhīm excelled even his forefathers in the scale of his charity to the poor and needy; the shrine had become so wealthy that its kitchens were stocked with dishes and vessels of gold and silver, and the Shaykh conducted himself like a king.

With the accession of Ibrāhīm's son, Junayd, to the leadership of the Safavid Order, the Safavid movement entered yet another important phase in the two centuries of patient preparation for the establishment of the Safavid dynasty. From his assumption of the leadership, Junayd gave clear indications of his desire for temporal power and kingship. It is no accident that he is the first Safavid leader to whom the term *sulṭān*, indicative of temporal authority, was applied. No importance should be attached to the fact that pious tradition liked to apply the title *sulṭān* retroactively to the early leaders of the Safavid family. No longer content with spiritual authority alone, Junayd introduced a militant note by inciting his disciples to carry on holy war against the infidel.[17]

These activities aroused first the suspicion and then the apprehension of the ruler of western Iran, the Qarā Quyūnlū chief Jahānshāh, whose authority extended from Āẕarbāyjān and the borders of Georgia to the Persian Gulf. Jahānshāh peremptorily ordered Junayd to disperse his forces, leave Ardabīl, and go wherever he pleased as long as it was outside his dominions. Should Junayd fail to comply with these demands, Ardabīl would be destroyed. Junayd fled from Ardabīl with a number of Ṣūfīs of the Safavid Order and, after some years in Asia Minor and Syria, was finally given sanctuary by Jahānshāh's enemy the Āq Quyūnlū ruler Ūzūn Ḥasan, whose base at that time was Diyār Bakr. Junayd spent three years in Diyār Bakr (1456–9), and cemented his political alliance with the Āq Quyūnlū ruler by marrying his sister, Khadīja Begum. Ūzūn Ḥasan saw Junayd as a useful ally in the event of an Āq Quyūnlū drive eastward into Iran against the Qarā Quyūnlū. Similarly, the decision of the Safavid leader to ally himself with the Sunnī Āq Quyūnlū was taken on the grounds of political and military expediency. Not only were the Qarā Quyūnlū too powerful militarily to permit any successful Safavid military *coup* in Āẕarbāyjān (Junayd had tacitly acknowledged this in abandoning Ardabīl, the nerve-centre of the Safavid movement), but the Qarā Quyūnlū were also rivals to the Safavids on the religious level too. Although the Qarā Quyūnlū were not militant Shī'īs, they had been "trying to unify their adepts on a shī'a platform",[18] and so they were much more likely to clash with the Safavids on ideological grounds than were the Āq Quyūnlū.

In 1460, Junayd led a force of 10,000 men into Shīrvān. According to some sources, this was a repetition on a larger scale of his earlier raids on Circassia, and he intended merely to march across the territory of the Shīrvānshāh in order to reach Circassia. Other sources, however, state that his object was the conquest of Shīrvān, which would then constitute a convenient base for a subsequent invasion of Iran. In view of the size of Junayd's army, this seems much more probable. The expedition ended in disaster, for Junayd was attacked by the Shīrvānshāh on the banks of the river Kur, near Ṭabarsarān on 4 March 1460, and was killed in the battle.

The value of the long years of patient ideological preparation by the Safavid organisation for the seizure of power in Iran now became apparent. Not only did the Safavid movement not disintegrate, but, with the succession of Junayd's son Ḥaydar, its drive to achieve temporal power accelerated. Ḥaydar's first move was to continue the political and military alliance with the Āq Quyūnlū by marrying Ūzūn Ḥasan's daughter 'Alamshāh Begum (also known as Ḥalīma Begum Āghā and Marta) whose mother, Despina Khātūn, was the daughter of Calo Johannes, the Emperor of Trebizond. Like his father, Ḥaydar wielded both spiritual and temporal authority: "inwardly, following the example of shaykhs and men of God, he walked the path of spiritual guidance and defence of the faith; outwardly, he was a leader sitting on a throne in the manner of princes".[19] It could only be a matter of time before Ḥaydar, like his father, would make a bid for a kingdom of his own. Before trying conclusions with the Qarā Quyūnlū, however, Ḥaydar, again like his father, gave his men battle experience by leading them in raids against the "infidels" of Circassia and Dāghistān – probably the Christian Alāns (Ossetes) living north of the Darial pass, and the Kabard Circassians. In order to reach these regions, it was necessary for Ḥaydar to cross the territory of the Shīrvānshāh, who had defeated and killed his father in 1460. The Shīrvānshāh allowed Ḥaydar's first two expeditions, in 1483 or 1486, and 1487, to cross his territory unopposed. In 1488, however, when Ḥaydar sacked the town of Shamākhī, the capital of Shīrvān, the Shīrvānshāh, Farrukhyasār, appealed for help to his son-in-law, the Āq Quyūnlū Sulṭān Ya'qūb: "At the moment," said Farrukhyasār, "Ḥaydar owns no territory, but he has mobilized a warlike army, and his ambitions will not be contained within the confines of the district of Ardabīl. Nor, if he succeeds in acquiring a kingdom such as mine, will he for long be satisfied with such a meagre empire. On the contrary, it will merely whet his appetite."[20] Sulṭān Ya'qūb, persuaded by these arguments, sent 4,000 men to the assistance of Farrukhyasār. This detachment played the decisive part in the defeat of Ḥaydar's army on 9 July 1488 at Ṭabarsarān, only a short distance from the place where his father had been killed in 1460. In the course of the battle, Ḥaydar received a mortal arrow-wound, and was buried on the battlefield by his followers.

What had brought about this *volte-face* in Āq Quyūnlū policy toward the Safavids? The great Āq Quyūnlū ruler, Ūzūn Ḥasan, had died in 1478, and had been succeeded first by his son Khalīl and, later the same year, by his younger son Ya'qūb. From the outset, relations between Ḥaydar and Ya'qūb were not smooth, and Ḥaydar recognised that he was no longer *persona grata* at the Āq Quyūnlū court. Whereas Ūzūn Ḥasan had seen Junayd as a useful ally against the Qarā Quyūnlū, and was prepared to continue to extend his friendship to Ḥaydar even after he himself

2. Court usher (*yasāvul*), a *qizilbāsh* officer

had destroyed the Qarā Quyūnlū empire in 1467, Ya'qūb increasingly saw the presence of a well-armed and trained Safavid force within his own kingdom as a potential danger to his own position.

Shortly before his third and fatal expedition to Shīrvān in 1488, Ḥaydar, instructed in a dream by the Imām 'Alī, had devised for his followers the distinctive scarlet headgear, with twelve gores commemorating the twelve Shī'ī Imāms, which henceforth was to be the distinctive mark of the supporters of the Safavid house, and which led the Ottomans derisively to dub them *qizilbāsh*, or redheads. This name, used by the Ottomans in a pejorative sense, was adopted as a mark of pride. Strictly speaking, the name *qizilbāsh* applied only to those Turcoman tribes inhabiting eastern Anatolia, northern Syria and the Armenian highlands which were converted by the Safavid *da'va*, or propaganda, and became disciples of the Safavid shaykhs at Ardabīl. Eventually, however, the term came to be applied loosely to certain non-Turcoman supporters of the Safavids. According to the anonymous history of Shāh Ismā'īl, when Ḥaydar first showed the Ṣūfī *tāj* (as this distinctive headgear came to be called) to Ūzūn Ḥasan, the latter kissed it and put it on his head. His son Ya'qūb, however, refused to wear it, and this was the origin of the enmity between Ḥaydar and Ya'qūb. This story, *se non e vero* (and it cannot be true if the date for Ḥaydar's invention of the *tāj* is correct, because Ūzūn Ḥasan died in 1478) *e ben trovato*. After the death of Ḥaydar, Ya'qūb is said to have forbidden his subjects to wear the *qizilbāsh tāj*. These evil actions, comments the Safavid chronicler piously, led to the destruction of the Āq Quyūnlū dynasty.

For the second time, the Safavid movement had lost its leader in battle, but its momentum continued to carry it forward inexorably. Of Ḥaydar's sons, only the three he had by 'Alamshāh Begum are of importance: 'Alī, Ibrāhīm and Ismā'īl. Of these, Ibrāhīm appears to have defected to the Āq Quyūnlū;[21] this would account for the silence of the Safavid historical tradition regarding his fate. The eldest son, 'Alī, succeeded his father as head of the Safavid Order, and the political aspirations of the Safavids were made even clearer by 'Alī's adoption of the title *pādishāh* (king). Ya'qūb Sulṭān's anxieties, temporarily stilled by the death of Ḥaydar, were aroused in a more acute form by reports that 'Alī was preparing to avenge his father's death. Ya'qūb sent a detachment of troops to Ardabīl and arrested the three brothers and their mother, who was his own sister; the prisoners were interned in the fortress of Iṣṭakhr in Fārs, and 'Alī's life was spared only at the intercession of his mother.

The prospects of a successful culmination of the Safavid plans to seize power in Iran appeared remote. In December 1490, however, Ya'qūb Sulṭān died, and the Āq Quyūnlū empire was torn by civil war as each of some half dozen claimants to the throne sought to eliminate all his rivals. One of these, Rustam, hit upon the plan of making use of the fighting *élan* of the Safavid supporters in his struggle against his rivals. Accordingly, in 1493, the Safavid brothers were released after four and a half years of imprisonment. ʿAlī was received by Rustam at the Āq Quyūnlū capital, Tabrīz, with a great display of respect, and Rustam said to the Safavid leader: "What has been done to you is past, and with God's help I will make amends for it. You are as a brother to me, and at my death you shall become King of Iran."[22] ʿAlī's forces played a vital part in Rustam's defeat of his principal rival, but the following year, 1494, Rustam in his turn grew alarmed at the obvious strength of Safavid support, and he re-arrested ʿAlī and his brothers. Hearing that Rustam planned to put him to death, ʿAlī escaped from Rustam's camp and made for Ardabīl, accompanied by the small band of seven devoted Safavid supporters known as the *ahl-i ikhtiṣāṣ*, or persons singled out for special duty, who played such a vital role in bringing the Safavid revolution to a successful conclusion. Rustam realised the urgent need to intercept the Safavid brothers before they made contact with their base at Ardabīl. "Should Sulṭān ʿAlī once enter Ardabīl," he said, "(which God forbid!) the deaths of 10,000 Turcomans would be of no avail." On the way to Ardabīl, Sulṭān ʿAlī had a premonition of his approaching death, and he designated his brother Ismāʿīl as his successor as head of the Safavid Order. "I desire you," he said, "to avenge me and your father and your ancestors upon the child of Ḥasan Pādishāh [Ūzūn Ḥasan]. For the die of Heaven's choice has been cast in your name, and before long you will come out of Gīlān like a burning sun, and with your sword sweep unbelief from the face of the earth."[23]

The small Safavid band was overtaken near Ardabīl by the Āq Quyūnlū troops, and ʿAlī was killed. Ismāʿīl reached Ardabīl in safety, and took refuge first at the Safavid shrine. Then, when Rustam instituted a house-to-house search for him in Ardabīl, Ismāʿīl was moved from one hiding-place to another by his devoted supporters for a period of six weeks. His mother was tortured by the Āq Quyūnlū, but without avail, since she was ignorant of her son's whereabouts. After eluding capture in Ardabīl for six weeks, Ismāʿīl was passed from hand to hand by devotees and sympathisers until he reached the court at Lāhījān in Gīlān of a local ruler named Kār Kiyā Mīrzā ʿAlī; there he was given sanctuary. The Āq Quyūnlū were still hot on his trail. A woman of the Ẕu'l-Qadar tribe who was one of the people who had sheltered him in Ardabīl, was seized and put to death after having revealed what she knew of the escape route followed by Ismāʿīl. Rustam sent spies into Gīlān disguised as Ṣūfīs of the Safavid Order, to try and ascertain Ismāʿīl's whereabouts. When they reported that Ismāʿīl was at Lāhījān, Rustam sent three successive envoys to Kār Kiyā Mīrzā ʿAlī, demanding that he surrender Ismāʿīl. Kār Kiyā Mīrzā refused these demands, though with considerable trepidation. An embellishment by pious tradition states that Kār Kiyā Mīrzā, when he swore on oath to Rustam's envoys that Ismāʿīl had no foothold on the soil of Gīlān, had Ismāʿīl suspended in a wooden cage in order not to perjure himself. Not satisfied with Kār Kiyā Mīrzā's denials, Rustam was making preparations to invade Gīlān with a large force, when his own territory was invaded by his cousin Aḥmad and he himself was killed (1497).

Further internecine struggles between rival Āq Quyūnlū princes gave Ismāʿīl a breathing-space at Lāhījān, and he and his close advisers made their final plans for their attempt to overthrow the Āq Quyūnlū state in Iran. It is often assumed that Ismāʿīl himself was solely responsible, by his charismatic leadership, for bringing the Safavid revolution to a successful conclusion. When one considers that Ismāʿīl was only seven years old when he took refuge in Gīlān; that he was only twelve when he emerged from Gīlān in 1499 to make his bid for power; and no more than fourteen when he was crowned Shāh at Tabrīz in 1501 as the first king of the Safavid dynasty, it is clear that this could not have been so. The responsibility for maintaining the momentum of the Safavid revolutionary movement lay primarily with the small band of seven close advisers known as the *ahl-i ikhtiṣāṣ*, already referred to. It was V. Minorsky who first observed that "the basic organisation of the early Safavids" was "very similar to the single party of a modern totalitarian state",[24] and the function of the *ahl-i ikhtiṣāṣ* is closely analogous to that of the small band of men through whom Lenin controlled the Bolshevik movement before the revolution, a group given formal status in 1919 as the Politburo.[25]

Throughout the almost five years spent by Ismāʿīl in hiding at Lāhījān, he maintained close contact with his disciples in Anatolia, the southern Caucasus and Āẕarbāyjān. Since his *qizilbāsh* supporters were in the main Turcoman tribesmen, who spoke a form of Turkish, Ismā'īl addressed to them simple verses in the Āẕarī dialect of Turkish, in order to make his propaganda more effective. In these poems, he adopted the pen-name (*takhalluṣ*) of "Khaṭā'ī". During the last half of the fifteenth century, before the establishment of the Safavid state, there is no doubt whatever that Safavid propaganda asserted that the Safavid leader was not merely the representative of the Hidden Imām but the Hidden Imām himself; the Safavid leader was even apotheosised as a divine incarnation. It is alleged that the disciples of Junayd (1447–60) openly addressed him as "God", and his son as "Son of God", and in his praise they said: "he is the Living One, there is no God but he".[26] When Ḥaydar became head of the Safavid Order in 1460, the Ṣūfī *khalīfas* "came from every direction and foolishly announced the glad tidings of his divinity".[27] The evidence of Ismā'īl's own poems is incontrovertible proof that he wished his followers to consider him a divine incarnation. To take just one example:

I am Very God, Very God, Very God!
Come now, O blind man who has lost the path, behold the Truth!
I am that *Agens Absolutus* of whom they speak.[28]

How was it that religious beliefs of such an extremist and antinomian character found such ready acceptance in Anatolia and Kurdistān in the fourteenth century? To answer that question one has to go back to the capture of Baghdād in 1258 by the Mongols, and the extinction of the caliphate. This event not only marks a watershed in the political history of the Islamic world, but had far-reaching effects on religious developments as well. For 600 years the caliphate had been the visible symbol of the unity of the Islamic world, and the upholder of the orthodoxy of the Islamic faith. The religious tolerance (some might say indifference) of the Mongol rulers deprived Sunnī or "orthodox" Islam of its dominant position, and created conditions which facilitated the development not only of Shi'ism but of popular religious beliefs of every kind. From the late thirteenth century onwards, a wide variety of extremist Shī'ī sects flourished in Anatolia and Kurdistān,[29] and many of these groups avoided persecution by the Ottoman government as schismatics only by placing themselves under "the all-embracing and tolerant umbrella of the Bektāshī organization".[30] Anatolia in particular became a veritable melting-pot of religious ideas. The two principal ingredients in this pot were Shi'ism and Sufism, and in the course of the fourteenth century these two ingredients became permanently blended. While I cannot concur entirely with Henri Corbin's dictum that: "True Shi'ism is the same as *Taṣavvuf* [*i.e.*, Sufism], and similarly, genuine and real *Taṣavvuf* cannot be anything other than Shi'ism",[31] this statement embodies in a rather extreme form a truth which is the key to the understanding of the history of Persia in the centuries during which Safavid propagandists were steadily making converts and preparing the ground for the Safavid revolution. Seyyed Hossein Nasr has pointed out that the connecting link between Shi'ism and Sufism is 'Alī, the 1st Imām: "in as much as 'Alī stands at the origin of Shi'ism, and is at the same time the outstanding representative of Islamic esotericism, the sources of Shi'ism and Sufism are in this repect the same and they have many elements in common".[32]

From the blending of these two ingredients was produced, after a period of fermentation, the heady brew of apotheosis of the Safavid leader, and those who quaffed this brew were inspired with the fanatical fighting spirit to which the account of a contemporary Venetian merchant bears independent testimony:

> This Sophy [Ṣūfī] is loved and reverenced by his people as a God, and especially by his soldiers, many of whom enter into battle without armour, expecting their master Ismael to watch over them in the fight. The name of God is forgotten throughout Persia and only that of Ismael remembered; if any one fall when riding or dismounted, he appeals to no other God but Shiac (Shaykh), using the name in two ways: first as God Shiac, secondly as prophet: as the Mussulmans say "laylla, laylla Mahamet resuralla" [*lā ilāha ilāllāhu wa Muḥammadun rasūlullāhi*], the Persians say "Laylla yllala Ismael velialla" [*lā ilāha ilāllāhu* (*va*) *Ismā'īl valī allāhi*]; besides this everyone, and particularly his soldiers, consider him immortal.[33]

The title *valī allāh* bestowed on Ismā'īl by his followers indicates that they accorded him a status equal to that of 'Alī himself as the "vicar" or "lieutenant" of God *par excellence*.

In August 1499, Ismā'īl, or more likely the *ahl-i ikhtiṣāṣ*, decided that the time was ripe for the supreme bid for power. This was indeed the moment of truth for the Safavid movement. By the loss of three successive leaders in battle, the movement had already suffered and overcome more serious setbacks than had been experienced by any other revolutionary movement in history. Not only would the morale of the *qizilbāsh* be unlikely to survive another disaster unscathed, but on this occasion the leader, Ismā'īl, had no successor; it was the Safavids themselves who had insisted that *pidar-farzandī*, that is, the dynastic principle, was the sole criterion to be used to determine the succession, and not *naṣṣ*, or designation; Ismā'īl as yet had no son, and his only surviving brother, Ibrāhīm, had defected to the Āq Quyūnlū. Kār Kiyā Mīrzā tried to dissuade Ismā'īl from his enterprise, emphasising his extreme youth (he was still only twelve), and reminding him of the fate of predecessors. Undeterred, Ismā'īl set out with the *ahl-i ikhtiṣāṣ* from Lāhījān to Ardabīl, and was joined en route by 1,500 men from Syria and Asia Minor. Threatened by the Āq Quyūnlū Governor of Ardabīl, Ismā'īl decided his forces were insufficient to risk a confrontation, and withdrew to the Ṭālish district on the borders of Āẕarbāyjān and Gīlān. During the winter of 1499/1500, both the Āq Quyūnlū and the Shīrvānshāh Farrukhyasār made unsuccessful attempts to seize or kill Ismā'īl.

Returning to Ardabīl in the sping of 1500, Ismā'īl dispatched heralds to his supporters in Syria and Asia Minor, instructing them to meet him at a rendezvous at Arzinjān in the Armenian highlands. On his way to the rendezvous, Ismā'īl was joined by a contingent of Turcomans of the Bāyburtlū tribe, and when he reached Arzinjān he found 7,000 men from the Ustājlū, Shāmlū, Rūmlū, Takkalū, Ẕu'l-Qadar, Afshār, Qājār and Varsāq tribes awaiting him. About the same time, the two Āq Quyūnlū princes who had survived a fresh outburst of dynastic strife, Alvand and Murād, had decided on an amicable partition of the Āq Quyūnlū empire: Alvand retained Āẕarbāyjān, Arrān, Muqān and Diyār Bakr (the north and west), and Murād 'Irāq-i 'Ajam, Kirmān and Fārs (the centre and south).

Ismā'īl did not immediately invade the Āq Quyūnlū empire; instead, he led his men against the Shīrvānshāh. Two motives may have influenced his decision: the practical desire to test his army against a less formidable enemy before risking a pitched battle with the Āq Quyūnlū; and a psychological motive, namely, the desire to avenge the deaths of his father and grandfather at the hands of the rulers of Shīrvān. In December 1500, Ismā'īl crossed the river Kur and brought Farrukhyasār to battle near Fort Gulistān; Farrukhyasār was defeated and killed. Ismā'īl proceeded to the coast and captured Bākū, but marched back toward Nakhchivān on hearing the news that Alvand had crossed the Aras and was marching to meet him. The two armies met at Sharūr. Ismā'īl had only 7,000 men against Alvand's 30,000, but Ismā'īl's victory was so complete that some 8,000 Āq Quyūnlū fell in the battle. This decisive victory gave Ismā'īl control of Āẕarbāyjān. He entered Tabrīz, where he was crowned in the summer of 1501. Although Alvand was collecting another army at Arzinjān, and Murād remained undefeated in the south with a large army, the battle of Sharūr was in fact decisive. Ismā'īl had captured the Āq Quyūnlū capital, Tabrīz, and the Safavid revolution, after two centuries of preparation, was an accomplished fact. Coins were minted in Ismā'īl's name, but his most important action was to pronounce that the official religion of the new Safavid state would be Ithnā 'Asharī, or "Twelver", Shi'ism. The implications of this pronouncement, which changed the whole course of subsequent Iranian history, will be considered in the next chapter.

2

Theocratic state: the reign of Shāh Ismā'īl I (1501–1524)

The announcement by Shāh Ismā'īl at Tabrīz in 1501 that the Ithnā 'Asharī, or "Twelver", form of Shi'ism was to be the official religion of the newly established but not yet consolidated Safavid state was the single most important decision taken by Ismā'īl. As previously noticed, Ithnā 'Asharī Shi'ism lay at the heart of one of the bases of the power of the Safavid leaders, namely, their claim to be the representatives on earth of the 12th Imām or Mahdī (if not the Imām himself); the cult of 'Alī had been inextricably bound up with the development of Iran of Sufism, or Islamic esotericism, from at least the thirteenth century, and the position of *murshid-i kāmil*, or perfect spiritual director, was the second basis of the power of the Safavid leaders; finally, by asserting that 'Alī's younger son, Ḥusayn, married the daughter of Yazdigird III, the last of the Sasanid kings, Shī'īs had linked the family of 'Alī with the ancient Iranian monarchical tradition, and the divine right of the Iranian kings, deriving from their possession of the "kingly glory", was the third basis of the power of the Safavid shahs. Ithnā 'Asharī Shi'ism was therefore the most important element in Safavid religious propaganda and political ideology.

Shi'ism was, in origin, a political movement, the Shī'at 'Alī (Party of 'Alī), which supported the claim to the caliphate of 'Alī, the cousin and son-in-law of the Prophet Muḥammad. Shi'is believe that Muḥammad formally designated 'Alī as his successor (*khalīfa*) at a ceremony at Ghadīr Khumm in the year 632. Shī'īs therefore regard the first three caliphs (Abū Bakr, 'Umar and 'Uthmān) as usurpers, and the ritual cursing of these persons has always been a proper duty of Shī'īs, although the emphasis placed on it varied from time to time. In the early days of the Safavid state, when revolutionary fervour was still strong, great emphasis was placed on this ritual cursing. Safavid supporters known as

3. Shāh Ismāʻīl I

tabarrā'iyān (those who have pledged themselves body and soul to the shah), walked through the streets and bazaars cursing not only the three "rightly-guided" caliphs mentioned above, but also all enemies of ʻAlī and the other Imāms, and Sunnīs in general. Anyone who failed to respond without delay, "May it [the cursing] be more and not less!", was liable to be put to death on the spot.[1]

Despite the two centuries of propaganda carried out by the Safavids, the promulgation of Shiʻism as the state religion was fraught with danger, and some of Ismā'īl's advisers were worried about the reaction to his announcement. "Of the 200,000–300,000 people in Tabrīz," they said, "two-thirds are Sunnīs...we fear that the people may say they do not want a Shī'ī sovereign, and if (which God forbid!) the people reject Shi'ism, what can we do about it?" Ismā'īl's reply was uncompromising: he had been commissioned to perform this task, he said, and God and the immaculate Imāms were his companions; he feared no one. "With God's help," he said, "if the people utter one word of protest, I will draw the sword and leave not one of them alive." Brave words indeed; but the political reality was that the Āq Quyūnlū prince Alvand, defeated at the battle of Sharūr, was mobilising a fresh army in the Anatolian highlands, and in the south, Sulṭān Murād, another Āq Quyūnlū prince, had an army of 70,000 men, a force nearly six times larger than anything Ismā'īl could put into the field. Whatever he might say in public, Ismā'īl was worried about the outcome, but he was reassured by 'Alī in a dream: "O son, do not let anxiety trouble your mind...let all the *qizilbāsh* be present in the mosque fully armed, and let them surround the people; if, when the *khuṭba* [formal address in a mosque] is recited, the people make any movement, the *qizilbāsh* will be able to deal with the situation, since they surround the people."[2]

The imposition of Shi'ism on a country which, officially at least, was still predominantly Sunnī, obviously could not be achieved without incurring opposition, or without a measure of persecution of those who refused to conform. Disobedience was punishable by death, and the threat of force was there from the beginning. As far as the ordinary people were concerned, the existence of this threat seems to have been sufficient. The '*ulamā* were more stubborn. Some were put to death; many more fled to areas where Sunnism still prevailed – to the Timurid court at Harāt and, after the conquest of Khurāsān by the Safavids, to the Özbeg capital at Bukhārā.[3]

What were the benefits deriving from Ismā'īl's action? First, it harnessed the driving power of a dynamic religious ideology in the service of the new state, and thus gave the latter the strength to surmount its initial problems, and the momentum to carry it through the serious crises which faced the state after the death of Shāh Ismā'īl I in 1524. Second, it clearly differentiated the Safavid state from the Sunnī Ottoman empire, the major power in the

Islamic world in the sixteenth century, and thus gave it territorial and political identity. It can, of course, be argued that the establishment of a militant Shīʿī state on the Ottoman border was an act of provocation which made conflict with the Ottomans inevitable, and to that extent militated against the interests of Iran. It is improbable, however, that Ottoman imperialist aspirations would not have embraced Iran during the sixteenth century, the period of the greatest expansion of the Ottoman empire, whether or not the Safavid revolution had succeeded; the fact that it did succeed gave the Safavid state at least a chance of survival against the most formidable military machine ever seen in the world of Islam. In short, the imposition by the Safavids of Ithnā ʿAsharī Shiʿism as the official religion of the state had the effect of producing a greater awareness of national identity, and thus of creating a stronger and more centralised government.

Once Ismāʿīl had declared that Ithnā ʿAsharī Shiʿism was the official religion of the Safavid state, there was an urgent need to impose doctrinal uniformity by directing and accelerating the propagation of the Shīʿī faith. We are told that there was an acute shortage of works on Shīʿī jurisprudence, and that a religious judge produced a copy of an ancient manual on the fundamentals of the faith which served as a basis for religious instruction. There was also a shortage of Shīʿī *ʿulamā*, and Ismāʿīl was forced to import some Shīʿī theologians from Syria. To supervise the propagation of the Shīʿī faith, and to act as head of all the members of the religious classes, Ismāʿīl appointed an officer termed the *ṣadr*. The office of *ṣadr* had existed in the Timurid and Turcoman states; the important difference in this office in the Safavid state was that the *ṣadr* was a political appointee, and the office of *ṣadr* was used by the Safavid shahs as a means of controlling the religious classes. Since the Safavids equated belief in the right religion with loyalty to the state, it was necessary to root out heresy, and this task was also part of the duties of the *ṣadr*. Upon the successful imposition of doctrinal uniformity depended the smooth operation of the temporal arm of government and the ability of the state to survive hostile attacks by its Sunnī neighbours. This task, initially the chief part of the *ṣadr's* duties, had been largely achieved by the end of Ismāʿīl's reign; thereafter, the energies of the *ṣadr* were devoted mainly to the overall administration of the religious institution and to the supervision of *vaqf* property. As a result, the political influence of the *ṣadrs* declined.

The administrative system of the early Safavid state was complex: on the one hand, the Safavids were the inheritors of a bureaucratic system which resembled the traditional bureaucracy of a mediaeval Muslim state; on the other hand, Shāh Ismā'īl was faced by the problem of how to incorporate into the administrative system of the new state the tightly-knit Ṣūfī organisation of the Ṣafaviyya Order which had prepared the ground for, and had been responsible for the success of, the Safavid revolution. One of the basic problems which face all revolutionary leaders is, how to stop the revolution once the opposition has been overthrown, how to cool what Trotsky called the "red-hot atmosphere" of the revolutionary struggle and how to repair the administrative fabric of the state, restore law and order and return to economic prosperity. Inevitably, there are always those among the ranks of the revolutionaries who do not want life to return to normal, who wish to live in an atmosphere of permanent revolution and who want the revolution units to continue in existence as "organs of struggle and preparation for a new insurrection". Those who hold the power in the new state, however, wish to transform such units into "organs for consecrating the victory", and to bring them under the control of the central administration.[4] The problem was exacerbated by the fact that, even after the establishment of the Safavid state in 1501, fresh recruits, who were aflame with all the revolutionary zeal possessed by those who had brought the Safavids to power, kept arriving in Iran from Anatolia. Ismā'īl, in order to siphon off this excessive revolutionary fervour, dispatched a number of military expeditions to Anatolia, culminating in the major expedition under Nūr 'Alī Khalīfa in 1512. This force penetrated deep into Anatolia, sacked the town of Tuqāt, and inflicted several defeats on Ottoman armies. These attacks on Ottoman territory were one of the factors which led to the Ottoman invasion of Iran in 1514.

Another factor which complicated the situation confronting Shāh Ismā'īl in 1501 was the mutual antipathy between the Tājīk, or Iranian, elements in Safavid society, and the Turkish, or more properly Turcoman, tribal forces (*qizilbāsh*) which had been largely reponsible for bringing the Safavids to power but which in many cases came from outside the borders of Iran. Friction between these two elements was inevitable because, as Minorsky put it, the *qizilbāsh* "were no party to the national Iranian tradition. Like oil and water, the Turcomans and Persians did not mix freely, and the dual character of the population profoundly affected both the military and civil administration of Persia."[5] The Iranian elements were, in general, the "men of the pen" of classical Islamic society. They filled the ranks of the bureaucracy, and represented the long Iranian bureaucratic tradition which antedated Islam and which, after the islamisation of Iran, had provided administrative continuity under a succession of foreign rulers – Arabs, Turks, Mongols, Tatars and Turcomans. In the opinion of the *qizilbāsh*, Tājīks, or "non-Turks", a pejorative term they applied to Iranians, were only fit to look after accounts and administrative matters generally. They had no right to exercise military command, and the *qizilbāsh* considered it a dishonour to be ordered to serve under an Iranian officer. They, the *qizilbāsh*, were the "men of the sword". The Iranian view of the *qizilbāsh* was equally stereotyped. If *qizilbāsh* officers were given political posts, or encroached on administrative areas which the Iranians considered to be their own preserve, the latter resented it. Iranians did not expect the *qizilbāsh* to have a taste for poetry or the fine arts. Such pursuits were the prerogative of cultured and civilised gentlemen, in other words, the Iranians.

The perception each ethnic group had of the other was, of course, a stereotype, but had enough underlying reality to cause a power struggle between the two groups in the early Safavid state. What steps did Shāh Ismā'īl take to try and effect a synthesis of these disparate elements and to combine them into one harmonious administrative system? In the first place, he created the new office of *vakīl-i nafs-i nafīs-i humāyūn*. This officer was to be the vicegerent of the shah, and to represent him both in his spiritual capacity as *murshid-i kāmil*, or perfect spiritual director, of the Safavid Order, and in his temporal function as *pādishāh*, or king. The creation of this office clearly represented an attempt on the part of Ismā'īl to bridge the gap between a theocratic form of government and a bureaucratic one. Since the *qizilbāsh* considered that it was merely a fitting reward for their services to the Safavid cause that they should fill the principal offices of the Safavid state, it was natural that the first holder of this new office, initially the most powerful in the new state, should be one of their number, and Ismā'īl selected one of the *ahl-i ikhtiṣāṣ*, the "nucleus staff" of the Safavid Order mentioned earlier, the *qizilbāsh* officer Ḥusayn Beg Lala Shāmlū. The second action taken by Ismā'īl in his attempt to build a bridge between Turcoman and Tājīk was to make the *ṣadr*, the head of the religious classes, a political appointee; in so far as this arrangement gave the *ṣadr* political influence, he formed a link between the largely Iranian ranks of the '*ulamā* and the political branch of the administration, dominated during the early Safavid period by *qizilbāsh* military commanders.

Reference has been made to the theocratic nature of the Safavid state during the reign of Ismā'īl I, and to the strongly military character of the administration. These are perhaps the two most important aspects of the Safavid state between 1501 and 1514. The shah was the apex of the whole administrative structure. His rule was in theory absolute. He was the living emanation of the godhead, the Shadow of God upon earth. Since the ruler was considered to be directly appointed by God, his subjects were required to obey his commands whether these be just or unjust. As the representative of the Mahdī, the Safavid shah was closer to the source of absolute Truth than were other men, and consequently disobedience on the part of his subjects was sin. The prevalent view was that the imperfections of the ruler did not invalidate his authority as the lieutenant of God, the vicar of the Prophet, the successor of the Imāms and the representative of the Mahdī during the occultation of the latter. As we have seen, many of the *qizilbāsh* believed that Ismā'īl was the manifestation of God Himself. The inevitable result was that the shah's power was absolute; indeed, that astute seventeenth-century observer, the Huguenot jeweller Chardin, considered the power of the kings of Iran to be greater than that of any other monarch in the world. As an apparent paradox, but in reality a logical consequence in a society devoid of powerful municipal and corporate institutions enjoying a considerable measure of autonomy, the absolute nature of the shah's authority was not a threat to, but rather a guarantee of, the individual freedom and security of the lower classes of society. Sir John Malcolm put it succinctly: "If the shah is not feared," he said, "the nation suffers a great increase of misery under a multitude of tyrants."[6] It was the persons who stood between the shah and the mass of his people, the nobility, the court functionaries and the serried ranks of officials, both civil and military, lay and ecclesiastic (to use Western terms), on whom the shah's anger might be vented without warning, and who stood in constant fear of their lives. Anyone who held office in the state was considered to be the slave of the shah; his property, his life and the lives of his children, were at the disposal of the shah, who held the absolute power of "loosing and binding", to use the terminology of the time.

The predominantly military character of the early Safavid state derived from the circumstances attending the rise of the Safavids to power. It was what Minorsky termed the "dynamic ideology" of the Safavid movement that made converts to the Safavid cause, but this cause would not have achieved political power without the cutting edge of *qizilbāsh* swords. As already noted, the *qizilbāsh* were conscious of the debt due to them. The use of such terms to describe the Safavid state as *qalamraw-i qizilbāsh* (the *qizilbāsh* realm), *dawlat-i qizilbāsh* (the *qizilbāsh* state) and *mamlikat-i qizilbāsh* (the *qizilbāsh* kingdom), make this abundantly clear. Similarly, the shah is commonly referred to as *pādishāh-i qizilbāsh* (the king of the *qizilbāsh*), a term which appears to exclude altogether from consideration the king's Iranian subjects![7] It should occasion no surprise, therefore, that the *qizilbāsh* demanded, and obtained, the principal offices of state after the accession of Shāh Ismā'īl. As already mentioned, a *qizilbāsh* was appointed to the new office of *vakīl-i nafs-i nafīs-i humāyūn*, and thus became the most powerful person in the state after the shah. *Qizilbāsh* officers naturally filled the two highest military posts, that of *amīr al-umarā*, or commander-in-chief of the army, and that of *qūrchībāshī*. The function of the *qūrchībāshī*, who ultimately superseded the *amīr al-umarā* as commander-in-chief of the *qūrchīs* or *qizilbāsh* tribal regiments, is initially obscure. Thus, of the five principal offices of state under Ismā'īl I, three – and these the most important – were held by *qizilbāsh* officers. Iranians filled the office of *ṣadr*, and also that of *vazīr*. The *vazīr*, traditionally the head of the bureaucracy and hence one of the most powerful officers of state, was reduced to subordinate status during the reign of Ismā'īl I as a result of first, the creation of the office of *vakīl*, who became a sort of "super-minister", and second, the tendency of the two powerful military officers, the *amīr al-umarā* and *qūrchībāshī*, to encroach on the preserves of other officials and in general to have a considerable say in political affairs.

During the reign of Shāh Ismā'īl I, then, the various branches of government, religious, political and military, were not rigidly separated compartments. There was considerable overlapping of authority, and the relative importance of the chief offices varied from time to time. When dealing with this period, therefore, such terms as "civil", "military", "religious" and "political" must be used with caution, and must be construed within the context of the actual powers, so far as these can be determined, of the official concerned. Perhaps the most striking illustration of the effect of the domination of the polity by the military is the way in which members of the religious classes, such as *ṣadrs* and *qāżīs*, frequently held not only military rank but also military command.

When Ismā'īl was crowned at Tabrīz in 1501, he was master only of the province of Āẕarbāyjān; it took ten years for him to conquer the rest of Iran. He also captured Baghdād, but that city was not destined to remain in Safavid hands for long. The main stages in the expansion of the Safavid empire were: the defeat of the remaining Āq Quyūnlū forces near Hamadān (1503) (this gave Ismā'īl control of central and southern Iran); the subjugation of the Caspian provinces of Māzandarān and Gurgān and the capture of Yazd in the south-east (1504); the pacification of the western frontier and the annexation of Diyār Bakr (1505–7); the capture of Baghdād and the conquest of south-west Iran (1508); the subjugation of Shīrvān (1509/10); and the conquest of Khurāsān (1510), which had been wrested three years previously from the Timurids by the Özbegs of Transoxania. All these campaigns entailed hard, sometimes bitter, fighting; the campaign in Māzandarān in 1503/4 was conducted with especial ferocity, which may be accounted for by the fact that Ismā'īl's opponent, a local ruler named Amīr Ḥusayn Kiyā Chulāvī, was a Shī'ī and was therefore seen by Ismā'īl as a rival on the religious plane as well as the political; certainly his political aspirations were not in doubt, since he had given sanctuary to a large number of Āq Quyūnlū troops after Ismā'īl's victory near Hamadān in 1503. Ismā'īl's greatest victory, however, was undoubtedly won at the battle of Marv, on 2 December 1510. After their conquest of Khurāsān in 1507, the Özbegs had taken to raiding the province of Kirmān. When Ismā'īl protested against this action, the Özbeg leader Muḥammad Shībānī Khān sent a derisive reply, bidding Ismā'īl return to his ancestral calling of *darvīsh* (i.e., Ṣūfī). In November 1510, Ismā'īl marched into Khurāsān, and on 2

December succeeded in luring the Özbegs, who had taken refuge behind the walls of Marv, into a pitched battle. Muḥammad Shībānī Khān and 10,000 of his men were killed. Ismā'īl sent the head of the Özbeg chief to the Ottoman Sulṭān Bāyazīd II, and this act is said to have aroused a strong desire for revenge in the latter's son, Selim "the Grim". As a result of this victory, the province of Khurāsān was brought under Safavid control, and the city of Harāt became the second city of the empire and the seat of the heir-apparent.

Since ancient times, the legendary frontier between Iran, the land of the Aryans or Iranians, and Tūrān, the land of the Turkish peoples, had been the Oxus river. The Safavids would have liked to have made the Oxus the frontier of their empire in the north-east, but they were unable to hold the key city of Balkh. At all events, after the disastrous adventure of Ismā'īl I in Transoxania, the Safavids renounced all territorial ambitions the other side of the Oxus. In 1511, Ismā'īl was drawn into an attack on Samarqand through the ambition of the Timurid prince, Ẓahīr al-Din Bābur, to recover his Transoxanian dominions, from which he had been driven by the Özbegs. In return for Ismā'īl's help, Bābur promised to have coins struck in his name and have his name included in the *khuṭba*. Ismā'īl sent a force to the assistance of Bābur, who succeeded in capturing Samarqand in October 1511, and Bukhārā shortly afterwards. At this point, Bābur made the mistake of sending the Safavid troops home. In May 1512, the Özbegs returned, drove Bābur out of Bukhārā and besieged him in Ḥiṣār-i Shādmān. Ismā'īl sent a large army to his assistance, under the command of the *vakīl* Amīr Yār Aḥmad Iṣfahānī. The events which followed seemed to underline the failure of one of Ismā'īl's basic policies, namely, his attempt to reconcile the two antipathetic ethnic groups in the state, the *qizilbāsh* and the Iranians.

It will be recalled that Ismā'īl had created the office of *vakīl-i nafs-i nafīs-i humāyūn*, with the idea that the *vakīl* would be his *alter ego*, with authority second to his own in both political and religious matters. The importance he attached to this office is shown by the fact that the man he chose to hold it in 1501 was Ḥusayn Beg Lala Shāmlū, a *qizilbāsh* officer and one of the "nucleus staff" of the Safavid Order, that small group of trusted companions who had saved Ismā'īl from being captured by the

Āq Quyūnlū during the four and a half years of his concealment in Gīlān. After he had held the office of *vakīl* for six years, Ḥusayn Beg Shāmlū was dismissed by the Shāh and replaced by Amīr Najm, a goldsmith of Rasht and, what is much more to the point, an *Iranian*. The only reason offered by any of the sources for the dismissal of Ḥusayn Beg Shāmlū, namely, that the Shāh had lost confidence in him because he had been surprised by Kurds during his campaign of 1507 and had lost 300 men, does not carry conviction, for in 1508, shortly after his dismissal from the office of *vakīl*, we find him in command of the Safavid army in the campaign which led to the capture of Baghdād. The inescapable conclusion is that the dismissal of Ḥusayn Beg Shāmlū was simply a question of policy. Apparently Ismāʿīl had already begun to be apprehensive of the power of the *qizilbāsh* chiefs who had raised him to the throne only seven years previously. The appointment of an Iranian to the office of *vakīl* in 1508 was obviously an attempt to curb the power of the *qizilbāsh* and to produce a better balance between *qizilbāsh* and Tājīk in the upper echelons of the administration. Unfortunately, the new policy was no more successful than the first. Amīr Najm held office for only two years, but even during that time there were ominous rumblings of discontent from the *qizilbāsh*, who felt that their position had been weakened in a manner unacceptable to them. The Shāh, however, held to his course, and, when Amīr Najm died in 1509/10, appointed another Iranian to this office: Amīr Yār Aḥmad Iṣfahānī. The resentment of the *qizilbāsh* rapidly increased, and came to a head when the new *vakīl* was placed in command of the expedition to Transoxania in 1512. After some initial successes, the combined armies of Amīr Yār Aḥmad Iṣfahānī and Bābur laid siege to the fort of Ghujduvān. When supplies began to run short, Bābur and some of the *qizilbāsh amīrs* suggested that they should go into winter quarters and resume the offensive in the spring. The *vakīl* refused to agree. On 12 November 1512, a large Özbeg army arrived to relieve the fort, and at once gave battle. Either immediately before the battle, or just after battle had been joined, many of the leading *qizilbāsh amīrs* deserted, because of their hostility toward the *vakīl* and because they considered it a dishonour to serve under him. Bābur also fled. The *vakīl*, whose personal courage was greater than his political acumen, fought on and was captured by the Özbegs and executed on the spot. The remains of his army were totally routed, and the Özbegs swept on into Khurāsān, capturing the cities of Harāt and Mashhad. The following year, Ismā'īl restored the situation on the north-east frontier, and an uneasy truce with the Özbegs existed for about eight years. When the Shāh reached Khurāsān, he subjected to public ignominy the *qizilbāsh* commander who had been the first to flee from the field of Ghujduvān. Dada Beg Ṭālish had his beard shaved off, was dressed in women's clothes and paraded round the camp mounted on an ass. Had Dada Beg Ṭālish not been one of the *ahl-i ikhtiṣāṣ*, the "nucleus staff" of the Safavid Order to whom Ismā'īl owed so much, his punishment would doubtless have been even more severe; as it was, later the same day he was pardoned and given a robe of honour.

Despite the fact that the *débâcle* in Transoxania had been caused primarily by the bad blood between the *qizilbāsh* chiefs and their Iranian commander-in-chief, Ismā'īl persisted with his policy of appointing Iranians to the office of *vakīl*. This can only mean that, in the Shāh's mind, given a choice between continuing friction between Turks and Iranians regarding the highest office of the state, and concentrating all power once again in the hands of the *qizilbāsh*, the former was the less dangerous course. Between 1512 and his death in 1524, Ismā'īl made three more appointments to the *vikālat* (office of *vakīl*): in each case, an Iranian was appointed. The first was killed in battle in 1514. The second, Mīrzā Shāh Ḥusayn Iṣfahānī, acquired what was, in the eyes of the *qizilbāsh*, undue influence over the Shāh, and this once more fanned their resentment to the point of fury; this fury, initially held in check by their fear of the Shāh, finally would brook no control, and they murdered the *vakīl* in 1523 after several unsuccessful attempts.

There can be little doubt that Shāh Ismā'īl originally decided to appoint Iranians to the *vikālat* because he was apprehensive of the power of the *qizilbāsh* chiefs. It was a deliberate attempt on the part of the Shāh to integrate the Turkish and Iranian elements in the newly formed Safavid state. The *qizilbāsh*, however, were not able to reconcile themselves to the idea of the most powerful office in the state being in the hands of a Tājīk, and did not hesitate to commit murder in order to remove from the scene Iranians appointed to this post. The fact that the *qizilbāsh* seized control of the state immediately after Ismā'īl's death in 1524 shows that the threat to the Shāh's authority was a very real one. The failure of Ismā'īl's policy in this respect had serious consequences for the Safavid state in the long term.

The setback in Transoxania was soon overshadowed by the much more serious threat of an Ottoman invasion. The establishment on the eastern frontiers of the Sunnī Ottoman empire of a state with a militantly Shī'ī ideology constituted in itself a grave challenge to that empire. This was particularly so because of the presence within the borders of the Ottoman empire of large numbers of Turcomans who sympathised with Shāh Ismā'īl's pretensions to quasi-divine status and supported his attempt to establish a Shī'ī state in Iran. They constituted what in more recent times would have been referred to as a "fifth column". The danger of their being seduced by Safavid propaganda was all the greater because the Ottomans had originally been backed by much the same kind of heterodox Sufism as constituted the basis of Safavid power. Although, during the fourteenth century, the Ottoman sulṭāns "gradually adopted a civilised palace life", and "came more and more under orthodox influences",[8] their subjects in the remote mountainous areas of eastern Anatolia, adjacent to the Iranian border, continued to belong to a wide variety of extremist Shī'ī sects which, in order to protect themselves from persecution by the Ottoman government as schismatics, later "gained the right of asylum under the all-embracing and tolerant umbrella of the Bektāshī organisation".[9] The Turcoman tribesmen who belonged to these Shī'ī groups had constituted fertile ground for Safavid propaganda; they venerated Ismā'īl and flocked to his standard in thousands. During the almost five years that Ismā'īl had spent in hiding in Lāhījān (1494–9), he had maintained constant contact with these *murīds* (disciples) in Anatolia by means of an extensive network of officers termed *khalīfa*, *dada*, *lala* and *pīra*. Disciples had constantly made their way to Gīlān to take gifts and offerings to their *murshid-i kāmil* (perfect spiritual director). In the late summer of 1499, when Ismā'īl had made his bid for power, the first contingents of troops to join him were Turcoman Ṣūfīs largely from Anatolia. In the spring of 1500, when Ismā'īl sent out his couriers from Ardabīl to summon his followers to the rendezvous at Arzinjān, his messengers were received with enthusiasm. The Ustājlū tribe, for example, "with one accord came with their wives and children, and they were

1,000 families...and when people from other districts heard that the Ustājlū tribe had come in this manner everyone became inclined [to follow their example]; they came, company by company, until their numbers reached 7,000".[10] There is no doubt that the active subversion of large numbers of Ottoman subjects in Anatolia by the politico-religious propaganda of the Safavids was the principal reason for the outbreak of war between the two states. "Had the Ottomans not put an abrupt and decisive end to this process their hold on vast areas in the Eastern parts of their realm would have been greatly jeopardised, and the Shi'a doctrine would have registered one of its most resounding successes."[11] Faced with the possibility that eastern Anatolia might be detached from allegiance to the Ottoman state, Bāyazīd II in 1502 ordered the deportation of large numbers of Shī'īs from Anatolia to the Morea. In 1511, a large-scale Shī'ī revolt at Tekke, on the Mediterranean coast of Asia Minor, emphasised that the danger still existed, and the same year a substantial number of Takkalū tribesmen from Karmiyān arrived in Iran to reinforce Ismā'īl's army. These two incidents show that the Safavid ideology had a strong hold, not only in eastern, but also in central, Anatolia.

The actual *casus belli* were two: the campaign in eastern Anatolia waged by Nūr 'Alī Khalīfa in 1512 with a Safavid force levied on the spot from among the Ṣūfīs of the Safavid Order; and the support given by Shāh Ismā'īl to Selim's rivals after the death of Sulṭān Bāyazīd in the same year. Ismā'īl supported first the legal heir, Aḥmad and, after Aḥmad had been put to death by Selim, Aḥmad's son Murād. Ismā'īl planned to use Murād to mobilise opposition to Selim but, when the expected support for Murād failed to materialise, the scheme was abandoned. Murād was granted asylum in Iran, and subsequently died at Kāshān. Sulṭān Selim, once firmly established on the Ottoman throne, immediately began preparations for the invasion of Iran with an army the size of which was remarkable in Middle East warfare of the period: 200,000 men. In order to secure his rear, before he marched he "proscribed Shi'ism in his dominions and massacred all its adherents on whom he could lay hands".[12] The number of Shī'īs put to death at that time is said to be 40,000, but this is probably a conventional figure merely indicating a large number. Those who were not put to death were branded and sent to Ottoman territory in Europe.

Sulṭān Selim reached Sīvās on 1 July 1514; there, he reviewed his troops and disbanded some of the less battleworthy units. Then he advanced slowly along the highroad to Arzinjān, through an area which had been systematically devastated by the Safavid Governor-General of Diyār Bakr, Muḥammad Khān Ustājlū. On 22 August 1514 the Ottoman army reached the plain of Chāldirān, north-west of Khvuy in Āẕarbāyjān, and the following day the Safavid army attacked.

Widely differing figures for the size of the opposing armies at the crucial battle of Chāldirān are given by both Iranian and Turkish sources, but the figures given by the Ottoman historian Ḥakīm al-Dīn Bitlīsī are probably close to the mark: Ottoman army, 100,000; Safavid army, 40,000. Shāh Ismā'īl possessed two commanders, Muḥammad Khān Ustājlū and Nūr 'Alī Khalīfa, who had had first-hand experience of Ottoman methods of warfare. Their advice was to attack at once, before the Ottomans had had time to complete their defensive laager. Muḥammad Khān Ustājlū also counselled against a frontal attack, because of the strength of the Ottoman artillery. Unfortunately for the Safavid cause, this sound advice was rejected both by a senior *qizilbāsh* commander, Dūrmīsh Khān Shāmlū, and by Ismā'īl himself. Dūrmīsh Khān Shāmlū had a privileged position at court because of his connections; his father had been one of the *ahl-i ikhtiṣāṣ*, or special companions, of Shāh Ismā'īl, and his mother was the Shāh's sister. He rudely rebuffed Muḥammad Khān Ustājlū with the words, "Diyār Bakr is *your* bailiwick",[13] and made the extraordinary proposal that, instead of attacking at once, the Safavid forces should wait until the Ottomans had completed their dispositions (presumably on the ground that it would not be sporting to attack them sooner). The Shāh, instead of treating his suggestion with derision, endorsed it: "I am not a caravan-thief," he said; "Whatever is decreed by God, will occur."[14] In later years, Ismā'īl's son, Shāh Ṭahmāsp, is said to have cursed the name of Dūrmīsh Khān whenever the battle of Chāldirān was mentioned.

The Ottomans were thus able to organise their laager or *wagenburg* at their leisure. Twelve thousand janissaries,[15] armed with muskets, were stationed behind a barrier formed of gun-carriages linked together by chains. This barrier presented an insuperable obstacle to the Safavid army, composed as it was almost entirely of cavalry. The sources give conflicting accounts of the course of the actual battle. It appears that the Safavid right wing, led by Shāh Ismā'īl in person, routed the Ottoman left and killed its commander, Ḥasan Pasha. The Ottoman centre, however, where the janissaries and the bulk of the artillery were stationed, remained intact. Ottoman firepower, consisting of 200 cannon and 100 mortars, was now brought into play with devastating effect. Muḥammad Khān Ustājlū, in command of the Safavid left, was killed, and his men fell back in disorder. Ismā'īl rallied his troops and led them in heroic, but vain, charges against the Ottoman laager; from behind cover the Ottoman gunners directed a deadly fire on the Safavid cavalry to which the latter had no answer. After suffering further heavy casualties, Ismā'īl was forced to break off the engagement. Casualty figures given by the sources are unreliable, but the extent of the disaster for the Safavids may be judged from the list of high-ranking *qizilbāsh* officers killed at Chāldirān: they included Ḥusayn Beg Lala Shāmlū, the former *vakīl-i nafs-i nafīs-i humāyūn*; Sārū Pīra Ustājlū, the *qūrchībāshī*; a number of provincial governors; the Amīr Niẓām al-Dīn 'Abd al-Bāqī, the *ṣadr*; and a former *ṣadr*. The Ottoman losses were not negligible: as Knolles puts it quaintly in his *General History of the Turks*, "besides his common footmen, of whom he made least reckoning, he [Selim] lost most part of his Illirian, Macedonian, Servian, Epirot, Thessalian and Thracian horsemen, the undoubted flower and strength of his army, which were in that mortall battel almost all slaine or grievously wounded".[16] When Shāh Ismā'īl left the battlefield, Sulṭān Selim, thinking that his withdrawal was a ruse, did not pursue him. Later, he marched to Tabrīz, the Safavid capital, which he occupied on 5 September 1514. He proposed to winter in Iran and complete the subjugation of Iran the following spring, but his officers mutinously refused to winter at Tabrīz and, eight days after he had entered Tabrīz, Selim marched out and went into winter quarters at Amasya.

Some authorities have seen the Ottoman victory at Chāldirān as primarily a triumph of logistics. It was, of course, an impressive feat to move such a large army, equipped with such a formidable number of guns, over a distance in excess of 1,000 miles from Istanbul to the plain of Chāldirān, the last part of the route passing through extremely mountainous terrain. Indeed, 60,000 camels are said to have carried the provisions for the army, and the commissariat department alone numbered 5,000 men. The decisive factor in the Ottoman victory was, however, their firepower, as the contemporary account by Caterino Zeno, Venetian ambassador to the court of Ūzūn Ḥasan, testifies:

The monarch [Selim], seeing the slaughter, began to retreat, and to turn about, and was about to fly, when Sinan, coming to the rescue at the time of need, caused the artillery to be brought up and fired on both the janissaries [*sic*] and the Persians. The Persian horses hearing the thunder of those infernal machines, scattered and divided themselves over the plain, not obeying their riders' bit or spur any more, from the terror they were in.... It is certainly said, that if it had not been for the artillery, which terrified in the manner related the Persian horses which had never before heard such a din, all his forces would have been routed and put to the edge of the sword.[17]

D. Ayalon writes:

Had the Ottomans not employed firearms on such a large scale in the battle of Chāldirān and in the battles which followed it, it is reasonably certain that their victory – even if they had been able to win – would have been far less decisive. In other words, the Ottomans would have acquired far less Safawid territory in that event and a much stronger Safawid army would have been left intact to prepare for a war of revenge.... At Chāldirān...Ottoman artillery and arquebuses wrought havoc among the ranks of the Safawis who had no similar arms with which to reply.[18]

Why was Shāh Ismā'īl's army not equipped with firearms? Unlike the Ottomans, who were the first Muslim state to adopt firearms and to use them on a large scale, the Safavids, at the time of Ismā'īl I, thought the use of firearms unmanly and cowardly. The Mamlūks of Syria and Egypt similarly remained wedded to their cavalry, and were similarly defeated by the Ottomans a few years after the battle of Chāldirān. Ismā'īl's failure to use cannon and hand-guns was certainly not due to ignorance of these weapons, although this is often asserted. The myth that firearms were first introduced into Iran nearly a century later, by two English gentlemen–adventurers, Sir Anthony Sherley and Sir Robert Sherley, has been a persistent one, but the evidence in both the European and the Persian sources makes it clear that this claim is entirely without foundation. In Europe, cannon were invented earlier than hand-guns. By the second half of the fourteenth century, artillery was being used by all the principal military powers in Europe, including England, Spain and Portugal. This new weapon, which revolutionised the whole art of warfare, was adopted by the Ottomans about 1420; by the time of the siege of Constantinople in 1453, they had become so adept in its use that they were casting cannon of gigantic size.

Contrary to the generally accepted tradition, the rulers of Iran were not ignorant of these developments, although their contacts with Europe were naturally not as close as were those of the Ottoman empire. In 1471, the Signory of Venice dispatched to the Āq Quyūnlū ruler Ūzūn Ḥasan a consignment of firearms which was intercepted at Cyprus. Two years later, in 1473, the Ottomans gave Ūzūn Ḥasan a practical demonstration of the use of artillery when they defeated him on the Upper Euphrates. Ūzūn Ḥasan appealed to Venice for assistance, and in 1478 the Venetians sent him "one hundred artillerymen of experience and capacity".[19] Possibly as a result of the efforts of these men, we find the Āq Quyūnlū prince Khalīl, in the same year, using cannon against a rival, and there are numerous references to the use of cannon in siege-warfare by the Āq Quyūnlū from that time on. The first recorded use of cannon by the Safavids is in 1488, when the Safavid leader Ḥaydar used siege-guns against the fort of Gulistān; this was twenty-six years before the battle of Chāldirān. The main points to note in regard to the use of cannon by the Iranians are, first, they adopted them with reluctance, and, second, unlike the Ottomans, they never made effective use of them in the field, but tended to restrict their use to siege-warfare. Hand-guns first appeared in Europe early in the fifteenth century, and were adopted by the Ottomans very soon afterwards. The early hand-guns were either matchlocks or arquebuses. Once again, the Ottomans had a clear lead over other Islamic states in the Middle East in the use of the new weapons. It is worth noting that, even in Europe, there was considerable resistance to their use. Hand-guns seem to have been in use in Iran by 1478; in other words, although a later invention than cannon, they may have reached Iran about the same time as the latter.

The inescapable conclusion, then, is that the Safavids did not use firearms at Chāldirān because they did not choose to use them. As a result of their attitude to firearms, they suffered a grave defeat at the hands of the Ottomans which might well have been fatal to the nascent Safavid state, then only thirteen years old. That their defeat did not result in the occupation of a large part, or perhaps the whole, of the Safavid empire, was due in part to the success of their scorched earth policy in the path of the Ottoman advance. The unwillingness of the Ottoman troops to winter at Tabrīz was due largely to the lack of provisions for themselves and their horses and baggage-animals. The lack of supplies was particularly serious because the Ottoman army was at the end of immensely long lines of communication which were stretched to the limit. As a result of their defeat at Chāldirān, the Safavids were thrown on to the defensive in their long-drawn-out struggle with the Ottomans, and did not regain the initiative for three-quarters of a century, until the reign of Shāh 'Abbās the Great. The crucial nature of the battle of Chāldirān was not lost upon contemporary observers: "if the Turk had been beaten, the power of Ismā'īl would have become greater than that of Tamerlane, as by the fame alone of such a victory he would have made himself absolute lord of the East".[20]

The immediate effect of the Safavid defeat at Chāldirān was the loss of the province of Diyār Bakr, which was annexed to the Ottoman empire in 1516/17. The Ottomans also put an end to the Ẕu'l-Qadar dynasty of Mar'ash and Albistān, and those regions too were absorbed into their empire. Far more serious than the loss of territory was the psychological effect of the defeat on Shāh Ismā'īl himself, and its effect on his relations with the *qizilbāsh*. Chāldirān was Ismā'īl's first defeat. "Since in his experience he had always been victorious, and his enemies defeated and conquered, he considered no adversary his equal, and thought himself invincible; the defeat at Chāldirān had a profound effect on Ismā'īl's character and behaviour; his egotism and arrogance were changed to despair and dejection"; so wrote Naṣr Allāh Falsafī, the principal Iranian historian of the Safavids in recent times.[21] According to Falsafī, Ismā'īl went into mourning after his defeat. He wore black robes and a black turban; the military standards were died black, and were emblazoned with the inscription *al-qiṣāṣ* (retribution). During the remaining ten years of his reign, Ismā'īl never once led his troops into action in person, despite the fact that both the Özbegs and his former ally Bābur, now a rising power and destined in 1526 to capture Delhi and Agra and found the Mogul empire in India, seized the key frontier cities of Balkh and Qandahār respectively. Nor did Ismā'īl devote his attentions to affairs of state as in the past. On the contrary, he seems to have tried to drown his sorrows by drunken debauches. As one Safavid chronicle puts it: "most of his time was spent in hunting, or in the company of rosy-cheeked youths, quaffing goblets of purple wine, and listening to the strains of music and song".[22]

Chāldirān shattered the belief of the *qizilbāsh* in their leader as a divine or semi-divine figure who was invincible. The mystical bond linking *murshid* (spiritual director) and *murīd* (disciple) had been snapped, and could not be repaired. Although the *qizilbāsh* continued to accord their leader the title of *murshid*, the title had become meaningless except for ritualistic purposes. Similarly, although traces of the original Ṣūfī organisation persisted in a fossilised form, they rapidly ceased to have any organic function within the Safavid body politic. The *qizilbāsh* tacitly dissociated themselves from the *murshid–murīd* relationship and began to behave like the mediaeval feudal barons whom they in some respects resembled. This view is supported by the fact that, only two years after Chāldirān, the *qizilbāsh* Governor-General of Khurāsān made a powerful challenge to Ismā'īl's authority, and by the fact that, within a year of Ismā'īl's death, civil war broke out between rival *qizilbāsh* tribes fighting for control of the state with little or no regard for the sancrosanct nature of the Shāh's person, and but scant appreciation of the supposedly absolute character of the Shāh's authority, in both its spiritual and temporal aspects. Iskandar Beg Munshī, the author of the greatest of all Safavid histories entitled *Tārīkh-i 'Ālam-ārā-yi 'Abbāsī*, written about a century after Chāldirān, makes the following fascinating comment on the Safavid defeat:

> Without doubt God, in His most excellent wisdom, had decreed that Shāh Ismā'īl should suffer a reverse at the battle of Chāldirān, for had he been victorious in this battle too, there would have been a danger that the belief and faith of the unsophisticated *qizilbāsh* in the authority of the Shāh would have reached such heights that their feet might have strayed from the straight path of religious faith and belief, and they might have fallen into serious error.[23]

This is indeed a valiant attempt to rationalise the Safavid defeat, but in the eyes of Sunnī Muslims, of course, the *qizilbāsh* had fallen into "serious error" long before Chāldirān.

Ismā'īl's abdication of his responsibilities in regard to the personal direction of the affairs of state after Chāldirān gave certain officials the opportunity to increase their own power proportionately. Many of the highest-ranking *qizilbāsh* officers had been killed at Chāldirān, and so *qizilbāsh* power was temporarily in eclipse. This allowed an official whose status had been downgraded by the creation of the office of *vakīl*, and by the dominant position of *qizilbāsh* military officers in the Safavid administrative system during the first decade of Ismā'īl's rule, to come to the fore: this official was the *vazīr*, the head of the bureaucracy and traditionally an Iranian. The evidence is contradictory as to whether Mīrzā Shāh Ḥusayn Iṣfahānī, appointed by the Shāh to succeed the *vakīl* Amīr 'Abd al-Bāqi, slain at Chāldirān, received the title of *vakīl* or was simply styled *vazīr*. What is certain is that there was a radical change in the character of the *vikālat* after Chāldirān. The original title of *vakīl-i nafs-i nafīs-i humāyūn*, indicating that the *vakīl* was the *alter ego* of the shah, is not recorded after Chāldirān; henceforth, the term used is simply *vakīl*, unembellished, or at best *vakīl-i salṭana*, a significant change indicating that the *vakīl*'s loyalty is now not so much to the person of the shah as to the state. The important development after Chāldirān is that what Minorsky called the "excessive prerogatives of a Vice-Roy" underwent considerable modification. The *vakīl*, even when so termed, was now regarded primarily as the head of the bureaucracy, in other words, as a *vazīr*. For a time, the *vakīl* continued to exist as a sort of superior *vazīr*, the *vazīr* proper still being regarded as inferior in rank. Once the *vakīl*'s *raison d'être* had ceased to exist, however, it was only a short time before the title itself fell into abeyance. This development marked a decisive step away from the original theocratic concept of the state, and toward a greater separation of religious and secular powers within the state. At all events, Mīrzā Shāh Ḥusayn took advantage of the Shāh's withdrawal from the day-to-day management of affairs to enhance his own authority. By becoming a boon companion of the Shāh in the drinking bouts in which Ismā'īl indulged with increasing frequency after Chāldirān, he acquired great – the *qizilbāsh* thought undue – influence over the Shāh. As a contemporary chronicle put it: "All the *amīrs* [military commanders] and pillars of the state, and all the *vazīrs* and nobles of the court, were ordered to obey him and, putting the saddle-cloth of obedience on their shoulders, were enjoined not to enter upon any affairs, whether important or trivial, without informing him and obtaining his advice."[24]

In 1521, Mīrzā Shāh Ḥusayn demonstrated his power by turning the tables on his former master, the high-ranking *qizilbāsh* chief Dūrmīsh Khān Shāmlū. It was one of the strengths of the administrative system of the early Safavid state that, when military officers were appointed to provincial governorships (as was the normal practice during the reigns of Shāh Ismā'īl and Shāh Ṭahmāsp), they proceeded to the seat of their governorate and personally administered the province under their jurisdiction. Dūrmīsh Khān Shāmlū was an exception. When he was appointed Governor of Iṣfahān in 1503, he had remained at court like any seventeenth-century French noble at Versailles, and had delegated one of his retainers, a certain architect at Iṣfahān named Mīrzā Shāh Ḥusayn, to act as his *vazīr* and deputy there and look after the administration for him. No doubt the fact that Dūrmīsh Khān Shāmlū was the Shāh's nephew gave him a privileged position at court, where he obtained the office of *ishīk-āqāsī* of the Supreme *Dīvān*, or Master of Ceremonies. In 1517, he was appointed *lala* (guardian) of Ismā'īl's second son, Sām Mīrzā. His continued presence at court was irksome to Mīrzā Shāh Ḥusayn, since it was a constant reminder of his own humble origins; but the former servant had now risen above his master, despite the fact that Dūrmīsh Khān was distinguished among the *qizilbāsh* chiefs by his close relationship to and intimacy with the Shāh, and in 1521 Mīrzā Shāh Ḥusayn succeeded in getting Dūrmīsh Khān sent to Harāt as governor. In the end, Mīrzā Shāh Ḥusayn overreached himself and, in April 1523, was assassinated by a group of *qizilbāsh*, thus adding his name to the list of those who had become victims of the struggle between Turk and Iranian in the early Safavid state.

A year later, on 23 May 1524, Shāh Ismā'īl I, the founder of the Safavid state, died, and was buried in the family mausoleum at Ardabīl. He was two months short of his thirty-seventh birthday at the time of his death, and had reigned for nearly twenty-three years. When he came to the throne in 1501, at the age of fourteen, he had been at once faced by problems of great complexity: the problem of how to incorporate the Ṣūfī organisation of the Safavid Order, of which he was the *murshid-i kāmil* (perfect spiritual director), in the administrative system of the new state, of which he was the king. There was the problem of how to reconcile the "men of the sword", the Turcoman military élite which had brought him to power, with the "men of the pen", the Iranian bureaucrats with a long tradition of professional expertise, on whom he depended for the smooth functioning of the state. There was the problem of how to encourage Shīʿī militancy while at the same time preventing the religious classes from becoming the dominant power in the state. There was the problem of first consolidating Safavid rule within the traditional boundaries of Iran, and then of defending these frontiers against powerful Sunnī neighbours to the east and to the west. Ismāʿīl possessed charismatic appeal, the gift of leadership and personal bravery, though as a general he lacked both the caution and the tactical and strategic brilliance of his descendant ʿAbbās I. He also possessed a high degree of statecraft and political wisdom. Although his imaginative and often ingenious solutions to the problems listed above were frequently successful in the short term rather than the long, this postulates not so much the inadequacy of the solutions as the intractability of the problems.

3

Internal dissensions and external foes: the Safavid state from 1524 to 1588

During the last decade of the reign of Ismā'īl I, there had been a movement away from the theocratic form of government which had been a distinctive feature of the early Safavid state. There had been a general trend toward the separation of religious and political powers, and toward the reduction of the influence of the *qizilbāsh* in state affairs. As noted in the previous chapter, there had been a change in the status of the *vakīl*. From 1508 onwards, the Shāh had not appointed a *qizilbāsh* chief to this high office. From 1514 onwards, there was a subtle change in the nature of the office; there was tendency to lay less emphasis on the special position of the *vakīl* as the vicegerent of the shah, and to regard him rather as simply the head of the bureaucracy, in other words, as a *vazīr*. Ismā'īl had also taken steps to reduce the status of the office of *amīr al-umarā*, or commander-in-chief, another of the principal offices of state held by the *qizilbāsh*. In 1509/10, Ḥusayn Beg Lala Shāmlū (who had initially combined this office with that of *vakīl*) was dismissed from his position as *amīr al-umarā*. Ismā'īl did not replace him by another high-ranking *qizilbāsh* chief, but awarded this important office to an unknown officer, Muḥammad Beg Ustājlū, who held the comparatively humble position of *sufrachī* (sewer). Muḥammad Beg was promoted to the rank of *sulṭān* and given the title of Chāyān Sulṭān, in order to give him a status more suitable to the holder of the position of commander-in-chief.[1] An even more significant fact is that Chāyān Sulṭān was given not only Ḥusayn Beg Shāmlū's office, but his tribal district (*ulkā*) and retainers as well. This action by the Shāh struck at the root of the *qizilbāsh* tribal organisation. The great *qizilbāsh* tribes, termed *ūymāq*, were subdivided into as many as eight or nine clans, and the basis of the fighting spirit of the *qizilbāsh* was their fierce tribal loyalty (*ta'aṣṣub-i ūymāqiyyat*; *ta'aṣṣub-i qizilbāshiyyat*). It would be impossible for the new *amīr al-umarā*, an Ustājlū, to command from Shāmlū tribesmen support in any way comparable to that which he naturally would receive from members of his tribe. The move appears to have been successful from Ismā'īl's point of view, for we hear nothing of note about Chāyān Sulṭān, though he held office until his death in 1523. The particular significance of Ismā'īl's action is that it foreshadows the methods used later by Shāh 'Abbās the Great to curb the power of the *qizilbāsh*.

Ṭahmāsp, Shāh Ismā'īl's eldest son, had been born on 22 February 1514. He was therefore only ten years and three months old when he succeeded his father on the throne. The *qizilbāsh* were not slow in seizing their opportunity to reverse the trend toward giving Iranians a larger share in the governance of the state. They took over control of the state and usurped the authority of the Shāh for a decade. A *qizilbāsh* chief, Dīv Sulṭān Rūmlū, summoned his fellow-*amīrs* to a gathering of the clans. At this gathering, Dīv Sulṭān Rūmlū displayed the testamentary disposition of the late Shāh appointing himself *amīr al-umarā* and guardian of the young Shāh Ṭahmāsp. To denote this latter function of regent, the old title of *atābeg*, used by the Seljuq Turks and the Turcoman rulers of Iran in the fifteenth century, was revived. The bulk of the chiefs of the Rūmlū, Takkalū and Ẕu'l-Qadar tribes agreed to recognise Dīv Sulṭān as their leader and elder (*rīsh-safīd*: literally, "grey-beard"). Two of the leading Shāmlū *amīrs*, Dūrmīsh Khān, Governor of Harāt, and Zaynal Khān, Governor of Astarābād, sent pledges of support and urged other Shāmlū chiefs to do the same. Some Ustājlū *amīrs* also joined Dīv Sulṭān, but the majority of the chiefs of that tribe, led by Köpek Sulṭān Ustājlū, the brother of the former *amīr al-umarā* Chāyān Sulṭān, ranged themselves against the new regent. The Ustājlūs had the advantage of being in control of the capital, Tabrīz. Some of Köpek Sulṭān's supporters urged him to challenge the regent in the field, but Köpek Sulṭān demurred: "We are both slaves of the Shāh," he said, "and devotees of the same threshold; we will not contend with each other."[2]

The regent, however, was not only an able military commander but an astute politician, and he completely outmanoeuvred the Ustājlū chief. In the autumn of 1525, the regent advanced on Tabrīz, and sent a message to the Ustājlūs to the effect that the late Shāh had entrusted him, Dīv Sulṭān, who was one of the veteran Ṣūfīs of the Ṣafavid house, with the care of the young Ṭahmāsp, and had taken solemn oaths from the other *amīrs* that they would not act contrary to his (Dīv Sulṭān's) judgement. It was therefore incumbent on them all, he said, to respect Shāh Ismā'īl's will, and he called on the Ustājlū *amīr* to come forth from Tabrīz and meet him. Otherwise, he said, civil war would break out, and the enemies of Iran would get the chance for which they had been waiting for years. The Ustājlū *amīrs*, reflecting on the dishonour which would attach to their name if they refused, agreed to meet the regent. Dīv Sulṭān at once put to death two *qizilbāsh* chiefs, one an Ustājlū and the other a Qājār, whom he accused of fomenting the dissension between himself and the Ustājlūs, and set up a triumvirate consisting of himself, Chūha Sulṭān Takkalū and Köpek Sulṭān Ustājlū. Not only was Köpek Sulṭān disappointed in his hopes of becoming a joint *de facto* ruler of the state with Dīv Sulṭān, but it rapidly became apparent that his role was to be like that of Lepidus in the celebrated triumvirate of Octavius, Mark Antony and Lepidus in 43 B.C. If Chūha Sulṭān affixed his seal to documents, this was held to signify the agreement of Köpek Sulṭān as well. Worse than that, Dīv Sulṭān and Chūha Sulṭān aimed to deprive the Ustājlū chiefs of the possibility of any effective opposition to themselves, by systematically dispersing them to their fiefs. Köpek Sulṭān, realising that, as a result of this underhand dealing, his position was untenable, withdrew to his fiefs at Nakhchivān and Erīvān; another version is that Dīv Sulṭān sent him with an expedition to raid Georgia. Whether Köpek Sulṭān's departure from centre stage was voluntary or not, his fellow-triumvirs took advantage of his absence to expropriate most of the lands which had been assigned to the Ustājlū tribe in the form of *tiyūl*.[3]

This arbitrary action on the part of the regent and Chūha Sulṭān precipitated the civil war. In the spring of 1526, only twenty-five years after the coronation of Shāh Ismā'īl at Tabrīz, the rival factions clashed near Sulṭāniyya in Āẕarbāyjān, and the Ustājlūs were put to flight and forced to take refuge in the forests of Gīlān. The following year, Köpek Sulṭān re-emerged, seized Ardabīl, where he killed the aged governor, Bādinjān Sulṭān Rūmlū, and marched on Tabrīz. In a pitched battle with his fellow-triumvirs near Sharūr,[4] he was defeated and killed, and the surviving Ustājlūs fled back to the forests.

The civil war had already been extremely detrimental to the state; as one chronicle puts it: "the body politic was destitute of administration and order, and confusion rent the country".[5] Many of the *qizilbāsh* chiefs stationed in Khurāsān had been drawn into the war, and the Özbegs, always eager to exploit any weakness on the north-east frontier, seized Ṭūs and Astarābād and roamed at will in other parts of Khurāsān. Much worse was to come. Chūha Sulṭān suggested to Ṭahmāsp that the regent, Dīv Sulṭān, was the real cause of the discord between the *qizilbāsh*, and it would be advisable to get rid of him. On 5 July 1527, when the regent entered the *dīvān*, the young Shāh shot an arrow at him which, despite Ṭahmāsp's lack of strength, struck the regent on the chest; at a signal from Ṭahmāsp, Dīv Sulṭān was then dispatched by the guards. Chūha Sulṭān thus emerged as the real ruler of the state. The administration of affairs was entirely in his hands, and Ṭahmāsp was king in name only. At first, Chūha Sulṭān's position seemed unassailable. He scored a diplomatic success by persuading some of the alienated Ustājlū chiefs to return to their allegiance to the Shāh; they were received at Qazvīn by the Shāh and each was assigned land and an office as befitted his position. The surviving triumvir handed out most of the land in the provinces in the form of assignments to members of his own tribe, the Takkalūs.

On the north-east frontier, the city of Harāt had been under siege by the Özbegs under 'Ubayd Allāh Khān for some months and, in the summer of 1528, with the civil war apparently over, Shāh Ṭahmāsp marched to its relief. Near Jām, the Safavid army was confronted by an Özbeg force overwhelmingly superior in numbers. According to one report, some of the *qizilbāsh* chiefs, including Chūha Sulṭān, in command of the right wing, were so overawed by the size of the Özbeg army that they fled from the field; another version states that Chūha Sulṭān remained on the field but exhibited cowardice later. The latter account states that the Takkalūs on the Safavid right were shattered by a charge made by the Özbeg commander Jānī Beg Sulṭān, and fled from the field followed by the troops forming the Safavid left. Ṭahmāsp alone stood firm, in the Safavid centre, thus demonstrating for the second time that he was not as malleable as some of *qizilbāsh* chiefs had thought. The Shāh ordered a counter-attack by the Safavid centre, composed of S̲h̲āmlūs and Z̲u'l-Qadars, and in the mêlée the Özbeg chief himself, 'Ubayd Allāh Khān, was wounded, and his men left the field in disorder. Meanwhile Jānī Beg Sulṭān, who had broken through the Safavid right and had been plundering in the Safavid rear, came near Ṭahmāsp's standard under the impression that it was that of 'Ubayd. Ṭahmāsp at once made to attack him but Chūha Sulṭān, kneeling in a most unmanly fashion, urged they should await the return of the *qizilbāsh* who had left the field.

Shāh Ṭahmāsp, though no doubt disgusted by Chūha Sulṭān's conduct, must have decided that his own personal position was as yet too insecure for him to make a move against the triumvir, because Chūha Sulṭān continued to direct the affairs of state. The situation at Harāt remained critical, because the Özbegs had resumed the siege of the city as soon as the royal army left Khurāsān. The Governor of Harāt, Ḥusayn Khān Shāmlū, whose conduct at the battle of Jām had been in marked contrast to that of Chūha Sulṭān, was desperately short of supplies; eventually, in the absence of any assistance from Tabrīz, he was forced to negotiate with 'Ubayd Allāh Khān. Chūha Sulṭān delayed the dispatch of a relief force to Harāt out of pure vindictiveness toward Ḥusayn Khān. Ultimately, Ḥusayn Khān was forced to surrender the city, but he obtained surprisingly generous terms: he, his ward Sām Mirza (the Shāh's brother), the *qizilbāsh* garrison and a number of Shī'īs from among the population of Harāt, were allowed to leave the city unmolested; they made their way via Sīstān to Shīrāz, where Ḥusayn Khān received a royal summons to proceed to court. Fearful of his reception at the hands of Chūha Sulṭān, the Shāmlū chief procrastinated, but finally, having received a pledge of safe-conduct, joined the royal camp near Iṣfahān and was received by the Shāh with great marks of affection.

This display of royal favour made Chūha Sulṭān detest Ḥusayn Khān Shāmlū even more, and he planned to murder the latter at a banquet. Forewarned of the plot, Husayn Khān decided to strike first, and made his way with a band of Shāmlū retainers toward Chūha Sulṭān's tent. Chūha Sulṭān fled, and took refuge in the royal tent, where a fierce struggle ensued. During this confused mêlée two arrows actually struck Ṭahmāsp's crown. At that moment the words of the Huguenot jeweller Chardin, writing in the second half of the seventeenth century, might have seemed to the Shāh to need some qualification: "le Gouvernment de Perse est monarchique, despotique et absolu, étant tout entier dans la main d'un seul homme, qui est le chef souverain, tant pour le spirituel, que pour le temporel...il n'y a assurément aucun souverain au monde si absolu que le roi de Perse".[6] Yet he was shortly to demonstrate his determination to rule *de facto* as well as *de jure*. The guards on duty happened to be Ẕu'l-Qadars; they sided with the Shāmlūs, and one of their number mortally wounded Chūha Sulṭān. The Takkalūs carried away his body and, returning in greater strength, overwhelmed the Shāmlūs, took 300 of them prisoner and promptly put them to death. The Takkalūs remained in a rebellious mood and, a few days later, fighting broke out again near Hamadān between them and the other *qizilbāsh* tribes. One of the Takkalū supporters misguidedly attempted to abduct the Shāh and carry him off to the Takkalū camp. Ṭahmāsp, his patience clearly exhausted, had the intruder put to death, and then gave the Draconian order for the general slaughter of the Takkalū tribe. Many were killed around the royal tent; others escaped to Baghdād, where the Safavid governor, himself a Takkalū, put some of them to death as a proof of his loyalty and sent their heads to the Shāh; some eventually defected to the Ottomans. The chronogram in Persian for this event gives the date of the event, 937 (1530/1), and the meaning "the Takkalū disaster"; the chronogram is particularly apt, for the Takkalū tribe never subsequently played any considerable part in the governance of the Safavid state.

Shāh Ṭahmāsp, still no more than sixteen or seventeen years of age, had given clear evidence that he did not intend to allow the usurpation of his royal prerogatives by the *qizilbāsh* to go on indefinitely, or to tolerate open rebellion by his *soi-disant* "disciples". Ḥusayn Khān Shāmlū, however, who succeeded Chūha Sulṭān as the most powerful *qizilbāsh* chief in the state, did not draw the appropriate moral from his predecessor's downfall. Ḥusayn Khān assumed office with the consensus of the *qizilbāsh* chiefs and the principal officers of state, who subsequently informed the Shāh of their decision. The four years of Takkalū supremacy were followed by three years of Shāmlū supremacy. Just as Chūha Sulṭān had appointed Takkalūs to office in preference to men from other tribes, so Ḥusayn Khān allotted the pick of provincial posts to Shāmlūs. Ḥusayn Khān repeated Chūha Sulṭān's mistake of not allowing the Shāh to have any say in the business of government, and he also repeated his predecessor's mistake of underestimating the Shāh. Having angered the Shāh by his arbitrary action in putting to death the *vazīr* Amīr Ja'far Sāvajī,[7] in 1533 he aroused Ṭahmāsp's suspicions that he was plotting to overthrow him and put his brother, Sām Mīrzā, on the throne; even worse, he was accused of contemplating desertion to and collaboration with the Ottomans, who had invaded Iran again. Ṭahmāsp had him summarily put to death. Since Ḥusayn Khān Shāmlū was a cousin of Ṭahmāsp himself, and was also the *lala* (guardian) of the Shāh's infant son Muḥammad Mīrzā, who had been born in 1531, his execution had a profound effect on the other *qizilbāsh* chiefs. It indicated not only that the Shāh had the will to take stern measures to put an end to *qizilbāsh* hegemony, but also that he had at his command a sufficient number of loyal officers to carry out his will.

The execution of Ḥusayn Khān Shāmlū marked the end of a decade of *qizilbāsh* rule (1524–33), and the reassertion of royal authority. The *qizilbāsh* interregnum had naturally caused some changes in the relative importance of the principal offices of state. The *vakīl*, whose position had been confused with that of the *vazīr* during the last decade of the reign of Shāh Ismā'īl, when the office was held by an Iranian, regained much of his former prestige and importance. Indeed, his military and political power was such that he is often confused in the sources with the *amīr al-umarā*, whose influence, as one would expect, was also greatly increased during the period of government by military commanders. The triumvirs are styled *vakīl* and *amīr al-umarā* indifferently, and during the *qizilbāsh* interregnum there seems to have been no clear distinction between these two offices in the minds of the historians of the period. When Shāh Ṭahmāsp succeeded in taking control of the affairs of state, both these titles fell into abeyance. We no longer hear of the *amīr al-umarā* as an officer of the central administration, and the office is not listed among the appointments by Shāh 'Abbās I at his accession in 1588. The title *vakīl*, too, almost disappeared from the scene. The reduction of the role of the military in the governance of the state necessarily led to a marked increase in the power of the head of the bureaucracy, the *vazīr*. The *qūrchībāshī*,[8] a military officer formerly subordinate to the *amīr al-umarā*, emerged as the chief military officer of the state, and continued to hold this position as long as the *qizilbāsh* troops constituted the whole or principal part of Safavid armies.

The civil war in Iran had critically weakened the state and had given an unexpected opportunity to the two most formidable enemies of the Safavid state, the Ottoman Turks in the west and the Özbegs in the east, to strike deep into Safavid territory. Reference has already been made to Özbeg attacks in the east and to the loss of Harāt. Between 1524 and 1538, the Özbegs, led by the vigorous and martial 'Ubayd Allāh Khān, launched five major invasions of Khurāsān; these were quite apart from the almost habitual annual raids across the north-east frontier. Even more dangerous were the four full-scale invasions of Iran between 1533 and 1553 by the Ottomans, then at the height of their power under the great Sulṭān Süleymān, known to the Ottomans as "the Lawgiver", and to the West as "the Magnificent". The remarkable thing is not that the Safavids suffered serious losses of territory as a result of these onslaughts, but that they were not overwhelmed. Shāh Ṭahmāsp, struggling against discord and disloyalty and treachery in high places, both on the part of *qizilbāsh* chiefs and on the part of his own brothers, managed to hold the Safavid state together for more than half a century. This postulates one of two things – or perhaps a little of both: either the institutional framework of the early Safavid state established by Shāh Ismā'īl, and its dynamic ideology, were strong enough, in spite of all, to enable the state to weather the storm; or else Ṭahmāsp possessed qualities with which he has not been credited by any source, Western or Oriental.

Shāh Ṭahmāsp reigned for fifty-two years, longer than any other Safavid monarch. His personal character seems to have made little impression on Western observers, and what impression it did make was wholly unfavourable. He is portrayed as a miser, so parsimonious that he sent his disused clothing to the bazaar to be sold. He is portrayed as a religious bigot, as a melancholy recluse who swung between extremes of abstinence and intemperance, as a man capable of great cruelty. He is said to have led the life of a "mere voluptuary", never leaving the *ḥaram*, "where he divides his time between dallying with his favourites and forecasting the future by means of lots".[9] He is not credited with any particular skill either in the arts of peace or of war.

This picture is obviously out of focus, even distorted. In the first place, Shāh Ṭahmāsp, whatever his faults, was not lacking in either physical or moral courage. At the battle of Jām in 1528, apparent total defeat at the hands of the Özbegs was converted into victory by Ṭahmāsp's personal bravery and powers of leadership. His moral courage was spectacularly demonstrated by his decisions to execute the regent Dīv Sulṭān Rūmlū in 1527 and the *amīr al-umarā* Ḥusayn Khān Shāmlū in 1533, and by his ordering of the general massacre of the rebellious Takkalūs in 1530. As a military commander, he was probably not in the same class as his father, Ismā'īl, or his grandson, 'Abbās I. On the other hand, Ismā'īl's flamboyance and dash, which achieved brilliant victories over the Özbegs, were if anything a handicap in warfare against the Ottomans, which called for a cool head, sure judgement and superior battle tactics. The shortcomings of Ismā'īl as a military commander were demonstrated by the Ottomans at Chāldirān, and after that defeat Ismā'īl retired to his tent, so to speak, to sulk rather in the manner of Achilles. Shāh Ṭahmāsp's military skills were essentially defensive in nature, but he had no choice but to fight defensive wars. For example, in 1533 he could muster only 7,000 men to meet an Ottoman invasion force of 90,000 men under the Grand Vizier Ibrāhīm Pasha, and the loyalty of many even of these 7,000 was suspect. The ability to survive in the face of such odds surely posits that Ṭahmāsp was a master of Fabian tactics. He made maximum use of a scorched earth policy. The frontier areas of Āẕarbāyjān through which invading Ottoman armies had to pass were systematically laid waste. When Ottoman forces reached the Iranian frontier, they were already at the end of a long line of communication, and the task of provisioning their men was a formidable one. The further they advanced into Āẕarbāyjān, the more difficult their position became. Frequently there was shortage of food for the troops, and their baggage-animals died because of the lack of pasture. When they were forced to beat a retreat, through the mountainous terrain of Āẕarbāyjān and Kurdistān, they were harassed by Kurdish and other tribes which made a living by raiding baggage-trains and cutting off stragglers; the severe winters of these areas also took their toll. Ṭahmāsp, realising that another defeat on the scale of Chāldirān would mean the end of the Safavid state, husbanded his meagre forces with the same parsimony with which he watched over his treasuries. The lessons of Chāldirān had been well learnt, and at no time did he commit his numerically far inferior forces to a pitched battle against the Ottomans. At the same time, within a few years of his accession, we find references to the presence of both gunners (*tūpchiyān*) and musketeers (*tufangchiyān*) in the Safavid armies. The use of cannon continued to be restricted in the main to siege-warfare. The one occasion on which the sources specifically record the use of cannon in the field by Ṭahmāsp is at the battle of Jām, and in that action the immobility of the cannon rendered them ineffective against swiftly moving light cavalry forces which constantly changed their point of attack; this was the case even though the guns employed on that occasion were not heavy field-guns, but light cannon (probably a type of mortar) mounted on wagons. The ineffectiveness of artillery in the field on that occasion merely increased the already considerable antipathy felt by the Safavids toward that weapon. In 1539, we hear for the first time of a new military office, that of *tūpchī-bāshī*, or commander-in-chief of artillery. In regard to hand-guns, detachments using arquebuses or muskets formed part of Safavid armies before the death of Shāh Ismā'īl, and after the accession of Ṭahmāsp references to them are frequent. Until his premature death in 1549 at the age of thirty-two, Bahrām Mīrzā, Ṭahmāsp's brother, gave the Shāh loyal support; Bahrām, a fearless and sometimes impetuous commander, in many ways resembled his father. Ṭahmāsp's two other brothers, however, Sām Mīrzā and Alqāṣ Mīrzā, were both guilty of treachery: the former, while Governor-General of Khurāsān, rebelled against the Shāh and carried on intrigues with the Ottomans; the latter, while Governor of Shīrvān, rebelled and threw in his lot with the Ottomans. In 1548, Sulṭān Süleymān equipped him with an army and sent him to Iran to overthrow Ṭahmāsp. The treachery of these two brothers was a source of great grief to the Shāh.

That Shāh Ṭahmāsp was a religious bigot is undeniable. The celebrated incident which occurred when Anthony Jenkinson, an Englishman in search of trade privileges, was received in audience by Ṭahmāsp in 1562, reveals the Shāh's attitude toward "infidels" in general (see Chapter 5). Shāh Ṭahmāsp certainly did not possess that dominant characteristic of pragmatism possessed by his grandson 'Abbās I who, when he realised that religious tolerance was good for trade, committed himself to a policy of religious tolerance. Ṭahmāsp's parsimony, too, is well attested. *A Chronicle of the Carmelites in Persia* asserts that:

> Every day, "for the sake of his soul", many kinds of tribute and imposts are removed and people made free of them; but for the most part such measures are not put into execution, because, when two or three years

have passed, he wants the whole sum at once, as he did at the time when I was with the court in the district of Julfā, inhabited entirely by Armenians, who had been exempted for 8 years from paying tribute, when all at once he determined to demand it for the whole time past, to the loss and ruin of those poor Christians.

Ṭahmāsp gave his cast-off clothing in lieu of payment, "what was worth '1' being reckoned as '10'". He often sold jewels and dealt in other merchandise, "buying and bartering with that subtlety which a passable trader might use".[10] The Shāh imposed a tax of one-seventh on all merchandise. A contemporary Persian source is uncompromising on the subject of his avariciousness:

Shāh Ṭahmāsp was extremely avaricious in regard to the accumulation of money, property and treasure. Of the rulers of Iran and Tūrān[11] since the invasions of Chingiz Khān – or even since the advent of Islam – no king at any period expended so much effort as Shāh Ṭahmāsp to accumulate treasure in the form of cash, cloths and stuffs, and articles like vessels of gold and silver.[12]

The need to fight on two fronts was a severe handicap for the Safavids. It meant that maximum Safavid strength could not be mobilised either in the west or the east, and in fact Safavid armies were regularly inferior in numbers to both the armies of the Ottomans and those of the Özbegs. At the battle of Jām in 1528, for example, Ṭahmāsp had 24,000 men against an Özbeg army of 80,000 seasoned veterans and some 40,000 skirmishers and irregulars, and the pitifully small force at Ṭahmāsp's disposal in 1534 at the time of the first Ottoman invasion has already been mentioned. The news that the Shāh had moved the bulk of his forces to Āẕarbāyjān to meet an Ottoman threat was a signal to the Özbegs to step up the pressure on the north-east frontier. Conversely, the Shāh was repeatedly prevented from taking any long-term measures against the Özbegs by Ottoman invasions in the west. In the winter of 1533/4, for instance, when Ṭahmāsp had just relieved Harāt after that city had endured a terrible siege by the Özbegs lasting eighteen months, during which the garrison and inhabitants had been reduced to eating cats and dogs, the Shāh was making plans for a major expedition to Transoxania when he received the news that Sulṭān Süleyman's army had invaded Āẕarbāyjān, and was forced to return to the west. There was no relaxation of the relentless series of attacks mounted by 'Ubayd Allāh Khān in the east until the death of that Özbeg leader in 1540.

The Ottomans were given considerable assistance in their efforts to conquer Iran by renegade *qizilbāsh amīrs* and by the traitor Alqāṣ Mīrzā, the Shāh's brother. Sulṭān Süleymān's first invasion of Iran in 1534 came about as the result of intrigues by the defector Ulāma of the Takkalū tribe. At the time when the triumvir Chūha Sulṭān was the *de facto* ruler of the state, Ulāma was commander-in-chief of the armed forces in Āẕarbāyjān. After the fall of Chūha Sulṭān, Ulāma had ambitions to succeed him as chief executive officer of the state. When Ḥusayn Khān Shāmlū was appointed to succeed Chūha Sulṭān, Ulāma forgot the debt of loyalty which he owed to the Safavid house, and defected to the Ottomans. It is true that many Takkalū officers fled in fear of their lives as a result of the stern action taken against the rebellious Takkalū tribe in 1530/1. There is, however, no evidence that the Shāh proscribed any Takkalūs who were not actually involved in the revolt at the time of the death of Chūha Sulṭān, and the fact that officers like Ulāma were prepared actually to enter Ottoman service shows the extent to which the *qizilbāsh* had abandoned in practice their unquestioning obedience to the Shāh as their *murshid-i kāmil*, whatever lip-service they might continue to pay to it in theory. It was Ulāma who alerted the Ottoman Sulṭān to the fact that north-west and central Iran lay undefended in 1533 when the Shāh was planning to invade Transoxania. Sulṭān Süleymān sent a force of 80,000–90,000 men under the Grand Vizier, Ibrāhīm Pasha, while he followed up with the main army. The Grand Vizier made contact with Ulāma, and dispatched him with a force in the direction of Ardabīl.

Shāh Ṭahmāsp marched back from the frontier of Transoxania to Rayy by forced marches, covering the distance in twenty-one days. The situation was a desperate one. Sulṭān Süleymān had joined forces with the Grand Vizier, and the vast Ottoman host had brushed aside a small force sent by the Shāh to try and hold Tabrīz. For the first time, the faith of some in the fortunes of the Safavid house wavered. More *qizilbāsh* officers defected, and the loyalty of some who remained was suspect. At this critical juncture, a heavy snowfall blanketed the plain at Sulṭāniyya, where the Ottomans were encamped, and many Turkish soldiers perished from exposure. Sulṭān Süleymān, unable to return by the route by which he had come, because no supplies were to be had in Āẕarbāyjān, was forced to withdraw through Kurdistān. The

Shāh went in pursuit of Ulāma and other renegades who had shut themselves up in the fortress of Vān, but meanwhile Sulṭān Süleymān had occupied Baghdād at the invitation of the Safavid garrison, which consisted of Takkalū troops. Only the commandant of the garrison and 300 men remained loyal to the Safavid cause. Thereafter Baghdād and the province of 'Irāq-i 'Arab, conquered by Shāh Ismā'īl in 1508, remained in Ottoman hands except for the short period between 1623 and 1638.

The second round of the Ottoman offensive opened the following year, and was directed by Sulṭān Süleymān from Baghdād. A number of engagements were fought at various points between Kurdistān and the Armenian highlands, and the Safavids were uniformly successful. The renegade Ulāma again took part in the fighting on the Ottoman side. The third Ottoman invasion occurred in 1548 and, like the first, was on a massive scale. Sulṭān Süleymān marched forth from Istanbul, with a vast army recruited from Anatolia, Syria, Egypt, Qarāmān, Diyār Rabī'a and 'Irāq-i 'Arab, accompanied by large quantities of artillery and countless janissaries. With him went the traitor Alqāṣ Mīrzā, Shāh Ṭahmāsp's brother. Alqāṣ Mīrzā, while Governor of Shīrvān, had rebelled against the Shāh, had been pardoned, rebelled again, and had finally sought refuge from Ṭahmāsp's wrath with the Ottoman Sulṭān. He had told the Sulṭān that, if he (Alqāṣ) were to enter Iran at the head of a large army, there would be a general uprising in his favour.

Ṭahmāsp made his usual preparations to meet the new onslaught. He had the entire area between Tabrīz and the Ottoman frontier laid waste, so that no trace of grain or blade of grass remained. The inhabitants of Tabrīz blocked up the underground water-channels, so that no drinking water could be found. Similarly, measures were taken to deny the enemy all forms of victuals. When Sulṭān Süleymān reached the Iranian frontier, he sent the renegade Ulāma Takkalū to lay siege to Vān, and dispatched Alqāṣ Mīrzā and 40,000 men in the direction of Marand. Once again the Ottomans occupied Tabrīz, but their forces soon began to suffer acutely from lack of provisions. When their pack-animals began to die like flies, Sulṭān Süleymān again beat the retreat, harassed at every step by the *qizilbāsh* forces. The Sulṭān detached Alqāṣ Mīrzā, who had ceased to be of use to him once his words had proved to be an empty boast, and Ulāma, hoping that they would draw off some of his pursuers. The move was unsuccessful. Alqāṣ Mīrzā penetrated deep into central Iran, passing through Qum to Kāshān; the people of Iṣfahān shut the gates of that city against him, and he moved south into Fārs, where Shīrāz also refused him admittance. After an equally unsuccessful attempt to rouse support in Khūzistān, Alqāṣ Mīrzā, in despair, returned to Baghdād. Now merely a source of embarrassment to the Ottomans, he was expelled from Baghdād, and fled into Kurdistān, where he was arrested by Safavid forces and taken before the Shāh, who upbraided him for his disloyal and dishonourable conduct. His life was spared, but he and the Shāh's other disloyal brother, Sām Mīrzā, were incarcerated in the remote fortress–prison of Qahqaha.

The suppression of Alqās Mīrzā's revolt was followed by four or five years of peace between the Safavid and the Ottoman empires. Minor acts of insubordination on the part of Kurdish chieftains along the frontier were overlooked, and Shāh Ṭahmāsp was encouraged to open negotiations for a more lasting peace. Before this was achieved, however, the acts of provocation committed by Iskandar Pasha, Governor of Vān and then Governor-General of Erzerūm, including attacks on Khvuy and Erīvān, led to the fourth and last invasion of Iran by the Ottomans during the reign of Sulṭān Süleymān. This time there was a change in the usual pattern of events. Instead of waiting for the arrival of the Ottoman army, Shāh Ṭahmāsp seized the initiative. The fact that he was able to divide his army into four army corps, and to send each in a different direction, indicates a significant increase in the strength of the Safavid army. Iskandar Pasha was soundly defeated outside Erzerūm, with the loss of 3,000 men. The Shāh captured a number of key forts along the frontier. When Sulṭān Süleymān finally reached Nakhchivān in the summer of 1533, he found it impossible to remain in the area because of the effectiveness of the Safavid scorched earth policy, and withdrew toward Erzerūm. In the course of his retreat, Sinān Beg, one of the Sulṭān's intimate companions and special favourites, was captured by a Safavid patrol, and this made the Sulṭān the more ready to enter into serious peace negotiations. Peace was finally signed at Amasya in 1555, and Iran obtained a much needed respite from Ottoman attacks which lasted for thirty years. Because Tabrīz had proved so vulnerable to Ottoman attack, the Shāh transferred his capital to Qazvīn.

Starting from a virtually hopeless position, Shāh Tahmāsp had achieved much during the first thirty years of his reign. He had maintained his position during a decade of civil war between those "turbulent praetorians", the *qizilbāsh* chiefs. With pathetically small resources, he had survived massive onslaughts from both east and west; not only had he survived, but he had gradually increased the strength of his armed forces and, aided by his one loyal brother Bahrām and by his son Ismāʿīl, had gone over to the offensive against the Ottomans in the campaign of 1553. As a result, when he opened peace negotiations with the Sublime Porte, he was able to do so from a position of relative strength, and the terms of the Treaty of Amasya were not unfavourable to Iran. Had Ṭahmāsp been forced to negotiate peace with the Ottomans in 1534, he would undoubtedly have been forced to cede large areas of territory in the north-west, including his capital, Tabrīz. As it was, by the Treaty of Amasya only minor territorial modifications were made along the Ottoman–Safavid frontier, and both sides made concessions. Georgia was divided into mutually agreed "spheres of influence". Peace remained unbroken for the remainder of Shāh Ṭahmāsp's lifetime. Sulṭān Selim II succeeded his father Süleymān on the death of the latter in 1566, and was succeeded in his turn by Sulṭān Murād who, during the lifetime of Ṭahmāsp and Ismāʿīl II, "did not deviate from the path of friendship and sworn peace".[13]

Between 1540 and 1553, Shāh Ṭahmāsp waged four campaigns in the Caucasus. In the course of these campaigns, Georgian, Circassian and Armenian prisoners were taken in large numbers and brought back to Iran. The introduction of these new ethnic groups profoundly changed the whole character of Safavid society, and had important repercussions on the military and political institutions of the state. Prior to the introduction of these new elements, there had been a struggle for power, for control of the principal offices of state, between the two "founding races", the Iranians and the Turks. By the end of the reign of Ṭahmāsp, the *qizilbāsh* found their privileged position as the military aristocracy challenged by members of the new ethnic groups. Moreover, the introduction into the royal *ḥaram* of Georgian and Circassian women, who were prized for their beauty, precipitated dynastic struggles of a completely new kind, as these women engaged in political intrigue with a view to securing the throne for their own sons.

Why did Shāh Ṭahmāsp wage these campaigns in the Caucasus, and was the introduction of these new ethnic groups from the Caucasus a conscious policy on his part in order to offset the power of the *qizilbāsh*? The answer to the first question is that Ṭahmāsp's motives in sending his troops into the Caucasian provinces were very probably the same as the motives of his forefathers Junayd, Ḥaydar and Ismā'īl, namely, the desire to give his troops battle experience, and the desire for booty. The Georgian churches constituted a rich source of gold, jewels and other luxury items, which found their way into the Safavid treasury. Since the Caucasian provinces were for the most part inhabited by Christian peoples, the launching of these attacks without any necessary provocation on the part of the victims could be given the convenient justification of *jihād*, or "holy war", against the infidel. The waging of these campaigns by Ṭahmāsp was probably part of a deliberate policy to try and restore the morale and fighting efficiency of the *qizilbāsh* after the double trauma of Chāldirān and the civil war of 1525–33. As a result of these campaigns,

> The governors of all the seven districts of Georgia were appointed by the Shāh and became his subjects, contracted to pay the poll-tax and the land-tax, and were instructed to have the name and exalted titles of the Shāh included in the *khuṭba*, and stamped on the coinage. Thus the infidels of those regions were reduced to submission by the sharp swords of the warriors of Islam.[14]

The answer to the second question is less certain. Shāh 'Abbās I, who came to the throne in 1588, gave official recognition to these "third force" elements by making the *ghulāmān-i khāṣṣa-yi sharīfa* (slaves of the royal household) an important part of both the civil and military administration. The *ghulāms*, on arrival in Iran, were required to become Muslims, though, particularly in the case of the Georgians, their conversion to Islam was fairly nominal. They were then given special training, on completion of which they were either enrolled in one of the newly created *ghulām* regiments, or given employment in the royal household or some other branch of the *khāṣṣa* administration. This was the situation as regularised by Shāh 'Abbās I. Were any elements of this situation visible during the reign of Ṭahmāsp? The answer, I think, is "yes", but the sources do not make it clear whether these changes were embodied in any formal structures or institutionalised forms; if they were, then it is safe to assume that they were the result of conscious policy decisions by Ṭahmāsp.

The majority of the prisoners brought to Iran from the Caucasus during the reign of Ṭahmāsp were women or children, and it was these children and their descendants, and the offspring of these women, who constituted the basis of the "third force" as institutionalised by ʻAbbās I. The number of people involved was considerable. For example, from the campaign of 1553/4, 30,000 prisoners were brought back to Iran. It should not be overlooked that some Georgian noblemen voluntarily offered their services to the Safavid crown. One nobleman, connected with the Georgian royal family, who had been sent to the Safavid court as an ambassador, entered Safavid service with all his retainers, and eventually became Governor of Shakkī, a province of Shīrvān. In 1585, during the reign of Sulṭān Muḥammad Shāh, we find a Georgian nobleman holding the office of *lala*, or guardian, to one of the Safavid princes. The office of *lala* had always been a jealously guarded preserve of the *qizilbāsh*, and the appointment of a Georgian to such a politically sensitive position is an indication that significant social changes had taken place before the accession of ʻAbbās I.

One of the most celebrated events of Ṭahmāsp's reign was the visit to Iran of the Mogul Emperor Humāyūn, the son of Bābur who had founded the empire in 1526.[15] At his accession, Humāyūn had to fight desperately against disloyal brothers and against strong Afghān forces. Defeated twice by the Afghāns, and with revolts on all sides, Humāyūn, made for Qandahār, on the frontier between the Mogul empire and the Safavid state, but was rebuffed there too, and threw himself on the mercy of Shāh Ṭahmāsp. The visit of this Sunnī ruler in 1544 clearly showed Ṭahmāsp's religious bigotry. He refused to give him any political assistance unless he became a convert to Shiʻism, and he let Humāyūn know that his own life and the lives of his 700-strong retinue were in jeopardy unless he agreed to become a Shīʻī. Reluctantly, Humāyūn signified his acceptance of the Shīʻī faith. After his return to India, he reverted to his Sunnī faith, but he was a man of liberal religious views and many Shīʻīs from Iran entered his service.[16] The *quid pro quo* which Ṭahmāsp demanded for giving sanctuary to the Mogul emperor was the strategically important city of Qandahār, which had been a bone of contention between the two states from the time of the founding of the Mogul empire. Humāyūn surrendered Qandahār to Ṭahmāsp, but the city did not remain in Safavid hands for long, and control of it continued to pass from one side to the other.

Another foreign dignitary to arrive at Ṭahmāsp's court, although of a rather different calibre, was the fugitive Ottoman prince Bāyazīd, who had rebelled against his father Sulṭān Süleymān. Bāyazīd attempted to persuade Ṭahmāsp to espouse his cause and to lead an army against the Ottomans, but Ṭahmāsp not surprisingly was averse to disturbing the hard-won peace which he had recently concluded with the Ottoman Sulṭān. Ultimately, the Shāh suspected that Bāyazīd, who had brought 10,000 fully armed men with him, was plotting a *coup* at Qazvīn, and Sulṭān Süleymān made it clear that the continuance of the existing peace was dependent upon the extradition of Bāyazīd. Ṭahmāsp thereupon handed over Bāyazīd and his four sons to the Ottoman delegation sent to fetch them, and the terms of the Treaty of Amasya were reconfirmed in 1562. On instructions from Sulṭān Süleymān, the five Ottoman princes were put to death as soon as they were taken into Ottoman custody.

In 1574, Shāh Ṭahmāsp fell ill. His illness lasted two months, and twice he was at the point of death. With the temporary removal of his firm hand from the helm, there was a recrudescence of dissension among the *qizilbāsh* chiefs. For forty years, since he reasserted the authority of the crown in 1533, Ṭahmāsp had achieved a satisfactory balance between the rival *qizilbāsh* and Tājīk elements in the state. Now that the Shāh was ailing, the *qizilbāsh* thought they could regain control of the state as they had after the death of Shāh Ismā'īl I when Ṭahmāsp himself was still a minor. In 1574, however, the situation was more complicated than it had been in 1524. In 1524, the struggle had been to determine which *qizilbāsh* tribe, or coalition of tribes, would govern a state in which the *qizilbāsh* tribes in general enjoyed a dominant and privileged position. In 1574, and particularly after the death of Ṭahmāsp in 1576, the struggle was to determine whether the *qizilbāsh* could fight off the challenge to this privileged position made by the Georgians, Circassians and Armenians who now constituted a "third force" within the state and society. The Safavid leaders Junayd and Ḥaydar had married wives of Turcoman stock, and Ṭahmāsp's mother was also a

Turcoman. With the question of the succession to Ṭahmāsp an imminent problem, the Georgian and Circassian women in the royal *ḥaram* who were the mothers of princes of the blood royal pushed the claims of their respective sons to the succession; had they succeeded in placing one of them on the throne, the power and influence of the "third force" elements in the administration of the Safavid state would obviously have been greatly enhanced.

Of Ṭahmāsp's nine sons who reached adolescence, seven were the sons of Circassian or Georgian mothers; only two were the sons of a Turcoman mother: Muḥammad Khudābanda, and Ismā'īl. The *qizilbāsh* problem was made more acute by the fact that neither of these princes was fitted to rule. Muḥammad Khudābanda's eyesight was so bad that he was virtually blind. Ismā'īl had had an auspicious start to his political career. Appointed Governor of Shīrvān in 1547, he had conducted several successful campaigns against the Ottomans in the Caucasus and eastern Anatolia, and in 1556 he was appointed Governor of Khurāsān. After only a few months at Harāt, however, Ismā'īl was suddenly arrested and sent to the remote prison of Qahqaha, usually reserved for dangerous political prisoners. Ismā'īl seems to have forfeited the Shāh's favour by certain actions at Harāt which made the Shāh suspect that Ismā'īl was plotting to overthrow him. These suspicions were played on by Ma'ṣūm Beg Ṣafavī, a powerful official descended from a side branch of the Safavid family, who had been appointed head of the bureaucracy in 1559 or perhaps earlier, and who was also the *lala* (guardian) of Ṭahmāsp's third son, Ḥaydar, whose mother was a Georgian slave. Ma'ṣūm Beg would naturally have aspirations for his own protégé to succeed Ṭahmāsp, and would therefore seize any opportunity to spoil Ismā'īl's chances. In his position of power in the central administration, Ma'ṣūm Beg was well placed to pour poison into the Shāh's ear. Whether Ṭahmāsp's suspicions were justified or not, Ismā'īl remained in jail for nearly twenty years, from the time of his incarceration in December 1556 to his release by the *qizilbāsh*, who proceeded to set him on the throne, in August 1576.

Before Ismā'īl II came to the throne, there was much jockeying for position on the part of the rival factions. It is clear that the *qizilbāsh* did not at once perceive the true nature of the threat to their own position from the Georgian and Circassian factions, because in 1574 certain *qizilbāsh* chiefs were plotting on behalf of Sulaymān Mīrzā, whose mother was the sister of a Circassian chief. By 1575, the *qizilbāsh* had split into two factions, one supporting Ismā'īl Mīrzā, the other Ḥaydar Mīrzā, whose mother was a Georgian and one of the Shāh's legal wives. Ṭahmāsp himself is said to have favoured Ḥaydar, but he kept his own counsel, and placed a special guard on Ismā'īl in case the pro-Ḥaydar faction should try to murder him. When Shāh Ṭahmāsp died on 14 May 1576, the Georgians and the Ustājlūs made an unsuccessful attempt to place Ḥaydar on the throne. Ḥaydar actually placed the crown on his head, and called himself "shah", but, as luck would have it, the guard on duty at the palace that day was composed of supporters of Ismā'īl – Afshārs, Rūmlūs and Bayāts – who effectively isolated Ḥaydar from his own supporters. In the fracas which ensued, Ḥaydar was killed. Next, the Rūmlūs and Circassians attempted to enthrone a prince whose mother was a Circassian slave, but this attempt, too, was frustrated. Finally, most of the *qizilbāsh* threw their support behind a "Turcoman candidate", Ismā'īl Mīrzā. Thirty thousand *qizilbāsh* assembled before the prison–fortress of Qahqaha. Ismā'īl, who consented to emerge from the security of the prison only after receiving the most solemn pledges of support, was enthroned at Qazvīn as Shāh Ismā'īl II, on 22 August 1576, at the age of forty.

Ismā'īl II early served notice that his mind had been affected by his long imprisonment. During the three months which elapsed between the death of his father and his enthronement, a delay which had been caused mainly by Ismā'īl's insistence on waiting for an auspicious date, Ismā'īl not only put to death many of those who had supported Ḥaydar, especially Ustājlūs, but also treated his own supporters in a hostile fashion. He executed those whose only crime was that they had held important office under his father. "The royal tents," he said, "cannot be held up by old ropes." It soon became clear that Ismā'īl II's only goal was to remain in power at all costs. To that end, he systematically killed, or blinded, any prince of the blood royal who might conceivably become the centre of a conspiracy against him. Five of his brothers, and four other Safavid princes, were murdered or blinded. The *qizilbāsh*, realising that he was not the sort of ruler they had hoped for, now conspired to assassinate him. The factor which gave a certain plausible justification to their action was that

Ismāʻīl II was a rather less than enthusiastic Shīʻī. Since Ismāʻīl was addicted to narcotics, his murder was an easy matter. With the connivance of Ismāʻīl's sister, Parī Khān Khānum, the conspirators placed poison in an electuary containing opium, which was consumed by the Shāh and one of his boon companions. Ismāʻīl died on 24 November 1577, having reigned for only slightly more than a year.

The only members of the Safavid royal house who had not been murdered or blinded by Ismāʻīl II during his brief reign were his elder brother Muḥammad Khudābanda and the latter's three sons: Ḥamza, Abū Ṭālib and ʻAbbās; and they had escaped Ismāʻīl II's purge only because he himself was murdered before orders issued for their execution had been carried out. The *qizilbāsh* therefore had little alternative but to place on the throne the prince whom they had passed over previously, namely, Muḥammad Khundābanda, and the latter reached Qazvīn from Shīrāz on 11 or 13 February 1578; he adopted the style Sulṭān Muḥammad Shāh. The new Shāh, who was of a mild, somewhat unworldly disposition, given to jokes and witticisms, who wrote poetry under the pen-name of "Fahmī", and who was, as will be recalled, almost blind, was at once caught up in the bitter rivalry between two ambitious and ruthless women: his own wife, Mahd-i ʻUlyā, and Ṭahmāsp's daughter, Parī Khān Khānum, who had aided the conspirators to murder Ismāʻīl II and had since his death managed the affairs of state through a council of *qizilbāsh* chiefs which she had set up. None of these chiefs dared to disobey her orders, and she confidently anticipated that her brother, Sulṭān Muḥammad Shāh, would submit to her will also. Her plans went awry when an experienced Iranian bureaucrat named Mīrzā Salmān, who had been appointed *vazīr* by Shāh Ismāʻīl II in June 1577, managed to obtain permission from Parī Khān Khānum to leave Qazvīn and travel to Shīrāz. With that innate sense of self-preservation bred in Iranian bureaucrats from long centuries of tradition, Mīrzā Salmān lost no time in ingratiating himself with Sulṭān Muḥammad Shāh and his wife by revealing to them the powerful position held at Qazvīn by Parī Khān Khānum. Mahd-i ʻUlyā immediately saw that either she or the Shāh's sister had to go, and she set about detaching as many *qizilbāsh* chiefs as possible from their allegiance to her rival. The night after the arrival of Sulṭān Muḥammad Shāh and Mahd-i ʻUlyā at Qazvīn, they had Parī Khān Khānum strangled; her uncle, the Circassian chief Shamkhāl, was executed, and Ismā'īl II's infant son was murdered.

Mahd-i 'Ulyā was now in complete control of the state. Her eldest son, Ḥamza Mīrzā, was appointed *vakīl* of the Supreme *Dīvān*, and was authorised to affix his seal to official documents above that of the *vazīr*, Mīrzā Salmān. For eighteen months, Mahd-i 'Ulyā reigned supreme. She was the daughter of a local ruler in Māzandarān whose family boasted of its descent from the 4th Shī'ī Imām, Zayn al-'Ābidīn. She was hostile to the interests of the *qizilbāsh*, and did all she could to strengthen the position of the Tājīks in the administration of the state; in this policy she naturally had the strong support of the *vazīr*. Mahd-i 'Ulyā was determined that her favourite son, Ḥamza, should succeed her husband. To prevent her younger son 'Abbās from constituting a threat to her plans, she tried repeatedly to get him sent to Qazvīn, but the Governor of Harāt, 'Alī Qulī Khān Shāmlū, refused to comply with her orders. Another of Mahd-i 'Ulyā's ambitions was to revenge herself on the man who had murdered her father in Māzandarān and expropriated her family's territory in that province. When her father's murderer died before she could achieve her object, she extended her feud to his son, Mīrzā Khān, who finally agreed to come to Qazvīn after receiving a solemn promise of safe-conduct. While Mīrzā Khān was on his way to Qazvīn with an escort of *qizilbāsh*, he was murdered by some of the Queen's men. The *qizilbāsh* chiefs felt great indignation at the Queen's violation of a sworn oath, particularly since it was they who had persuaded Mīrzā Khān to throw himself on the Queen's mercy in the first place.

Sulṭān Muḥammad Shāh tried to win the favour of his subjects by a policy of lavish grants from the treasury. All the *qizilbāsh* chiefs who were appointed to provincial posts received their pay and allowances for one year and in some cases for two. The large stock of robes of honour which had been accumulated in the treasury were distributed to the *amīrs*, to office-holders, to financial agents, *kalāntars* (mayors) and other provincial dignitaries. The troops of the royal bodyguard, who had received no pay for ten years, were paid all the arrears due to them. New positions of the status of *amīr* were added to the establishment of each *qizilbāsh* tribe. Since all the provinces had already been assigned as fiefs (the normal form of payment), the payment of these newly created *amīrs* constituted yet another drain on the royal treasury, which rapidly became exhausted. This royal largesse did not produce good government. The civilian population complained of a lack of security. The *qizilbāsh*, seeing that new offices and perquisites were apparently there for the asking, demanded more.

The general impression created abroad by the administration of Sulṭān Muḥammad Shāh and his Queen was one of weakness and discord within the state. The traditional enemies of the Safavids, the Ottomans and the Özbegs, were not slow in attacking Iran to see whether this impression was correct. The Özbegs again ravaged Khurāsān, and, in the west, the Ottomans, in league with some Kurdish chiefs, probed the Safavid defences in Āẕarbāyjān. The long period of peace with the Ottomans was definitively broken when Sulṭān Murād sent an army of more than 100,000 men, which included a large force of Crimean Tatars, to invade Āẕarbāyjān in 1578. The Safavid forces suffered defeat after defeat. A large part of Georgia was overrun. In 1579/80 Ḥamza Mīrzā and the *vazīr* Mīrzā Salmān made a successful counter-attack in Shīrvān and Qarābāgh, and the Tatar chief, 'Ādil Girāy Khān, was taken prisoner. 'Ādil Girāy was treated with honour, in the hope of weaning him from his allegiance to the Ottomans, and he was lodged in the state apartments in the royal palace at Qazvīn. The *qizilbāsh amīrs* pressed the Shāh to transfer the Tatar khān to one of the fortress–prisons, on the grounds that it was too dangerous to leave him at Qazvīn while most of the *amīrs* were away on campaign against the Ottomans.

The hostility between the Queen and the *qizilbāsh* chiefs was rapidly coming to a head. The *qizilbāsh* resented the Queen's pro-Tājīk policies; those who had persuaded Mīrzā Khān to go to Qazvīn on the Queen's guaranteeing his safe-conduct were outraged when the Queen violated her oath; those of the royal bodyguard who carried out the murder of Mīrzā Khān were disgruntled because the Queen failed to reward them adequately; they were angered by the Queen's rejection of their advice in regard to 'Ādil Girāy Khān; in short, they disliked Mahd-i 'Ulyā and everything she stood for, and in particular they disliked her hold over the Shāh and the fact that she missed no opportunity to humiliate the *qizilbāsh*. A group of *qizilbāsh* conspirators banded together to remove Mahd-i ʿUlyā from her position of power. They sent a message to the Shāh:

Your Majesty well knows that women are notoriously lacking in intelligence, weak in judgement, and extremely obstinate. Mahd-i ʿUlyā has always opposed us, the loyal servants of the crown, and has never agreed with us on matters of state policy; she has acted contrary to the considered opinions of the *qizilbāsh* elders, and has constantly attempted to humiliate and degrade us. We have not been safe from her actions, even though up to the present time we have not been guilty of improper conduct, nor have we done anything to cause her alarm. So how can we feel secure now, when our basic incompatibility has come out into the open, when she has lashed with her tongue the elders of the *qizilbāsh* tribes, has called us mutinous, and has uttered dire threats against us? In short, we do not consider it proper that word should get around among neighbouring rulers that no member of the royal family still remains in the care of the *qizilbāsh*, because a woman has taken charge of the affairs of state and is all-powerful. Mahd-i ʿUlyā's power and influence in the government of the realm is objectionable to all the *qizilbāsh* tribes, and it is impossible for us to reach a *modus vivendi* with her. If she is not removed from power, in all probability revolts will occur which will be to the detriment of both religion and the state.[17]

The Shāh, a pious, ascetic and mild soul, offered to exile his wife to Qum, or to send her back to Māzandarān, or to abdicate himself, leaving the choice of his successor to the *qizilbāsh* chiefs. The Queen despised his attempts to appease the *qizilbāsh*; she would not swerve a hair's breadth, she said, from the line of conduct she had followed so far. When they heard this, a group of the conspirators burst into the *ḥaram* and strangled the Queen. A few days later, the *qizilbāsh amīrs* assembled at the palace, and reaffirmed their fealty to Sulṭān Muḥammad Shāh and, after him, to Ḥamza Mīrzā. The impotence of the Shāh and Ḥamza Mīrzā, starkly revealed by their inability to call the murderers of the Queen to account, encouraged the *qizilbāsh* to give full rein to inter-tribal rivalries in a manner reminiscent of the factionalism rampant at the beginning of the reign of Ṭahmāsp. In the case of Ṭahmāsp, they had been able easily to dominate a ten-year-old boy; in the case of Sulṭān Muḥammad Shāh, they were able to impose their will on a good, well-meaning, but pathetically weak and almost blind middle-aged man. At Qazvīn, the Turkmān and Takkalū tribes were in control; in Khurāsān, an Ustājlū–Shāmlū coalition raised the standard of revolt in 1581 and swore allegiance to the Shāh's son 'Abbās, then ten years of age. In November 1582, the Shāh and Ḥamza Mīrzā led the royal army to Khurāsān to suppress the revolt, but their attempt brought them further humiliation at the hands of the *qizilbāsh*. At first, all went well. The Ustājlū leader, Murshid Qulī Khān, declared his allegiance to Ḥamza Mīrzā, and received the royal pardon. The Shāmlū chief, 'Alī Qulī Khān, was isolated and besieged at Harāt. Then the bad blood between the *qizilbāsh* chiefs in the royal army, and the *vazīr* Mīrzā Salmān, formerly the right-hand man of the Queen, Mahd-i 'Ulyā, came to a head. Since the *qizilbāsh* in the royal army were less than enthusiastic about prosecuting a siege against their fellows within the walls of Harāt, the *vazīr* openly accused them of dereliction of duty and sedition. The *qizilbāsh* already hated the *vazīr* because he had supported the pro-Tājīk policies of the late Queen, and because he had been granted military rank and had taken a leading part in the campaigns of 1579/80 against the Ottomans. In other words, the *qizilbāsh* were no more reconciled in 1583 to the idea of a Tājīk having military pretensions than they had been in 1512 when their animosity toward the Tājīk *vakīl* had led to the defeat and death of the latter. They now denounced Mīrzā Salmān in violent terms. He was, they said, the destroyer of the state and the enemy of the *qizilbāsh*, and they demanded his dismissal from the office of *vazīr*. Mīrzā Salmān had every reason to expect that his patrons, the Shāh and Ḥamza Mīrzā (the prince was additionally his son-in-law) would protect him, but they surrendered him tamely to the *qizilbāsh* *amīrs*, who put him to death after appropriating all his possessions.

After the murder of Mīrzā Salmān, Ḥamza Mīrzā, then about nineteen years of age, directed the affairs of state, but he lacked the maturity of judgement and political experience required by such turbulent times. Not only was he impulsive and hot-tempered, but he was a heavy drinker, and he made the fatal mistake of making some of the younger *qizilbāsh* officers stationed at Qazvīn his drinking-companions. As a result, he soon became embroiled in *qizilbāsh* factionalism. The military situation continued to deteriorate, and the Ottomans occupied Tabrīz in 1585. This time, they were to remain in occupation of the former Safavid capital for twenty years. The same year, Ḥamza had to suppress a plot in favour of his brother Ṭahmāsp. On 6 December 1586, Ḥamza Mīrzā was murdered in mysterious circumstances while campaigning in Qarābāgh.

In July 1585, the leader of the Ustājlū faction in Khurāsān, Murshid Qulī Khān, had outwitted his rival Shāmlū chief and had secured possession of the person of ʻAbbās Mīrzā, then about fourteen years of age. The death of Ḥamza Mīrzā the following year, and a massive invasion of Khurāsān in December 1587 by the Özbegs under their new leader ʻAbd Allāh Khān, who laid siege to Harāt and threatened to engulf the whole province, made Murshid Qulī Khān decide to risk a *coup* at Qazvīn. When he reached Qazvīn, a public demonstration in favour of ʻAbbās decided those among the *qizilbāsh* chiefs in the capital who still wavered, and on 1 October 1588 Sulṭān Muḥammad Shāh handed over the insignia of kingship to his son, who was crowned Shāh ʻAbbās I. The kingmaker, Murshid Qulī Khān Ustājlū, was for the moment the most powerful man in the Safavid state, and he assumed the title of *vakīl* of the Supreme *Dīvān* as a token of that fact. As in 1534, the existence of the Safavid state was at stake. Harāt, after a heroic defence lasting nine months, fell to the Özbegs in February 1589, and the Özbegs swept on to Mashhad and Sarakhs. In the west, all efforts to dislodge the Ottoman garrison at Tabrīz had failed. The situation called for a strong and astute ruler; fortunately for the Safavid state, and indeed for the future of Iran, the seventeen-year-old ʻAbbās was such a man.

4

The Safavid empire at the height of its power under Shāh ʻAbbās the Great (1588–1629)

The gravity of the situation facing ʻAbbās I at his accession in 1588 was extreme. In the west and north-west, almost all the provinces lying along the border with the Ottoman empire had been occupied by the Ottomans; in the east, half the province of Khurāsān had been overrun by the Özbegs. On the domestic scene, the twelve years that had elapsed since the death of Ṭahmāsp had witnessed a dramatic loss of authority on the part of the ruler; in fact, after the murder of the Queen by *qizilbāsh* conspirators in 1579, the Shāh and his son, Ḥamza Mīrzā, had been reduced to total impotence. Not only had there been a recrudescence of *qizilbāsh* inter-tribal factionalism in an extreme form, but the incident of the murder of the *vazīr*, Mīrzā Salmān, showed that the fundamental dichotomy in the Safavid state between Turk and Iranian was as sharp as it had been at the establishment of the state eighty years earlier. In the absence of a firm, controlling hand, the principal officers of state looked each to his own interests alone, and the result was a situation bordering on anarchy. The treasury, as a result of the prodigality of Sulṭān Muḥammad Shāh, was empty.

With the resources at his disposal, such numerous and grave problems could not be dealt with simultaneously; it was necessary to set priorities. ʻAbbās at once displayed the strong sense of pragmatism which was one of his dominant characteristics. His order of priorities was to be: first, the restoration of internal security and law and order, reorganisation of the army and reform of the financial system; second, expulsion of the Özbegs from Khurāsān; third, recovery of territory occupied by the Ottomans. In order to free his hands to deal with the domestic situation, and to restore the discipline and morale of the armed forces with a view to taking the offensive on the eastern front, ʻAbbās took the painful but decisive step of signing a peace treaty with the Ottomans in 1589/90 which ceded to the enemy some of Iran's richest provinces: Āẕarbāyjān, Qarābāgh, Ganja, Qarājadāgh and parts of Georgia, Luristān and Kurdistān. The acceptance of such humiliating peace terms was an indication of the weakness of 'Abbās's position at his accession.

One matter was of the greatest urgency: he had to make it clear to the *qizilbāsh* chiefs that, though they had made him shah, he had no intention of being their puppet. The very manner in which he had come to the throne, by means of a *coup d'état* which overthrew his father, the legal ruler, made it obvious that the *qizilbāsh* might conspire to overthrow him in the same way if he failed to govern in accordance with their wishes. The events of 'Abbās's formative years had left him with a deep and abiding distrust of the *qizilbāsh* chiefs. In 1581, when he was too young to have any real say in the matter, he had been proclaimed king in Khurāsān by a group of *qizilbāsh* chiefs, although he had no wish to be the centre of a revolt against his father. He had been a pawn in the struggle between his own guardian, 'Alī Qulī Khān Shāmlū, Governor of Harāt, whose aim was to unite all the *qizilbāsh* chiefs in Khurāsān behind 'Abbās Mīrzā, and Murshid Qulī Khān Ustājlū, the Governor of Mashhad, whose ambition would not allow him to accept a position subordinate to that of 'Alī Qulī Khān. Finally, in 1585, in a battle between the two factions, 'Abbās was taken prisoner by Murshid Qulī Khān's men and carried off in triumph to Mashhad. 'Abbās had been brought up since infancy among the Shāmlū tribe, and this turn of events was abhorrent to him. His captor, Murshid Qulī Khān, assumed the role of his guardian, and arrogantly gave himself the title of *vakīl*.

However much 'Abbās might wish to take punitive action against the *qizilbāsh* for their disloyalty to the state, he had to recognise that they still constituted the backbone of the fighting forces and that too drastic a purge of their ranks would militate against his objective of increasing the strength of the army. 'Abbās had made one basic decision: there was to be no going back to a situation in which the *qizilbāsh* chiefs held a dominant position in the state, or even to the situation which obtained between 1533 and 1574, when Shāh Ṭahmāsp adroitly maintained a delicate balance between the Turcoman and Tājīk interests. The punishment of the *qizilbāsh* for their disloyalty and factionalism was to be the forfeiture of their privileged position in the state. Yet one of the bases of the power of the Safavid kings had been the unquestioning obedience and devotion accorded to them by their *qizilbāsh* Ṣūfī disciples. Although the actions of the *qizilbāsh* since the battle of Chāldirān in 1514 had made it abundantly clear that they no longer believed in their leader as a divine or quasi-divine person, nevertheless the dynamic ideology which had motivated the early Safavid movement had not entirely disappeared. The Shāh was, in theory at any rate, still their *murshid-i kāmil*, their perfect spiritual director, and they were his *murīds* (disciples). At moments of crisis, an appeal to those *qizilbāsh* who were *shāhī-sevän*, that is, who loved the shah, was still an effective rallying-cry. The original Ṣūfī organisation of the Safavid party was still in existence, though its existence was a shadowy one and it had no organic function within the administrative framework of the state. Nevertheless the head of this organisation, the *khalīfat al-khulafā*, still considered himself a person to be reckoned with, and in 1576 had even made a direct challenge to the authority of Shāh Ismā'īl II. Ismā'īl, in order to test the loyalty of the *khalīfat al-khulafā*, Ḥusayn Qulī Khulafā Rūmlū, told him that he would appoint him *vakīl* of the Supreme *Dīvān* if he was willing to relinquish the position of *khalīfat al-khulafā*. Ḥusayn Qulī replied: "I will not surrender the position of *khalīfa*. If the office of *vakīl* be added to that, well and good; but if not, I will not be satisfied with the *vikālat* [alone]."[1] He said this because he considered his power as *khalīfa* to be superior to that of a *vakīl*. While one cannot help thinking that Ḥusayn Qulī was exaggerating the importance of his office, given the realities of the situation in 1576, it is clear that Shāh 'Abbās could not afford lightly to dispense with the devotion to his person which was inherent in the Ṣūfī ideology, even though by 1588 perhaps only a minority of the *qizilbāsh* subscribed to this ideology wholeheartedly.

The question, therefore, was what source of support could 'Abbās find which would place loyalty to himself above sectarian interests? For an answer, 'Abbās turned to the "third force" which Shāh Ṭahmāsp had introduced into the state, namely, the Circassians, Georgians and Armenians termed the *ghulāms* (slaves) of the shah, who, after conversion to Islam, had been trained for service either in the army or in some branch of the administration of the royal household. The term *ghulām* invites an obvious comparison with the Ottoman *qapî-qullarî*, or slaves of the Porte: indeed, the term *qullar* soon entered into Safavid usage too. ʻAbbās immediately set about levying, from the ranks of the *ghulāms*, several regiments which constituted the nucleus of a standing army. The concept of a standing army was in itself an innovation in Iran in Islamic times. Throughout the mediaeval Islamic period, armies had been levied on a tribal basis in times of need, and mobilisation was a relatively lengthy and cumbersome process. The ruler, who might or might not possess a small bodyguard, had to maintain his position by his personal prestige and whatever other factors constituted the basis of his own particular authority. By creating new *ghulām* regiments, ʻAbbās formed an army which was always available, was able to go into action at short notice and, most important of all, owed no allegiance except to the Shāh in person. The existence of the new standing army enabled ʻAbbās to deal ruthlessly with the slightest sign of recalcitrance on the part of the *qizilbāsh*.

The new *ghulām* regiments created by ʻAbbās consisted of cavalry, armed with muskets in addition to the usual weapons, and numbered 10,000–15,000 men. These regiments did not make up the whole of the standing army. In addition, ʻAbbās created a corps of musketeers (*tufangchiyān*), composed mainly of Iranians, who were originally intended to be infantry but were gradually provided with horses, and an artillery corps (*tūpchiyān*); each of these corps was 12,000 strong. Finally, the size of the royal bodyguard was increased to 3,000 men, and it was drawn exclusively from the ranks of the *ghulāms*, another clear indication of the Shāh's distrust of the *qizilbāsh*. All in all, the Shāh thus had at his command a standing army of about 40,000 men.

ʻĀbbās, having created a standing army, was faced by the problem of how to pay it. Prior to Shāh ʻAbbās I, the *qizilbāsh* troops constituted by far the larger part of the total forces available. The government of the provinces was allotted to the *qizilbāsh* chiefs in the form of assignments known as *tiyūl*. The governor of the province was allowed to consume the greater part of the revenue of the province on condition that he maintained, and mustered when required to do so by the shah, a stated number of troops. Provinces organised in this way were termed *mamālik* or "state" provinces; only a small part of the revenue from such provinces was given to the king, usually in the form of presents and dues. The amount of cash in the royal treasury was therefore small and totally inadequate as a source of funds to pay a standing army of some 40,000 men. "Crown" lands constituted the principal source of income for the shah, the revenues from such lands being collected by the shah's stewards or bailiffs. The solution to the problem which was adopted by Shāh 'Abbās was the conversion of a number of *mamālik*, or "state" provinces, into *khāṣṣa*, or "crown" provinces. The "crown" provinces were administered by a comptroller or intendant of the Crown, and these officials were often drawn from the ranks of the *ghulāms*. This policy thus at the same time reduced the number of powerful *qizilbāsh* provincial governors who acted like petty princes in the area under their jurisdiction, and enhanced the prestige of the *ghulāms*. The policy therefore seemed doubly attractive to 'Abbās, and in the short term it solved his problems. In the long term, however, it was open to serious objections. In the first place, in the case of the old-style *qizilbāsh* provincial governors, self-interest militated against extortion; if they tried to levy undue amounts in the form of taxes and extraordinary dues of various kinds, they damaged the province's economy and the law of diminishing returns came into effect. In the *khāṣṣa* provinces, on the other hand, the intendant of the Crown had only one interest, to retain his job by remitting to the royal treasury if possible more than the amount of the tax assessment; since he had no vested interest in the province concerned, he did not mind if the burden of taxation caused its level of prosperity to decline. In the second place, this policy weakened the state militarily in the long term, particularly under 'Abbās's successors, Shāh Ṣafī (1629–42) and 'Abbās II (1642–66), who accelerated the process of the conversion of *mamālik* into *khāṣṣa* provinces. Ultimately, even the frontier provinces were made "crown" provinces, except in time of war, when *qizilbāsh* governors were reappointed. The fact that *qizilbāsh* governors were reappointed in times of crisis was in itself an admission that they were better able to defend them. The *qizilbāsh* chief to whom a province had been assigned as a fief was likely to have more interest in defending it than a government appointee with no long-term commitment to the region. An additional point is that the *ghulām* troops, although they performed creditably enough in campaigns against the Ottomans and elsewhere, and although some outstanding military commanders emerged from their ranks, did not in the last analysis possess that irresistible fighting *élan*, based on a strong tribal *esprit de corps*, which had made the *qizilbāsh* the only troops in the Middle East to win the grudging admiration of the Ottoman janissaries. The *qizilbāsh*, in fact, despised the *ghulāms*, whom they dubbed *qarā-oghlū*, or sons of black slaves. In the long term, then, the policy of converting "state" into "crown" provinces impaired the economic health of the country and weakened it militarily.

The reduction of the number of *qizilbāsh* provincial governorships was by no means the only measure devised by 'Abbās to curb the power of the *qizilbāsh*. He embarked on a systematic policy of transferring groups of *qizilbāsh* belonging to one tribe, to an *ulkā*, or tribal district, held in fief by another tribe. This was just one of a number of ways in which 'Abbās sought to weaken the close tribal bonds which were the source of *qizilbāsh* strength: in some cases, he would deliberately place an officer in charge of a tribe who was not himself a member of that tribe; in other cases, he would allege that the tribe did not possess an officer capable of leading it, and would appoint a *ghulām* to act as chief of the tribe. Such measures succeeded in their short-term objective, but the continuance of these policies by his successors ultimately undermined the military strength of the Safavid empire.

The effect of these policies on the Safavid polity should not be underestimated. Within a short time, Georgians, Armenians and Circassians were appointed to the highest offices of state. Minorsky has calculated that, by the end of the reign of Shāh 'Abbās, they filled one-fifth of the high administrative posts. In some cases, notably that of the celebrated Allāhverdī Khān, these *nouveaux riches* of Safavid society attempted to found their own family dynasties. By 1595, Allāhverdī Khān, a Georgian, had become one of the most powerful men in the Safavid state. He held not only the office of *qullar-āqāsī*, or commander of the *ghulām* regiments, an office which was one of the five principal offices of the state at that time, but he was Governor-General of the rich province of Fārs. This appointment signalled a radical change of policy on the part of Shāh 'Abbās I. Hitherto, all important provinces had been governed by *qizilbāsh amīrs*. By his appointment as Governor-General of Fārs, Allāhverdī Khān achieved equality of status with the *qizilbāsh amīrs*, and became the first representative of a new *ghulām* aristocracy. His power reached its peak in 1598, when he was appointed commander-in-chief of the armed forces. His rise to such eminence in so short a time can only be described as meteoric. One has only to contrast the situation which obtained ten years earlier to be amazed at the rapidity with which 'Abbās had brought about this transformation. These new *ghulām* aristocrats were subject to the same risks in regard to their lives, the lives of their families and their property, as were the members of the old *qizilbāsh* aristocracy. On the death of Allāhverdī Khān in 1613, Shāh 'Abbās appointed his son, Imām Qulī Khān, to succeed him as Governor-General of Fārs, but in 1633 Imām Qulī Khān and his whole family were executed by Shāh Ṣafī (see Chapter 10).

Before any of these policies could be formulated, 'Abbās had to meet an immediate challenge to his authority by the *qizilbāsh*. In the first place, the powerful *qizilbāsh* chief Murshid Qulī Khān, the head of the Ustājlū tribe which had been decimated by Shāh Ismā'īl II and the man responsible for placing 'Abbās I on the throne, assumed that, as in the past, he would be able to bend the young Shāh to his will. As an indication of the role he intended to play, he arrogated to himself the title of *vakīl-i shāh*, or *vakīl-i salṭana*, i.e. vicegerent of the shah, or vicegerent of the state. This was a clear echo, if not of the original concept of *vakīl-i nafs-i nafīs-i humāyūn*, the vicegerent of the shah in both his spiritual and temporal capacity, at least of the *vakīls* of the period of *qizilbāsh* supremacy between 1524 and 1533. Murshid Qulī Khān no doubt intended to return to the "excessive prerogatives" of a viceroy, and to establish a special relationship with the Shāh. 'Abbās had never liked Murshid Qulī Khān as his guardian, nor had he enjoyed being among the Ustājlū tribe. After his accession, 'Abbās liked even less his *vakīl*'s ever-increasing power. He was not alone in his dislike of the *vakīl*'s power; within a short time a group of *qizilbāsh* chiefs had formed a conspiracy to assassinate the *vakīl*. Murshid Qulī Khān was forewarned of the plot, and took refuge in the palace with the Shāh. The conspirators stormed past the palace guards and into the audience-hall, with their weapons, riding-boots and all. 'Abbās, much as he would have liked to rid himself of the *vakīl*, realised that if he failed to visit condign punishment on the conspirators for their effrontery in breaking into the palace fully armed, he would condemn himself to the same sort of subordinate position as had been endured by his father. It was a test case. 'Abbās made an appeal for assistance to "those who love the shah" (*shāhī-sevān*), and a number of *qizilbāsh* rushed to the palace. The conspirators demanded that 'Abbās establish a council of *amīrs*, similar to the one which had existed in the time of Sulṭān Muḥammad Shāh. 'Abbās would have none of it. When one of the conspirators lost his temper and started abusing Murshid Qulī Khān, the Shāh flew into a rage: "You seditious little man!" he shouted. "You, and people like you, are thorns in the side of the body politic!"[2] The thorns were speedily removed; invoking the aid of the *shāhī-sevāns*, 'Abbās had all the ringleaders of the plot executed. Having survived this test, 'Abbās felt strong enough to rid himself of the *vakīl* as well, and he had him assassinated on 23 July 1589, nine months after his own accession. These displays of summary royal justice caused some *qizilbāsh* to desert in fear of their lives, but 'Abbās had made his point. "Now that I am king," he said, "we are going to forget about the practice of Sulṭān Muḥammad Shāh; the king is going to make the decisions now."

The reorganisation and rebuilding of his armed forces could not take place overnight, and the situation on the eastern front continued to deteriorate. The Özbegs overran the province of Sīstān, lying to the south of Khurāsān, which was normally immune from their attacks. Qandahār, which had been in Safavid hands intermittently since 1537, was lost to the Moguls in 1590. 'Abbās took an army to Khurāsān, but hesitated to commit his forces to a pitched battle. From the beginning, he displayed as a military commander that caution which was to be one of his outstanding characteristics in later campaigns. It was not until 1598, ten years after his accession, that the death of the formidable Özbeg leader 'Abd Allāh II precipitated dynastic struggles and gave 'Abbās his opportunity in the east. He marched from Iṣfahān on 9 April 1598, the Özbegs abandoning city after city as he advanced into Khurāsān. On 29 July the Shāh made a pilgrimage to the shrine of the 8th Shī'ī Imām, 'Alī al-Riżā, at Mashhad. He found the shrine in a bad way. It had been stripped of its gold and silver chandeliers, and nothing remained of the ornaments donated to the shrine except the gold railing round the tomb of the Imām. Leaving Mashhad on 1 August, the Shāh marched toward Harāt in the hope of bringing the Özbegs, now led by

Dīn Muḥammad Khān, to battle. This was never an easy task. The Özbegs preferred to avoid pitched battles, and to retire across the Oxus into the trackless wastes of Transoxania, into which a regular army pursued them at its peril. Biding their time until the royal army retired, they would then resume their traditional pattern of warfare, bottling up the Safavid garrisons in the cities and ravaging the countryside. In the event, 'Abbās used the same ruse which had been employed by Ismā'īl I at his great victory over the Özbegs at Marv in 1510. He ordered his advance guard to retire, and to spread word that the Shāh had been forced to return to the west because of a crisis there. Dīn Muḥammad Khān was lured out from behind the fortifications of Harāt, and the Shāh, covering ten days' journey in four and a half days, caught the Özbegs in the open on 9 August 1598. The horses of many of the Shāh's men were jaded, and in his forced march he had so far outstripped his main army that he had no more than 10,000 men with him; the Özbegs numbered 12,000. The battle was fierce, and the outcome still hung in the balance when the Shāh's bodyguard of 200 men suddenly saw the gleam of the helmets, chain-mail and breastplates of riders advancing through a reed-bed; it was Dīn Muḥammad Khān himself with 1,000 picked men he had kept in reserve. A wave of panic went through the Shāh's bodyguard. "Attack like men," the Shāh shouted, "for a valiant death is preferable to a life of shame!"[3] A determined charge by his bodyguard broke the Özbeg ranks and, when Dīn Muḥammad Khān was wounded by a spear-thrust, the Özbegs began a general retreat. The Safavid forces pursued them until their horses foundered under them, and the Özbegs lost 4,000 men. Dīn Muḥammad Khān, faint from loss of blood, seems to have been set upon and murdered by tribesmen in the course of his retreat. By his victory at Rabāṭ-i Pariyān, 'Abbās not only liberated Harāt, but was able to stabilise the north-east frontier with a reasonable measure of success through a series of alliances with local Özbeg chiefs. This enabled him, in 1602, to begin a series of campaigns against the Ottomans in the west.

Shortly before his expedition to Khurāsān, 'Abbās had transferred his capital from Qazvīn to Iṣfahān. The more central location of Iṣfahān made it easier to move troops to any part of his dominions. The imaginative exercise in town-planning which transformed Iṣfahān into one of the world's most beautiful cities will be described in a later chapter. On his return to Iṣfahān after his victory over the Özbegs, the Shāh signalled the event by remitting taxes to the value of 100,000 'Irāqī *tumāns*. This tax remission was made up as follows: tax on sheep and goats (*chūpān-begī*): 20,000 *tumāns*. In consideration of the fact that the people of Khurāsān, throughout the period of the Özbeg occupation, had assisted with their lives and property the troops of the royal army, their fellow-Khurāsānīs and all manner of official guests, and had suffered great hardship in so doing, the Shāh ordered a permanent remission of the tax on flocks in Khurāsān; abolition of fees illegally collected by governors in excess of the tax assessment: 50,000–60,000 *tumāns*; remission of all taxes at Iṣfahān for one year, as a reward for the loyal services of the people of that city: 20,000 *tumāns*.[4]

In 1589/90, 'Abbās had signed away large areas of Iranian territory in order not to have to fight on two fronts, and in order to have his hands free to deal with urgent problems at home. In 1602, with the eastern front stabilised at least for the time being, and with internal security restored, the Shāh's thoughts turned to the recovery of Āẕarbāyjān and Shīrvān, two of the most important provinces which had been conquered by the Ottomans. Whenever he had discussed with his advisers the possibility of recovering his lost territory, they had reminded him of the power of the Ottoman sulṭāns, and the numerical superiority of their armies. 'Abbās's first act was to raze the fort at Nihāvand, which had been left by the Ottomans as an advance base for future invasions of Iran. The Shāh did his best to allay Ottoman suspicions that he was planning an attack on Āẕarbāyjān, by announcing that he was going on a hunting expedition to Māzandarān. Nevertheless, rumours reached the commandant of the Ottoman garrison at Tabrīz, Vakīl Pasha. The story goes that Vakīl Pasha was discussing the matter with an astrologer, and they decided to refer to the poems of Ḥāfiẓ for an augury. At the top of the right-hand page was the following line:

> O Ḥāfiẓ! You have captured 'Irāq and Fārs by your poetry;
> Now it is the turn of Baghdād and Tabrīz![5]

The Shāh left Iṣfahān on 14 September 1603, and marched north to Kāshān, as though he were going to Māzandarān. From Kāshān, he doubled back to Qazvīn, and then marched from

Qazvīn to Tabrīz in six days. When the Shāh's troops were some 12 miles from the city, the local inhabitants donned their distinctive Safavid headgear, which they had kept hidden during the Ottoman occupation, and rushed to greet them. When the Safavid vanguard entered Tabrīz, some of the Ottoman garrison had left the citadel and were busy making purchases in the market. Hearing the cheering of the townsfolk, they rushed back into the citadel and closed the gates.

The city presented a desolate sight, because the populace had initially fled at the time of the Ottoman occupation, and the Ottomans had done much damage to buildings and houses. During the twenty years of Ottoman occupation, people had gradually trickled back into the city, many of them having lost all their possessions, but the physical destruction remained. Of every hundred houses, scarcely a single house was in even a third as good a condition as formerly. The inhabitants of Tabrīz were implacable in their reprisals. If an Ottoman soldier had taken a Tabrīzī girl into his house and had had children by her, the girl's relatives would make no allowances for that, but would drag the Ottoman off and kill him.

'Alī Pasha, the commandant of the Ottoman garrison, had been absent from the city with 5,000 men when the Shāh's forces reached the city. He marched back to Tabrīz but his force was routed by a Safavid force which, for once, had superiority of numbers. The Ottoman garrison in the citadel then surrendered. Many of the garrison took advantage of double the pay and allowances they had received in Ottoman service, and entered the Safavid army. From Tabrīz, the royal army marched to Nakhchivān, which they captured; this caused all Ottoman forces south of the Aras river to withdraw and congregate at Erīvān. The Ottoman forces in the area numbered about 12,000, and the fortifications at Erīvān, consisting of three separate forts, constituted one of the strongest defensive positions in the area. The three forts, supporting each other and well garrisoned with seasoned troops and amply stocked with provisions and supplies, constituted a formidable problem, particularly as the Safavids, in their wars with the Ottomans, had rarely succeeded in taking a fortress by storm. The siege proceeded throughout the winter of 1603/4, but made little progress because of the extreme cold; the ground was so hard that it was impossible to dig trenches. The fort finally surrendered in June 1604, and Safavid forces made several forays into Qarābāgh. An Ottoman diversionary attack from Baghdād was repulsed, and its commander taken prisoner. The news that the Ottomans were mounting a major counter-attack from Istanbul led the Shāh to devastate the area of Qārṣ and Erzerūm in eastern Anatolia, and to transfer to ʿIrāq-i ʿAjam some 2,000–3,000 Armenian families who normally spent the summer in that area. Jeghāl-oghlū Pasha, in command of the Ottoman army, marched as far as the river Aras but, because of the lateness of the season, retired to Vān for the winter. The Shāh's reputation for making forced marches had the effect of making the Ottoman force nervous about moving too far from its base at Vān, and a year passed in manoeuvre and counter-manoeuvre. Eventually, the Shāh sent Allāhverdī Khān against Vān; the commander-in-chief scored some brilliant successes against both Jeghāl-oghlū and a relief force sent from Sīvās, and Jeghāl-oghlū Pasha had to slip away across Lake Vān in a boat to mobilise a new army. The decisive battle in this campaign was fought at Ṣūfiyān, near Tabrīz, on 6 November 1605. In this battle, ʿAbbās displayed his outstanding talents as a commander in the field. Before the battle, he had not intended to risk everything on one pitched battle, but had planned rather to wear down the enemy's strength by daily, but limited engagements. However, the faithful adherence to his orders not to precipitate an action, on the part of another of his brilliant *ghulām* commanders, Qarchaqāy Beg, was interpreted as a sign of weakness by the Ottomans, who launched an attack which led to a general action which ended in an overwhelming victory for the Shāh's forces. By 1607, less than five years since the Shāh began his counter-offensive against the Ottomans, the last Ottoman soldier had been expelled from Iranian territory as defined by the Treaty of Amasya in 1555.

The Ottomans were not yet ready to negotiate a new peace settlement on the basis of that Treaty, and sporadic clashes between Ottoman and Safavid forces continued for some years. When Naṣūḥ Pasha succeeded Murād Pasha as Ottoman commander-in-chief on the eastern front, serious peace negotiations were resumed. The Safavid ambassador, Qāżī Khān, who held the office of *ṣadr*, was received in audience by Sulṭān Aḥmad I. After a lot of discussion, it was agreed to negotiate peace on the basis of the Treaty of Amasya. During the sixty years that had elapsed since the signature of that Treaty, many changes had taken place in the frontiers. For example, the Meskhia region of Georgia, and the forts in the Akhesqa district, which under the Treaty of Amasya had been defined as Iranian territory, had in the meantime been occupied by the Ottomans; on the other hand, some forts in the 'Arabistān and Baghdād regions which had been defined as Ottoman territory, were now in Safavid hands. It was recognised that it was going to be hard for either side to surrender the territory it had occupied, and so it seemed easier for each side to keep the territory actually in its possession at the time the new peace treaty was signed. To demarcate the new frontiers in Āẕarbāyjān and 'Irāq-i 'Arab, each side appointed plenipotentiaries. The work of these officers was frustrated by the activities of the Georgians and Kurds, and border incidents provoked by them led to a resumption of hostilities between the Ottomans and the Safavids. In 1616, a large Ottoman force laid siege to Erīvān; when the attack failed, the Ottoman commander, Muḥammad Pasha, once again raised the question of peace talks. The Shāh replied that he was willing at any time to reopen talks on the basis of the preliminary agreement worked out between Qāẓī Khān and Naṣūḥ Pasha, and on the basis of the work of the two boundary commissions, the authenticated text of whose report was in the hands of both parties. At Erzerūm, the preliminary peace treaty was reaffirmed on the same basis as before, and the Ottoman army withdrew. The preliminary treaty was renounced by Sulṭān Aḥmad I, who accused Muḥammad Pasha of dereliction of duty, and dismissed him. His successor, Khalīl Pasha, was ordered to prepare to invade Iran, once again in co-operation with the Crimean Tatars. The Shāh ordered Qarchaqāy Khān, an Armenian *ghulām* who had risen rapidly in the Shāh's esteem and had been appointed commander-in-chief after the death of Allāhverdī Khān in 1613, to devastate the whole of the Erīvān–Vān region through which the invasion army would have to march. This action delayed the Ottoman advance, and, before Khalīl Pasha could bring up his main force, the death of Sulṭān Aḥmad I and the accession of the less belligerent Sulṭān Muṣṭafā again opened up possibilities of peace talks; although no definitive peace was concluded, there was a lull in the warfare between the two sides until 1623, when 'Abbās, taking advantage of internal discord in the Ottoman province of Baghdād, invaded it and captured the city of Baghdād, which had been taken from Shāh Ṭahmāsp by Sulṭān Süleymān in 1534. The Safavid historian Iskandar Beg Munshī, recording the fall of the city on 14 January 1624, uttered the pious hope: "May Baghdād remain in Safavid hands until the end of time!"[6] This hope was not fulfilled, for the city was recaptured by the Ottomans only fourteen years later, under 'Abbās's incompetent successor, Shāh Ṣafī.

The fall of Baghdād destroyed the morale of the Ottoman garrisons at Mosul, Kirkuk and Shahrazūr, and the troops began to desert; all three forts were captured by the Safavids. The Shāh visited the Shī'ī shrines at Karbalā, Najaf, Kāẓimayn and Sāmarrā. Ḥāfiẓ Aḥmad Pasha was appointed Grand Vizier and commander-in-chief of the Ottoman forces along the Iranian frontier, with orders to recover Baghdād. After ordering that the land along the Ottoman line of march from Vān be stripped of all supplies, the Shāh reinforced the Safavid garrison at Baghdād and himself marched to defend it. Ḥāfiẓ Aḥmad Pasha's army reached the city in November 1625, and blockaded the citadel on three sides. The Ottoman lines extended along the east bank of the Tigris for a distance of some 4 miles, and a force had thrown a bridge across the Tigris near the tomb of Abū Ḥanīfa and had occupied Old Baghdād. The Ottoman besieging force was well provisioned, because the harvest had just been gathered in. A task force of 1,000 Safavid volunteers slipped through the Ottoman lines carrying supplies of gunpowder and lead for shot for the garrison. Nevertheless, the Ottomans were prosecuting the siege with vigour, and the Shāh's relief force, approaching from Hārūnābād, had been held up by the necessity of bridging numerous watercourses which were in spate. Ḥāfiẓ Aḥmad Pasha's aim was to take the city by assault before the Shāh could arrive. Working night and day, his men charged through the breach, only to be confronted by inner defence walls which the Safavid garrison had constructed against this eventuality. The Ottomans lost 5,000 men in this abortive assault.

When 'Abbās finally reached Baghdād, the siege was in its seventh month. The Ottoman plan was not to give battle to the Shāh, but to sit tight behind their lines, which were protected not only by a ditch, but also by barricades of gun-carriages and by palisades, behind which were stationed the cannon and musketeers. While refusing to give battle to the Shāh's relief force, they could continue to lay siege to the citadel. 'Abbās decided that a frontal attack on the Ottoman lines would be too costly, and he determined to try and cut the Ottoman supply-lines both by land and by water. He sent a force to intercept supplies reaching the Ottomans by boat from Diyār Bakr and Mosul; another force crossed the Diyāla river and constructed a fortified camp west of the river; a third force crossed the Tigris south of the city on rafts and in boats, and established another bridgehead on the west bank. This last force was able to intercept supplies reaching the Ottomans from the south, from Ḥilla and Baṣra. Yet another force was dispatched to block the main Ottoman supply-route from Aleppo to Fallūja. These moves were highly successful, and a whole caravan from Aleppo was captured. By June 1626, however, the Safavid garrison in the citadel was running short of food. A daring body of men from the garrison ferried boats down the Tigris to the Shāh's camp under cover of darkness. There, they were loaded with flour, wheat, barley, rice, cooking-fat, chickens, sheep and other foodstuffs including desserts, sherbets, sugar, sugar-candy and the like. This cargo had to run the gauntlet of Ottoman troops who, for a distance of about 2 miles, lined both banks of the Tigris as a result of their occupation of Old Baghdād. Part of the cargo was sent up by boat, and the rest by camel caravan along the west bank, the way for this caravan being cleared by a strong escort of Safavid troops.

The re-provisioning of the citadel was a major setback to Ottoman plans, and Ḥāfiẓ Aḥmad Pasha decided to risk a pitched battle against the relief force. The Shāh's forces drove the Ottomans back behind their defences with heavy losses. The Safavid blockade of the Ottoman supply-lines was now having its effect; not only were the besiegers short of food, but sickness had broken out in their camp. On 4 July 1626, Ḥāfiẓ Aḥmad Pasha was forced to withdraw his forces, abandoning his cannon because of a lack of animals to pull them. Several thousand sick and dying men were abandoned in the Ottoman lines. The relief of the siege of Baghdād, like the battle of Ṣūfiyān in 1605, was an example of Shāh 'Abbās's brilliant tactical sense. A letter written by a senior Ottoman officer to a friend of his at Istanbul gives a vivid account of what conditions were like for the Ottoman besiegers when the Safavid blockade of their supply-lines took effect:

Those of delicate constitution who were dainty in their food, now are thankful when they see horse-flesh! Those elegant and dandified fellows who were ashamed to wear a shirt of Egyptian cotton, now are glad to get shirts of old tent canvas which do not cover their knees! Those conceited heroes who in the coffee-houses have mocked at the *qizilbāsh* for their cowardice, now when they behold the most insignificant of them three miles away on the road, compare him with Rustam the son of Zāl![7]

The last comment illustrates very well the military achievement of 'Abbās I. Early in his reign, he had been forced to surrender to the Ottomans the richest provinces of Iran. By the end of his life, the Ottomans no longer looked for easy conquests of Safavid territory.

We have seen that the period from the establishment of the Safavid state in 1501, up to the accession of Shāh 'Abbās I in 1588, was one of change and experiment. An attempt was made to incorporate the original Ṣūfī organisation of the Safavid Order in the administrative structure of the state. An attempt was made to prevent the Turcoman elements in the state from assuming a dominant position at the expense of the Tājīk elements. Both these attempts failed. The failure of the first attempt meant a steady movement away from the theocratic origins of the Safavid state and toward a greater separation of religious and secular powers. The failure of the second attempt led Shāh Ṭahmāsp to introduce, as a "third force", elements which were neither Turcoman–*qizilbāsh* nor Tājīk–Iranian; these Caucasian Christian elements, termed *ghulāms* or *qullar*, were a major factor in the administrative reorganisation of the state, and in the concomitant social revolution, brought about by Shāh 'Abbās I. In the new social order, loyalty and obedience to the shah, and not membership of the *qizilbāsh* élite, were to be the sole criterial for advancement.

The changed social and political basis of the Safavid state under 'Abbās I was naturally reflected in its administrative structure. After the initial attempt by the kingmaker Murshid Qulī Khān Ustājlū to revive the outmoded concept of *vakīl*, the offices of *vakīl* and *amīr al-umarā*, relevant to a situation which no longer obtained, both lapsed. The *amīr al-umarā* was commander-in-chief of the armed forces at a time when the *qizilbāsh* were, to all intents and purposes, the armed forces. Once the *qizilbāsh* regiments became only part of the total armed forces, the term *qūrchī* became the common term to denote the old *qizilbāsh* tribal cavalry, and their commander, the *qūrchībāshī*, whose authority in both the political and military fields had steadily increased under Ismā'īl II and Sulṭān Muḥammad Shāh, continued to be one of the principal officers of state under 'Abbās I, and his counsel carried great weight in public affairs. The fall of the *qizilbāsh* from their dominant position meant the rapid increase of the power of the *vazīr*, the head of the bureaucracy and traditionally an Iranian. The greater centralisation of the administration under 'Abbās I gave the bureaucracy even more work to do than it had before, and the enhanced status of the *vazīr* was indicated by the titles now commonly conferred on him: *i'timād al-dawla* (trusty support of the state), and, less frequently, *ṣadr-i a'ẓam* (exalted seat of honour, which was also the title of the Ottoman Grand Vizier). To replace the *vakīl* and the *amīr al-umarā* in the top echelon of the Safavid administration, we find the commanders of two of the new corps: the *qullar-āqāsī*, or commander of the corps of *ghulāms*; and the *tufangchī-āqāsī*, or commander of the musketeers. Neither of these two officers, however, replaced the *amīr al-umarā* as commander-in-chief of all the Safavid armed forces. To serve this function, Shāh 'Abbās created a new office, *sardār-i lashkar*, and later the ancient Iranian title *sipahsālār* was revived in the same sense. These names suggest the triumph of the Tājīk elements in the state, but, ironically, the office went first to a Georgian *ghulām*, Allāhverdī Khān, and then to an Armenian *ghulām*, Qarchaqāy Khān. By this policy, 'Abbās avoided the dissension which would inevitably have resulted from the appointment of either a Turk or an Iranian to the office of supreme commander, and was able to weld his now heterogeneous forces into a cohesive body. It is interesting to note that the *tūpchī-bāshī*, or commander of the artillery corps, is not listed among the principal officers of state, and this undoubtedly reflects the general Safavid antipathy toward artillery. The last member of the reconstituted group of principal officers of state was the *ishīk-āqāsī-bāshī*, or Grand Marshal, whose duties were largely ceremonial, but who nevertheless was influential in the councils of state because of his inside knowledge of the royal household; this office was usually filled by a *qizilbāsh*. The administrative reforms of 'Abbās I gave the Safavid state new strength and vigour. He placed the administration on such a firm footing that the machine continued to function for nearly a century after his death, despite the fact that most of his successors, with the exception of 'Abbās II, were incompetent rulers. Toward the end of the Safavid period, the machine was running more or less under its momentum. The secret of 'Abbās's success was that he maintained a delicate balance between the various elements of the system – Turks, Iranians and Caucasians. The failure of his successors to maintain this balance led ultimately to the decline of the dynasty.

The increasing secularisation of the state under 'Abbās I was reflected in the eclipse of the *ṣadr*, the head of the religious classes and, during the early period of the Safavid state, one of the principal officers of state. The influence of the *ṣadr*, who was a political appointee, decreased once doctrinal uniformity had been imposed throughout the Safavid empire. As a corollary, the power of the *mujtahids*, the most eminent doctors of Shī'ī law and theology, tended to increase. The Safavids had used institutionalised Sufism to attain power; once in power, they used institutionalised Ithnā 'Asharī Shi'ism to maintain it. As Sanson somewhat cynically, but nevertheless realistically, declared: "The care that Chiek-Sephi (Shaykh Ṣafī al-Dīn) took to establish a particular sect, which was so very different from the other Mahometans, was an admirable invention to prevent the people from revolting, through the solicitations of either the Turks, Tartars, or Indians, who are all their neighbours."[8] With the increasing crystallisation of Ithnā 'Asharī theology, the *mujtahids* became the most powerful members of the religious classes. This necessarily posed a threat to the position of the Shāh himself, because, as will be recalled, the Safavid shahs claimed to be the representatives on earth of the Mahdī or Hidden Imām. In making this claim, they had usurped the prerogatives of the *mujtahids*, who were the real and legal representatives. They had allowed the shahs to usurp this prerogative (although grudgingly), because the establishment of a state in which Shi'ism was the official religion had enormously enhanced the power of the religious classes in general. There were, however, during the reign of Shāh Ṭahmāsp, several instances of friction between the *ṣadr*, who represented political authority, and the *mujtahids*, and, as the influence of the *ṣadr* declined, it was only the authority of the Shāh himself which kept the power of the *mujtahids* within bounds. During the last half century of Safavid rule, when the shahs were weak, the potential danger that the religious classes would acquire a position of dominance in political affairs became a reality. Under a strong ruler like 'Abbās I, the *mujtahids* knew their place.

Reference has already been made to the way in which the *ḥaram* emerged as a source of political power during the succession struggles before and after the death of Shāh Ṭahmāsp, and after the death of Sulṭān Muḥammad Shāh. During the reign of Shāh 'Abbās I it began to exert its influence on the future of the Safavid state in a way which was even more pernicious than the fostering of dynastic intrigue. To begin with, 'Abbās I had followed the traditional Safavid practice of appointing the royal princes to provincial governorates, in the care of a *qizilbāsh* chief who, while the prince remained a minor, was the *de facto* governor of the province and also, as *lala*, the guardian and tutor of the prince, responsible for his welfare and physical and moral education. Under this system, the royal princes received a thorough training in administrative skills and the art of statecraft. Their physical training was taken care of by a programme of lessons in such manly pastimes as archery, horsemanship and swordsmanship. The revolt of one of his sons, however, caused 'Abbās to abandon this traditional policy, and to give orders that henceforth the royal princes should be closely confined within the *ḥaram*, where their only companions were the court eunuchs and the women of the *ḥaram*. They were cut off from all access to the outside world, and to cultivate their friendship was to risk one's life. They left the capital only to accompany the Shāh on his campaigns, and then only because 'Abbās feared that, if they remained in the capital, they might become the centre of a plot against him. The event which soured the Shāh's relationship with his sons was the revolt in 1589 of the *qizilbāsh* chief who was the guardian of his second son, Ḥasan, who was Governor of Mashhad. This event seems to have awakened dark memories of his own youth in Khurāsān, and the way in which he had been used by the *qizilbāsh* as a pawn in the *coup* against his father. He went to extraordinary lengths to segregate his sons from political and military leaders in the state, and his morbid suspiciousness caused him to lend too ready an ear to informers. In 1614/15, his eldest son, Muḥammad Bāqir, was alleged to be the centre of a plot against the Shāh involving certain Circassian elements at court. When the Shāh executed some of the Circassians who were under suspicion, other Circassian chiefs came out openly in support of Muḥammad Bāqir, and in February 1615 the Shāh had his son assassinated. Muḥammad Bāqir may well have been the innocent victim of Circassian intrigue, and 'Abbās was filled with remorse at his action. Unhappily, this second plot against him merely increased 'Abbās's fears of assassination. In 1621, when 'Abbās fell ill, his third son Muḥammad, known as Khudābanda after his grandfather, prematurely celebrated his death, and openly solicited support among the *qizilbāsh*. When 'Abbās recovered, he had Muḥammad blinded. A similar fate befell his fifth son, Imām Qulī Mīrzā, in 1626/7. As his second son, Ḥasan, and his fourth son, Ismā'īl, predeceased him, 'Abbās I had no son capable of succeeding him. Apart from the personal tragedy of this situation for the Shah, his policy of confining the royal princes to the *ḥaram* gave rise to the degeneration of the dynasty which later became a principal cause of its decline. Moreover, control of the royal princes by the court eunuchs and the women of the *ḥaram* gave the latter an undue and altogether pernicious influence in political affairs, as the mothers of royal princes, aided and abetted by court officials, intrigued endlessly to secure the succession of their particular candidate for the throne.

The military and political achievements of 'Abbās I, great though they were, represent only one aspect of this multi-faceted ruler. His reign marks a high point in that remarkable flowering of the arts which occurred in Safavid times. Under his patronage, carpet-weaving was elevated from the status of a cottage-industry to that of a fine art. The textiles produced during his time at the great weaving centres of Iṣfahān, Yazd, Kāshān and Rasht were never excelled in brilliance of colour and design, and Persian silks, damasks and brocades were equally renowned. It was Shāh 'Abbās who made the manufacture and sale of silk a royal monopoly. The "art of the book" – the illumination and illustration of manuscripts, calligraphy and bookbinding – reached a peak during the reign of 'Abbās. In the markets of Europe, Safavid ceramics rivalled the products of China. Safavid mosques, *madrasas* (theological seminaries), shrines and other buildings, were clad in glazed polychrome and mosaic tiles of incomparable beauty. Safavid artistic achievements will be discussed in greater detail in Chapter 6.

Iṣfahān, which 'Abbās I made his capital in 1598, was essentially his creation. Not since the development of Baghdād in the eighth century A.D. by the Caliph al-Manṣūr had there been such a comprehensive example of town-planning in the Islamic world, and the scope and layout of the city centre clearly reflect its status as the capital of an empire. The core of the new city was the Naqsh-i Jahān, a magnificent piazza seven times the size of the Piazza di San Marco. Grouped round this piazza were the 'Ālī Qāpū palace, the vast Qayṣariyya, or Royal Bazaar, and two of the greatest masterpieces of Safavid architecture, the Masjid-i Shāh, or Royal Mosque, and the Shaykh Luṭf Allāh Mosque. From the south, the broad, tree-lined avenue known as the Chahār Bāgh (Four Gardens), approached the city, bisecting an extensive area of luxurious residences belonging to court officials and other dignitaries, set in terraced gardens; the avenue then crossed the Zāyanda-rūd by the Allāhverdī Khān bridge, and became the main commercial and residential thoroughfare of the city. Shāh 'Abbās's Iṣfahān will be discussed at greater length in Chaper 7. 'Abbās's building activities were by no means confined to Iṣfahān. The extension and restoration of the shrine of the 8th Shī'ī Imām at Mashhad, and the construction of the celebrated stone causeway along the marshy littoral of the Caspian Sea, were among his more notable achievements. All over the country, he build caravanserais along the main highways for the convenience of merchants and travellers, and numerous bridges, hospitals and public baths were other examples of his energy in the field of public works. One of his most celebrated engineering projects, which unfortunately ended in failure because of the inadequacy of the technology then available, was his attempt to link the headwaters of the Zāyanda-rūd and Kūhrang rivers (see Chapter 7).

Shāh 'Abbās's love of the Caspian province of Māzandarān, which Thévenot thought "the only lovely Province of all Persia",[9] led him to build there two winter palaces: Ashraf and Faraḥābād. As he grew older, he spent more and more time at these retreats, and each spring he returned with greater reluctance to his state duties and the rigours of military campaigns. Formerly known as Ṭāhān, the site of Faraḥābād was renamed by 'Abbās I when, in 1611 or 1612, he ordered the construction of a royal palace there. Around the palace were built residences, gardens, baths, bazaars, mosques and caravanserais. Faraḥābād was linked

4. Özbeg ambassador to Shāh Sulṭān Ḥusayn, 1700

to the town of Sārī, 17 miles away, by 'Abbās's famous stone causeway. Pietro della Valle, who visited Faraḥābād in 1618, declared that the circuit of the walls was equal to, if not greater than, that of Rome or Constantinople, and that the town contained streets of more than a league in length. The new town, he said, was peopled by the Shāh with colonies of different

5. Royal travel, 1671

nationalities, including Christians from Georgia, which had been moved there from territory overrun by Safavid forces. The buildings were destroyed by the Cossacks in the course of a raid by the latter in 1668. Ashraf lay some 26 miles to the south-east, at the foot of a wooded spur of the Alburz range and commanding a fine view over the bay of Astarābād to the north. The new town of Ashraf was founded by 'Abbās I about 1612. Intended initially to be a simple rural retreat, it consisted of a group of farmhouses surrounding the royal palaces, but eventually the royal residences extended over a considerable area. Spacious accommodation was provided for guests and travellers. The gardens were laid out with walks bordered by pines and by orange and other citrous trees, and were watered by an elaborate system of reservoirs, cisterns and channels fed by a spring which also supplied numerous fountains and cascades. Ashraf was severely damaged by the Afghāns and during the Zand–Qājār civil war which followed the collapse of the Safavid dynasty and the death of Nādir Shāh. Faraḥābād in particular became a sort of second capital. When the Shāh was not actually on campaign, he would retire to Faraḥābād; from this base he carried on the affairs of state, and foreign envoys who wished to see him had to visit him there.

Under 'Abbās I, Iṣfahān became a prosperous city. Merchants from China, India, Central Asia, Arabia, Turkey and Europe flocked to Iṣfahān to buy the luxury items produced by Safavid craftsmen. Thousands of skilled Armenian artisans were transferred from Julfā on the present Irano-Soviet border in Āẕarbāyjān to "New Julfā", a suburb of Iṣfahān on the right bank of the Zāyanda-rūd. In addition to merchants seeking trading privileges, many other Europeans came to Iṣfahān: ambassadors from Spain, Portugal and England; representatives of foreign monastic orders such as the Carmelites, the Augustinians and the Capuchin friars, who were given permission to proselytise and establish convents in Iran; gentlemen–adventurers such as the Sherley brothers, one of whom, Sir Robert, distinguished himself in the Shāh's service against the Ottomans, and was appointed "Master General against the Turks"; and travellers such as Pietro della Valle, who left valuable accounts of Safavid Iran. Intense commercial rivalry in the Persian Gulf and the Indian Ocean between the Dutch, the Portuguese and the English meant the development of diplomatic relations between Iran and the west (see Chapter 5). In all things a pragmatist, 'Abbās I realised that an attitude of religious tolerance toward Christian fathers would establish a climate in which trade with Europe could flourish. Similarly, his development of Mashhad as a major centre of Shī'ī pilgrimage kept in Iranian coffers large sums of money which might otherwise have been spent at the other principal Shī'ī shrines, Karbalā, Najaf, Kāẓimayn and Sāmarrā, all of which are located in Mesopotamia and were for a large part of 'Abbās's reign in Ottoman hands. The restoration and embellishment of Shī'ī holy places such as Mashhad, and the constituting of lands and other property as *awqāf*, or property held in mortmain, for the benefit of the shrine, also enhanced the prestige and wealth of the religious classes, and made them more prepared to acquiesce in the usurpation by the Safavid rulers of their own prerogative of acting as the general agency on earth of the Mahdī or Shī'ī messiah.

This is not to say that 'Abbās's personal piety was not genuine. Whenever he was in Khurāsān, he would visit the shrine of the 8th Imām and keep vigils and perform various menial tasks, such as sweeping the carpets and snuffing the candles, to indicate his devotion. In 1601, he made his celebrated pilgrimage on foot from Iṣfahān to Mashhad in twenty-eight days. The Shāh decreed that any of the *amīrs*, principal officers of state and court attendants who wished to make the pilgrimage with him, could ride, since the vow to make the journey on foot applied to himself alone; several of his attendants, however, accompanied him the whole way on foot. If these were gestures indicative of the importance 'Abbās I attached to fostering the Shī'ī element of Safavid ideology, he was equally concerned, in his capacity of *murshid-i kāmil* (perfect spiritual director) of the Safavid Order, to maintain the cult of the Safavid shaykhs at Ardabīl. He invariably made a visit to the tombs of his ancestors at Ardabīl before embarking on a military expedition or taking a decisive step of any sort; on these visits, he would enlist the spiritual aid of the holy shaykhs of the Safavid Order through prayer and supplication.

Shāh 'Abbās I possessed in abundance qualities which entitle him to be styled "the Great". He was a brilliant strategist and tactician whose chief characteristic was prudence. He preferred to obtain his ends by diplomacy rather than war, and showed immense patience in pursuing his objectives. A charismatic leader, his presence in the field induced his men to perform feats beyond

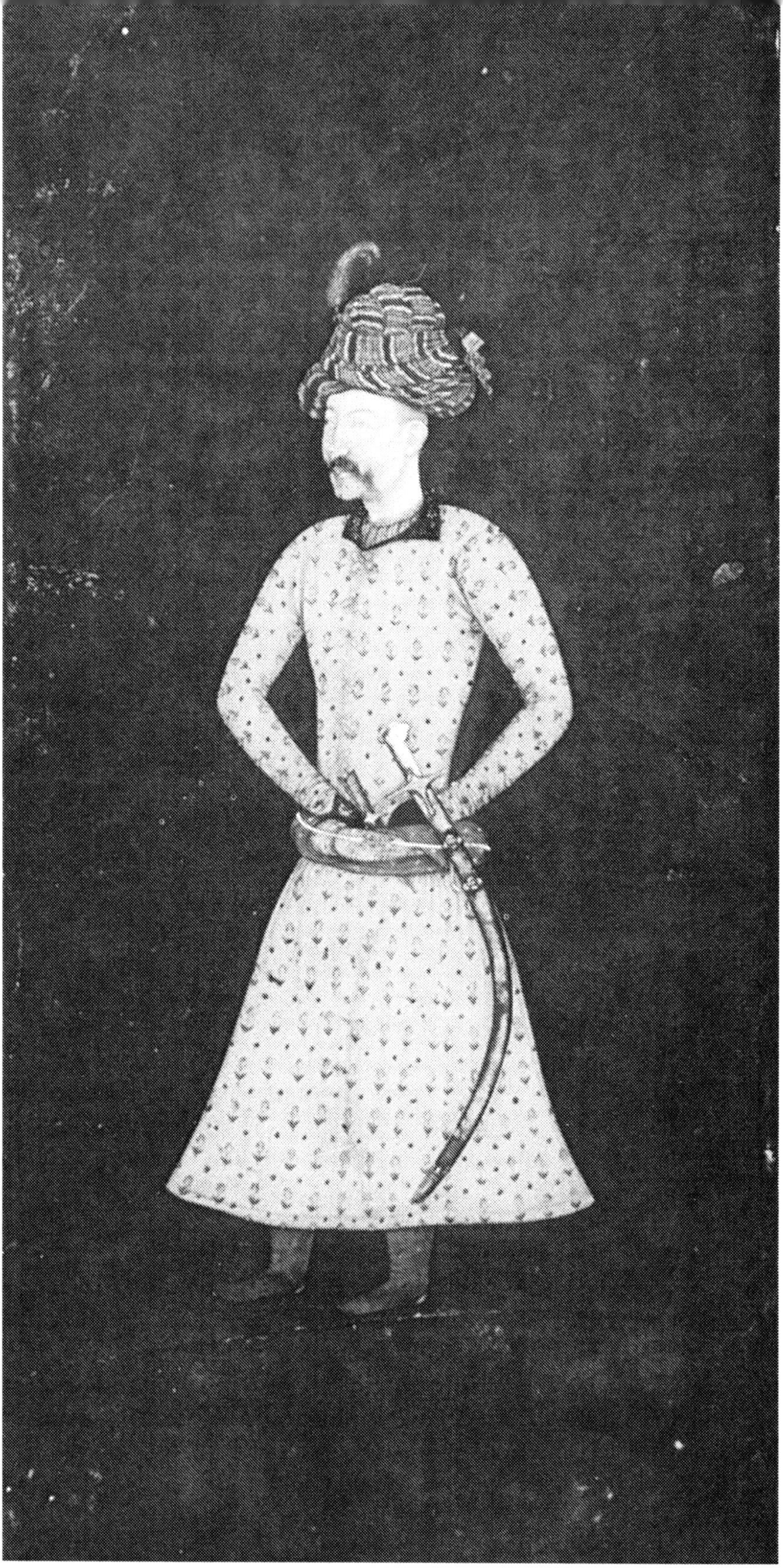

the limits of their endurance; a spectacular example of this is his famous forced marches with small bodies of troops, in the manner of Julius Caesar, which frequently gave him the advantage of surprise. Implacable in his punishment of disloyal officers, his affection for old and trusted retainers was strong and lasting. He ordered that special acts of heroism in battle should be reported to him so that the men concerned might be suitably rewarded. To men he trusted, 'Abbās was ready to delegate a large degree of independence of action. Above all, he was beloved by his people because he possessed the common touch. He spent much time walking incognito through the streets and bazaars of Iṣfahān, and conversing with people in tea-houses. He had a strong sense of humour. His manner of dress was simple and unadorned. Malcolm, after describing the richness and luxury of the state apartments and the royal audience hall, says: "'Abbās was clothed in a plain dress of red cloth. He wore no finery about his person; his sabre alone had a gold hilt. Those high nobles who sat nearest him were also plainly attired; and it was evident that the king, surrounded as he was with wealth and grandeur, affected simplicity."[10] As to his personal appearance, Malcolm again has the best description: 'Abbās

> had a fine face, of which the most remarkable features were a high nose and a keen and piercing eye. He wore no beard, but had large mustachios, or whiskers. In his stature he was rather low, but must have been uncommonly robust and active, as he was celebrated throughout life for the power of bearing fatigue, and to the last indulged in his favourite amusement of hunting.[11]

Perhaps Chardin's verdict is the most fitting epitaph for 'Abbās I: "When this great prince ceased to live, Persia ceased to prosper!"[12]

6. Shāh 'Abbās I: portrait by Bishn Das

5

Relations with the West during the Safavid period

From earliest times, relations between Iran and the West have existed on a number of different levels: diplomatic, political and military contacts; trade relations; and the mutual interchange of religious ideas. Under the first head, the contacts between the Greeks and the Achaemenids, between the Parthians and the Romans and between the Sasanids and the Romans are well known. Under the second head, Iran, as the land-bridge between Europe, Asia Minor and the Mediterranean lands on the one hand, and Central Asia, the Indies and the Far East on the other, was from ancient times involved in the transit trade between East and West; for example, the famous silk route from China passed through Iranian territory, and the transit dues charged on this trade were a lucrative source of income to the rulers of Iran. Under the third head, the traffic was initially all east–west. In Parthian times, the cult of Mithras exerted an influence on the Roman legionaries and, as a result, spread to Rome and further west. By Sasanid times, however, Christianity began to penetrate Iran from the west. The process was accelerated when Shāpūr I transplanted to Iran large numbers of the inhabitants of Syria and other eastern provinces of the Roman empire; many of these people were Christians. After Christianity became the state religion of the Roman empire, the loyalty of the Christian inhabitants of Iran became suspect and they were subject to persecution. In return for Christianity, Iran exported to the West the dualistic religion of Mani, in which elements of Christianity and Zoroastrianism were blended. Though suppressed in Iran as a heresy, Manichaeism penetrated westwards as far as France, and even the great Bishop of Hippo, St Augustine, was a Manichaean in his early years.

In the seventh century A.D., the Arabs conquered Iran, and gradually the whole of Iran adopted the new religion of the conquerors, Islam. Iran, from being a world-power (in terms of the then known world), with many centuries of imperial history behind it, was relegated to the position of being just one part of a vast Islamic empire whose centre of power was at first Medina, then Damascus, and finally Baghdād. As the Arabs rapidly extended their control over the eastern Mediterranean and North Africa, and as the Turks, from the eleventh century onwards, gradually brought Asia Minor under their control, this Islamic empire placed an impenetrable barrier between Iran and the West. As a result, Iran became a forgotten land. The Crusaders, filled with zeal for the conquest of the Holy Land, had little interest in the countries which lay further to the east. The strength and persistence of the legend of Prester John, the powerful Christian potentate living somewhere in Central Asia, who, it was thought in the West, would be a useful ally against the Saracens, indicates the extent of Western ignorance of Asia in mediaeval times.

The invasion of the eastern Islamic world by Chingiz Khān in 1219, and the subsequent establishment of the *pax Mongolica* from China to the Balkans, brought Iran back into contact with the West, and the Mongol rulers of Iran made repeated but unproductive attempts to form an alliance with European monarchs against the Mamlūk sulṭāns of Egypt and the Levant. After 1335, the Mongol state in Iran broke up into a number of small units which in most cases followed old provincial boundaries. There was a general lessening of cohesion and security, and at times a situation not far removed from anarchy; these conditions were naturally not attractive to merchants, and the Venetians and Genoese who were rash enough to venture into Āẕarbāyjān were usually robbed and in many cases lost their lives. The campaigns of Tīmūr (Tamerlane) in Iran (1381–1405) again brought Iran to the notice of the West, but, shortly after his death in 1405, the whole of north-west and central Iran came under the control successively of two Turcoman dynasties, the Qarā Quyūnlū, or Black Sheep Turcomans, and the Āq Quyūnlū, or White Sheep Turcomans. Both dynasties made Tabrīz their capital, and, under the great Āq Quyūnlū ruler Ūzūn Ḥasan (died 1478), internal security so far improved as to encourage the Italian city-states to resume diplomatic and commercial contacts with Iran. A decade after the death of Ūzūn Ḥasan, the Portuguese sea-captain Bartolomeu Dias rounded the Cape of Good Hope, and ten years after that, his fellow-countryman Vasco da Gama reached India. The sea-route from western Europe to the East, for so long the dream of Prince Henry the Navigator, had thus been opened three years before the establishment of the Safavid dynasty in Iran. The Portuguese had outflanked not only the intervening Islamic countries which had for so many centuries virtually cut Iran off from contact with the West, but also the Venetians and other European mercantile powers which had traded with Iran via the Mediterranean ports.

The Portuguese were not long in following up their advantage. In 1507, a Portuguese fleet under the command of Afonso de Albuquerque arrived off the island of Hurmūz in the Persian Gulf. The Portuguese Viceroy immediately perceived the immense strategic and commercial importance of the site, which commanded the entrace to the Persian Gulf and from which Portuguese communications with India could be protected. The Portuguese captured the island, and the twelve-year-old King of Hurmūz became a vassal of the King of Portugal and agreed to pay an annual tribute. This caused friction with Shāh Ismā'īl I, whose envoy reached Hurmūz shortly afterwards also to demand tribute. A threatened mutiny on the part of his captains forced Albuquerque to sail from Hurmūz in 1508, but he fully intended to recover it as soon as an opportunity arose, and in 1513 he sent the envoy Miguel Ferreira to Shāh Ismā'īl with a friendly message. In 1515, Albuquerque returned to Hurmūz, where he was met by Miguel Ferreira and an envoy from Ismā'īl. The Shāh, not possessing a navy, and with an army much weakened by his disastrous defeat at Chāldirān the previous year, had to accept the occupation of Hurmūz as a *fait accompli*. Albuquerque concluded a treaty with Ismā'īl which confirmed the King of Hurmūz as a Portuguese vassal. To sweeten the pill, Albuquerque sent the Shāh's envoy back with gifts worth double the ones he had received from Ismā'īl. The Portuguese also contracted under the treaty to help the Shāh recover the Bahrein islands from the Arab Jabrid dynasty; to enter into an alliance with Iran against the Ottomans; and to help Iran to put down a revolt by a Balūchī tribe in Makrān.[1] Some years later the Portuguese occupied the Bahrein islands but, instead of handing them over to Iran as they were bound to do under the 1515 Treaty, they retained possession of them for eighty years.

The Portuguese soon tightened their grip on Hurmūz by occupying and fortifying the coastal strip on the mainland north and north-west of the island. A second Portuguese embassy in 1523, under Balthasar Pessoa, was well received by Shāh Ismā'īl, and an Ottoman challenge to Portuguese naval supremacy at the approaches to the Persian Gulf probably led the Portuguese to supply Shah Ṭahmāsp in 1548 with cannon and men at the time of Sulṭān Süleymān's second invasion of Iran.[2] In the second half of the sixteenth century, an Augustinian mission from Portugal established itself at Hurmūz. A Jesuit named Francisco da Costa encouraged Pope Clement VIII to believe that there was some hope that Shāh 'Abbās I might become a Christian, and the Pope promptly despatched Costa with a layman named Diego de Miranda to express his joy at the Shāh's "ready inclination toward the Christian religion". The Pope also made an eloquent plea for joint action against "the unceasing and most hostile enemy the Turk, who with unbearable pride and insatiable desire to rule, longs most eagerly to oppress all kingdoms and all territories and to lay them under the yoke of most hard slavery".[3] This part of the Pope's message at least might have evoked a sympathetic response from the Shāh, had not most unseemly quarrels between Costa and Miranda, in the course of which Costa stole Miranda's clothing and Miranda got Costa put in chains, brought the whole mission into disrepute.[4] In 1602, three Augustinian fathers arrived in Iran from Goa; all three made an excellent impression on Shāh 'Abbās, who gave them permission to establish a convent at Iṣfahān and also to build a church there; the Shāh even offered to defray part of the cost of decorating the church. The Prior of the Augustinians at Iṣfahān, in addition to his religious duties, represented the King of Spain (between 1580 and 1640 the thrones of Portugal and Spain were united under the King of Spain), and thus became the first permanent diplomatic representative of the West in Iran. Also in 1602, 'Abbās I showed his determination to be master of his own house by expelling the Portuguese garrison from the Bahrein islands. The expulsion of the Portuguese from Hurmūz had to wait for twenty years, until he was able to persuade the English to provide the requisite naval assistance.

The Portuguese had been first in the field in regard to developing a political empire and commerical interests in the Persian Gulf. Their discovery of a sea-route to the East had severely damaged Venetian and Genoese trade with the East, and Italian commercial contacts with Iran during the sixteenth century consequently declined. The accounts of various Italian merchants who were in Iran between 1500 and 1520, which were published by the Hakluyt Society in *A Narrative of Italian Travels in Persia in the Fifteenth and Sixteenth Centuries*, contain many inaccuracies but are valuable as giving something of the "flavour" of the period. Of more interest are the attempts by a number of European powers to conclude an alliance with the Safavid shahs against their mutual enemy, the Ottoman Turk. Despite a considerable amount of goodwill on both sides, the slowness of communications proved an insurmountable difficulty. As in the thirteenth century, when the Mongol rulers had similarly tried to conclude alliances with Western rulers against the Mamlūks, it proved impossible to synchronise any joint activity. It took a minimum of two years for an exchange of diplomatic notes to take place, and it was impossible to project joint plans far enough ahead to allow for this time-lag. It was also quite probable that circumstances, either in Iran, or in the European country, or in both, would have changed during the interval. For example, in 1529 the Emperor Charles V sent a letter to Shāh Ismā'īl I, apparently unaware that the latter had died *five* years previously! Both parties remained incurable optimists, however, and the tempo of diplomatic activity increased during the sixteenth century.

The first European monarchs to suggest an alliance with the Shāh against the Sulṭān were King Charles I of Spain and Ludovic II of Hungary. In 1523, Ismā'īl I sent a letter in Latin to Charles, now the Emperor Charles V, in which he expressed astonishment that the European powers, instead of combining to crush the Turks, were fighting among each other. The policy of the French government at this period was to be on friendly terms with the Turks. In 1548, the French ambassador to the Sublime Porte, Baron et Seigneur d'Aramon et de Vallabrègues, accompanied Sulṭān Süleymān on the latter's expedition to Iran; at the siege of Vān, M. d'Aramon interpreted his ambassadorial function rather liberally by giving advice to the Turkish gunners directing fire against the fort; his advice on the placing of the guns, followed by the Turks, proved so effective that the Safavid garrison surrendered. After the establishment of the Levant

Company in 1581, England, too, wished to further her commercial enterprises by improving relations with the Ottoman Sulṭān.

In 1598, when 'Abbās I returned to Qazvīn after his great victory over the Özbegs, he found waiting for him a party of twenty-six Europeans, headed by two English soldiers-of-fortune, Sir Anthony and Sir Robert Sherley. The Shāh took these brothers with him to Iṣfahān, his new capital, and in May 1599 he dispatched Sir Anthony Sherley to Europe, bearing letters of friendship from the Shāh to the Pope and to various European princes, including the Holy Roman Emperor Rudolf II, King of Bohemia (1552–1612), King Henry of France (1589–1610), Philip III of Spain (1598–1621), the King of Scotland, the King of Poland, the Queen of England, the Seigneur of Venice and the Grand Duke of Tuscany. Sir Anthony was charged with enlisting the support of these princes against their common enemy, the Ottomans; he was accompanied by a *qizilbāsh* officer, Ḥusayn 'Alī Beg Bayāt, and by another Iranian, who was to remain in Moscow as ambassador to the court of Tsar Boris Godunov. Sir Robert Sherley remained behind at the Safavid court as a hostage for Sir Anthony's good behaviour; in view of the latter's subsequent conduct in Europe, it says much for Shāh 'Abbās's sense of justice that he took no retaliatory action against Sir Robert.

Once again, human frailties were to be the undoing of a diplomatic mission. Sir Anthony Sherley was also accompanied by a Portuguese Augustinian friar named Nicolao de Melo, who was on his way to Rome. They had hardly entered Russian territory before violent quarrels broke out between Sir Anthony and Melo, and it is alleged that Sir Anthony tried to drown the friar in the Volga. After six unproductive months in Moscow, marked by quarrels over precedence between Sir Anthony and his Iranian colleagues, Sir Anthony and Ḥusayn 'Alī Beg Bayāt embarked at Archangel early in 1600, sailed to Emden, and in October 1600 reached Prague by a somewhat circuitous route dictated by the existence of the Ottoman empire. At Prague, the mission was well received by the Emperor Rudolf, but at Rome, which was reached in April 1601, a disastrous quarrel over precedence between Sir Anthony and Ḥusayn 'Alī Beg Bayāt led to the latter's dissociating himself from Sherley and going on alone to Spain. In March 1602, Sir Anthony went to Venice, and carried on a correspondence with the King of Spain. Some of his letters were intercepted by English agents, and were held to be treasonable. He was refused permission to return to England, and English ambassadors abroad were instructed to repudiate him. In April 1603, he was arrested in Venice and imprisoned – whether as an insolvent debtor or as a seditious person is not clear. After the accession of King James I, he was released from jail and granted a licence to "remain beyond the sea some time longer".[5] Anthony's failure either to return to Iran or report the progress of his mission led Shāh 'Abbās temporarily to withdraw his favour from Anthony's brother Robert, but the latter was soon reinstated and, in 1608, nearly ten years after Sir Anthony had left Iran, was sent to Europe by the Shāh on a similar mission, with the additional task of finding his brother and reporting to the Shāh on the success or otherwise of his mission.

After parting from Sir Anthony, Ḥusayn 'Alī Beg Bayāt proceeded to Valladolid, where he was received by Philip III. There, the Safavid ambassador, who had already experienced the embarrassment of having three of his servants announce their conversion to the Catholic faith in Rome, suffered a far worse shock, when his own nephew, 'Alī Qulī Beg, and one of his secretaries, both adopted Christianity. King Philip and Queen Margarita acted as their godparents, naming them respectively Felipe and Juan.[6] The ambassador was so upset by this development that he tried to have Don Juan assassinated. History does not record the fate of Ḥusayn 'Alī Beg Bayāt when he returned to Iran and related this disgraceful state of affairs to the Shāh.

Sir Robert Sherley caught up with his brother in 1611 at Madrid, where Sir Anthony was living in abject poverty. After fruitless recriminations with his brother, Robert went on to England, where he was received by James I. However, all his efforts to establish trade relations between England and Iran were frustrated by the powerful lobby mounted by the Levant Company, then engaged in a bitter struggle with the English East India Company, founded in 1600, for control of trade with the Middle East and Indies. Robert returned to Iran in 1615, and the same year was sent back to Europe on a second mission which lasted until 1627. This long absence from Iran enabled his enemies there to undermine the Shāh's confidence in him and, when he returned to Iran from his second mission, he found himself out of favour, and he eventually died in Iran in a state of poverty.

In terms of the concrete results obtained by Western nations from contact with Iran, the sixteenth century must be conceded to the Portuguese. The English made a determined attempt to turn the northern flank of the Ottoman empire, just as the Portuguese had turned its southern flank by rounding the Cape, but the attempt ended in failure. Early in 1553, "the Mysterie and Companie of the Merchant Adventurers for the Discoverie of Regions, Dominions, Islands and Places Unknown" was formed in London with Sebastian Cabot as its first Governor. The original object of this company was to discover a north-east passage to China, but, after the discovery of the route to Archangel, the company was renamed successively "The Muscovy Company" and "The Russia Company". It was the first of the English joint-stock companies formed for foreign trade. Two of the three ships sent out in 1553 were lost in stormy weather north of Norway, but the third, under the command of Richard Chancellor, reached Archangel. Chancellor went to Moscow, and obtained trading privileges from Ivan the Terrible. On his return from his second trip to Archangel, Chancellor himself and his ship were lost.

Despite this discouraging beginning, in 1557 Anthony Jenkinson and two brothers, Richard and Robert Johnson, made another attempt. They reached Archangel safely, and were also received affably by Ivan the Terrible. They travelled to Astrakhan, and crossed the Caspian Sea to Bukhārā. Although Jenkinson was mistaken in thinking that he and his band were the first Christians to sail on the Caspian Sea – the Genoese had done so some two and a half centuries earlier – it was nevertheless a pioneering effort, and they had discovered a route to Central Asia. In 1561, Jenkinson made a second voyage, bearing letters from Queen Elizabeth to Tsar Ivan the Terrible and to Shāh Ṭahmāsp, who was addressed as "the Great Sophie".[7] In 1562, Jenkinson again took ship to cross the Caspian, this time landing on Safavid territory on the west coast, in Shīrvān. There, he was hospitably received by the governor, 'Abd Allāh Khān Ustājlū, who was the Shāh's brother-in-law and cousin, and sent on to Qazvīn. On 20 November 1562, Jenkinson was received in audience by Ṭahmāsp, and handed to the Shāh the Queen's letter, the purpose of which was "to treate of friendship, and free passage of our Merchants and people, to repaire and traffique within his dominions, for to bring in our commodities, and to carry away theirs to the honour of both princes, the mutual commoditie of both Realmes, and wealth of the Subjects". All went well until the Shāh discovered that Jenkinson was a Christian: "Oh thou unbeleever," he said, "we have no neede to have friendship with the unbeleevers." Jenkinson was abruptly dismissed from the royal presence, and was disconcerted to notice that, as he left, a servant followed him "with a bassinet of sand, sifting all the way that I had gone within the said pallace".[8] All was not lost, however, for 'Abd Allāh Khān not only interceded with the Shāh, who so far relented as to give Jenkinson a handsome gift when he left, but the Khān himself granted important trading privileges to the Muscovy Company. The hazards of this route proved too great, and in 1581 it was abandoned; apart from the appalling risks involved in the sea-route round the north of Scandinavia to the White Sea, attacks by Tatar bandits in the Volga region, and other troubles, resulted in too great a loss of lives and goods.

A few years after Jenkinson's visit to the court of Shāh Ṭahmāsp, Ivan the Terrible himself was considering the possibilities of joint military action with the Shāh against the Ottomans. In 1569, he sent an envoy named Dolmet Karpivicz to Ṭahmāsp; as gifts for the Shāh, the Russian envoy brought 30 cannons of varying sizes, and 4,000 muskets; accompanying him were 500 "good musketeers", "who would be able to instruct and drill his subjects in marksmanship". If the Shāh liked those cannon and the musketeers, the Tsar promised to sell him all kinds of guns which he (the Tsar) could obtain from Germany. Shāh Ṭahmāsp was very satisfied with this embassy and these gifts, and offered to aid the Tsar to the best of his ability. Although Moscow was less remote than western Europe, nothing came of this *démarche*.[9]

In the same year that the decision was taken to abandon the north-east passage route, an English merchant named John Newberie arrived at Hurmūz: he was the first Englishman to travel the overland-route to the Persian Gulf. On his return to London, he contacted other merchants such as Edward Osborne, who in 1581 had become the first Governor of the Levant Company, which had just obtained a royal charter which gave it the exclusive right to trade with Turkey for seven years. On hearing Newberie's news, the Levant Company merchants decided to extend their operations to Iran and India, using the overland-route through Syria and Mesopotamia. In 1583 Newberie set off again with a group of other merchants, intending to set up a factory at Hurmūz as the Venetians had succeeded in doing. A few days after their arrival at Hurmūz, however, their Venetian rivals denounced them to the Portuguese Capitão as spies and heretics; they were thrown into jail, and shipped to Goa to stand trial, but were eventually released on the intercession of an English Jesuit and two Dutchmen.

In 1600, a London merchant named John Mildenhall, accompanied by a Protestant minister named John Cartwright, set out from Aleppo for India. Cartwright did not go further than Iran, but Mildenhall went on to India. The English attempt to establish an overland trade route to the Persian Gulf had met with no more success than had the route via the north-east passage and overland across Russia. Clearly, if the Portuguese hold on the Persian Gulf trade was to be broken, naval power superior to that of the Portuguese would be required. It was shortly to be provided by the English East India Company and the Dutch East India Company, which at first co-operated to defeat the Portuguese, and then became bitter rivals.

In 1615, the English East India Company made its first attempt to break into the Iranian market. A factor of the Company, Richard Steele, had noticed that Iranian winters are cold, and thought that there would be a market for good English broadcloth. The Company sent him and John Crowther to Iṣfahān, where they obtained a *farmān*[10] from 'Abbās I, in which the Shāh instructed his subjects

> unto what degree soever...to kindly receive and entertaine the English Frankes or Nation, at what time any of their ships or shipping shall arrive at Jasques [Jāsk], or any other of the Ports in our Kingdome: to conduct them and their Merchandize to what place or places they themselves desire: and that you shall see them safely defended about our Coasts, from any other Frank or Franks whatsoevere.[11]

Steele and Crowther, after examining several ports, chose Jāsk, on the Makrān coast east of Hurmūz. In December 1616, the Company sent Edward Connock in the *James* with a cargo of cloth; the *James* reached Jāsk despite Portuguese attempts to intercept her. Connock took the cloth to Shīrāz, and opened factories both in that city and in Iṣfahān. 'Abbās issued another *farmān* in more specific terms, giving the English East India Company the right to trade freely throughout the country. An English ambassador was to reside permanently in Iran, and was empowered to appoint agents and factors as and where necessary. English nationals were guaranteed free exercise of their religion; in legal matters, they were to be under the jurisdiction of their ambassador. Moreover, the Shāh promised to supply the Company with between 1,000 and 3,000 bales of silk annually at a given rate, and the Company might ship this silk from Jāsk free of duty.

The East India Company might well be gratified by this display of royal liberality. There was, however, a small string attached. In return for these concessions, 'Abbās I expected the English to assist him in expelling the Portuguese from Hurmūz. 'Abbās I had always, quite naturally, regarded the Portuguese forts on the island of Hurmūz and on the mainland, and the fact that the King of Hurmūz was a Portuguese tributary, as infringements on his own sovereignty. In default of a navy, however, he, like his predecessors, had been powerless to drive the Portuguese out of

7. House and garden; the East India Co. director's residence

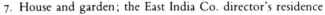

Hurmūz Island, although, as already mentioned, he had expelled the much smaller Portuguese garrison from the Bahrein islands in 1602. The advent of the English East India Company's fighting ships seemed to give him the opportunity he was seeking.

Relations between 'Abbās and the Portuguese had been deteriorating for a number of years. In 1608, 'Abbās had sent the Portuguese Augustinian Antonio de Gouveia on a mission to King Philip of Spain, accompanied by the *qizilbāsh* officer Dengīz Beg Rūmlū. Apart from the usual presents for King Philip, the Shāh, who was never one to miss the chance of a good deal, sent with them 50 bales of silk, the proceeds of which were to be brought back for the royal coffers. As usual, the objectives of the mission were part political, to persuade King Philip to wage war on the Ottomans, and part commercial, to promote trade relations between Iran and Spain and Portugal. The mission was a complete failure, and when its members returned to Iran in 1613, Shāh 'Abbās had Dengīz Beg summarily executed. 'Abbās had various causes for complaint against this officer: the most serious were that he had broken the royal seal on the letter he was bearing to the King of Spain – a sacrilegious act – and had communicated its contents to the governor of Cadiz; that he had paid some merchant a sum of money to deliver the letter from the Shāh to the Pope which he was commissioned to deliver in person; and that certain members of his staff had embraced Christianity and remained in Europe. It was considered that the only possible reason why they would have renounced Islam was the ill-treatment accorded to them by Dengīz Beg. Gouveia, who had been appointed Apostolic Delegate to Iran while he was in Spain, was charged with having given the bales of silk to King Philip instead of selling them on the Shāh's behalf. Gouveia, in fear of his life, fled to Shīrāz, where he was detained for a time by the Governor-General of Fārs, Imām Qulī Khān; the latter, not receiving instructions on the matter, allowed Gouveia to proceed to Hurmūz. The Shāh's orders commanding Imām Qulī Khān to detain Gouveia at Shīrāz arrived too late. 'Abbās was angry with the Governor-General for allowing Gouveia to escape,[12] and Imām Qulī Khān, in order to regain the Shāh's favour, decided to attack the territory on the mainland held by the Portuguese opposite Hurmūz. Toward the end of 1614, he captured the small port of Jarūn (later renamed Bandar 'Abbās), landed troops on the island of Qishm, and thus effectively cut off the supply of fresh water from the Portuguese garrison at Hurmūz (there was no fresh water on the island of Hurmūz), and drove the Portuguese from their *pied-à-terre* at Ra's al-Khayma on the southern shore of the Persian Gulf.

Shāh 'Abbās had let it be known that he was tired of receiving friars as ambassadors, and he had asked the King of Spain to send him some gentleman of note; by such a gentleman, he considered, the King of Spain's interests would be better served, because "a religious man out of his cell was like a fish out of water".[13] In 1613, therefore, King Philip sent as his ambassador to Iran Don García de Silva y Figueroa, who reached Goa in October 1614. Although the Spanish grandee had some Portuguese blood in his veins, he was *persona non grata* to the Portuguese authorities at Goa, who detained him there on one pretext or another for more than two years. When he eventually reached Hurmūz in April 1617, again he encountered strong hostility from the Portuguese authorities. Due to the further delay at Hurmūz, he had ample time to inspect the Portuguese defences, on which he commented unfavourably. Don García reached Iṣfahān in the summer of 1617, but did not receive an audience with 'Abbās I until the summer of 1619, more than five and a half years from the time he left Spain. When he did meet the Shāh, his arrogant and tactless demands infuriated the latter, who dismissed him. Don García had demanded the restitution of the Bahrein islands and of the coastal strip north of Hurmūz, recently seized by Imām Qulī Khān; he also demanded the expulsion from Iran of the English East India Company factors. Having ruined his chances of achieving anything in Iran, Don García set sail for Spain, but died on the return voyage.

The Shāh's experiences with the Gouveia mission and with Don García had soured his relationship with the Portuguese (he did not make any clear distinction between them and the Spaniards and indeed, there was no good reason why he should, for the thrones of Spain and Portugal were still united). In June 1620, a Portuguese squadron under Ruy Freyre de Andrade reached Hurmūz with the intention of ejecting the English from the Persian Gulf, but was defeated in two naval battles with ships of the English East India Company on Christmas Day 1620 and 7 January 1621. In May 1621, Ruy Freyre de Andrade landed a force on the island of Qishm with the object of regaining control of the wells which provided the water-supply for the Portuguese garrison on Hurmūz island. Hardly had Ruy Freyre completed a fort designed to protect the wells before it was attacked by a Safavid force and, in February 1622, was captured. Ruy Freyre became the prisoner of the English. Portuguese attacks on Iranian coastal towns and villages had caused so much damage that in 1621 Imām Qulī Khān had requested the English East India Company captains, Blyth and Weddel, to assist him in expelling the Portuguese from the island of Hurmūz; should they refuse, their trade privileges in Iran and the Persian Gulf would be cancelled.

The English captains were reluctant to agree, because Portugal and England were officially at peace, but they allowed themselves to be persuaded by Edward Monnox, who had been the Company's Agent in Iran. The main points of the agreement with Imām Qulī Khān were: the spoils to be equally divided; the English to have the fort at Hurmūz; the English to be allowed to import or export goods via Hurmūz free of duty; the English to receive half the customs dues levied on other merchandise passing through Hurmūz; the Christian captives to be handed over to the English; Imām Qulī Khān to pay half the cost of the provisions consumed by the Company's ships while in service against the Portuguese. The first joint action by the English and Imām Qulī Khān's forces was the capture of the Portuguese fort at the eastern end of the island of Qishm. One of the few English casualties was Captain William Baffin, the discoverer of Baffin's Bay. As the chirurgeon with the flotilla wrote: "Master Baffin...received a small shot from the Castle into his belly, wherewith he gave three leapes, by report, and died immediately."[14] The landing on the island of Hurmūz itself followed. Imām Qulī Khān's men were transported to the island in English ships. The Portuguese and the vassal King of Hurmūz, Maḥmūd Shāh, retreated inside the fort. The English flotilla anchored on the side of the fort where the fortifications ran down to the water, and the Safavid troops began the work of digging trenches and pushing their breastworks forward up to the walls of the fort; they then began mining operations. Charges of gunpowder destroyed part of the tower, and a general assault began. When the attackers began to get the upper hand, the Portuguese laid down their arms and were taken on board the

English ships. The fort surrendered on 3 May 1622. Among the weapons which fell into the hands of the besiegers were several large cannon, and siege guns of various sizes, "cunningly wrought by skilled Portuguese craftsmen. Each one was a masterpiece of the art of the Frankish cannon-founders".[15]

The unique experiment in Anglo-Iranian co-operation at Hurmūz in 1622 was followed by the dispatch by Charles I in 1627 of the first official English ambassador to the Iranian court, Sir Dodmore Cotton, a gentleman of King Charles I's Privy Chamber. Sir Dodmore was accompanied by Sir Robert Sherley, who had been away in Europe since 1615, and whose position high in the Shāh's favour had been undermined during his absence by enemies at the royal court. Both envoys reached the Shāh's palace at Faraḥābād in May 1627. Publicly repudiated by the Shāh, Sir Robert retired to Iṣfahān where he died on 13 July 1627, a broken man. Only ten days later, Sir Dodmore Cotton also "bade the world Adieu"; in the words of Sir Thomas Herbert, a member of his suite: "Like discontents, long conflict with adverse dispositions, and fourteen days consuming of a flux (occasioned, as I thought, by eating too much fruit, or sucking in too much chill air upon Taurus), brought that Religious Gentleman, Sir Dodmore Cotton, our Ambassadour, to an immortal home."[16]

The fall of Hurmūz marked the beginning of the end of Portuguese dominance in the Persian Gulf. The Portuguese attempt to recapture Hurmūz in 1625 failed, and the English East India Company were able not only to maintain their factories on the coast but to expand their commercial operations in the interior. As the Portuguese Viceroy Albuquerque had shrewdly observed in the early sixteenth century, Hurmūz was one of three strategic points possession of which would give their owner control over the whole of the Persian Gulf, Indian Ocean and Red Sea, and thus of the East Indies trade. The Portuguese developed Muscat, on the southern shore of the Persian Gulf, to compensate for the loss of Hurmūz, but Muscat was vulnerable from the rear where it was open to attack by the Arab tribes of Oman. Although Portuguese power had been broken, a new rival to the English appeared on the scene, in the form of the Dutch East India Company which had been founded in 1602, having grown out of "The Society for Trade to Distant Countries" formed in 1597. Immediately, there was conflict with the English over the spice trade from the East Indies, and by the middle of the seventeenth century the Dutch had driven the Portuguese out of Malacca and Ceylon and had established a colony on the Cape of Good Hope. In 1635, the Dutch had helped the English defeat the Portuguese attempt to recapture Hurmūz, but from then on they began to challenge the English position in Iran. Under the agreement between the English East India Company and Imām Qulī Khān, the English were to receive half the customs dues levied on merchandise passing through Hurmūz. The Dutch refused to pay. The death of Shāh 'Abbās I in 1629 gave the Dutch their chance to obtain a share of the silk trade. The privileges of the English East India Company were not renewed and confirmed until 1632, and meanwhile the Dutch established a factory at Bandar 'Abbās for the import of pepper, nutmeg, cloves and other spices. In 1645, the Dutch attacked the island of Qishm, and extorted from 'Abbās II a licence to purchase silk in any part of Iran and export it free of customs duty, thus effectively breaking the royal monopoly of the silk trade which had been established by 'Abbās I. Dutch pressure became so great that the English moved their factory from Bandar 'Abbās to Baṣra in 1645, but the Dutch immediately sent ships to Baṣra and almost ruined the new factory. The value of Dutch trade in the Persian Gulf in the middle of the seventeenth century has been estimated at £100,000; English commerce had been almost swamped.

The rivalry between the English and Dutch in the Persian Gulf, Indian Ocean and the East Indies, was just part of the world-wide struggle between the two powers for commercial pre-eminence. The 1651 Navigation Act, designed to destroy the Dutch carrying trade, precipitated war in Europe, and the celebrated Dutch admirals Van Tromp and Ruyter fought it out with the equally famous English admirals Black and Monk. In 1653 and 1654, vessels of the English East India Company were captured or sunk in the Persian Gulf. When peace was concluded later in 1654, the English East India Company was awarded £85,000 damages.

The failure of the Stuart kings to support commercial enterprises in the Indies contrasted strongly both with the previous policies of Cromwell and with the strong support given by the Dutch government to its merchants. Thévenot, Fryer and Chardin all testify to the supremacy of Dutch trade in the Persian Gulf during the second half of the seventeenth century. In 1664, another rival appeared on the scene in the shape of the French East India Company. France, which hitherto had had little contact with Iran, decided that it must follow the example of the Dutch and the English and obtain overseas interests as well as being a European power. Both Cardinal Richelieu and Père Joseph disliked the fact that the Augustinians in Iran were exclusively Portuguese, and that there was a preponderance of Spaniards and Italians in the Carmelite missions there. In 1627, Richelieu sent a mission to Iran to obtain permission from 'Abbās I for the establishment of Capuchin missions at Iṣfahān and elsewhere. The mission was successful, and Capuchin missions were founded at Iṣfahān and Baghdād, the latter city recently taken from the Ottomans. The Superiors of the Capuchins were considered to represent the King of France, and to constitute a diplomatic counterweight to the Augustinians. The most famous of them was Père Raphael du Mans, who went to Iran in 1644, spent the rest of his life there, and died at Iṣfahān in 1696 at the age of ninety-three. He learnt Persian well, and was much esteemed as a mathematician by 'Abbās II and Shāh Sulaymān. He wrote *Estat de la Perse en 1660* for the guidance of the French minister Colbert, who, with characteristic thoroughness, was collecting information on Iran prior to forming the Compagnie Française des Indes in 1664. French influence in Iran was also increased by the establishment in 1653 of Jesuit missions at Julfā, the Christian suburb of Iṣfahān, and Shīrāz, headed by Père François Rigordi. This brought to five the number of foreign religious Orders operating in Iran: Dominicans, Franciscans, Augustinians, Carmelites and Jesuits.

Immediately after the formation of the French East India Company, three representatives of the Company and two envoys to the Shāh from Louis XIV set out for Iran. On reaching Iṣfahān in November 1665, they at once indulged in the quarrels of the type which had plagued more than one diplomatic mission. Despite the bad impression created by these squabbles, and the even worse impression created by the failure of either Louis XIV or the Company to send gifts to the Shāh, the Shāh granted the Company exemption from tolls and customs dues for three years, and trading privileges similar to those already granted to the English and Dutch. Toward the end of the seventeenth century, the French East India Company stepped up its activities in Iran, and de Châteauneuf, the French ambassador to the Sublime Porte, sent a capable merchant from Marseilles named de Canseville to Iṣfahān. Ostensibly acting as secretary to the Capuchin mission there, he was actually engaged in gathering information on economic matters for the Company. After returning briefly to France in 1705 to report, he went back to Iran. In March of that year, the French government sent a mission to Iran with the hope of concluding a commercial treaty, but its choice of a head of mission, Jean-Baptiste Fabre, was a curious one. Fabre was so short of funds that he had to borrow money from his mistress, who kept a gaming-house in Paris, before he could make his preparations for the voyage. When the expedition got under way in March 1705, one of its members was a "cavalier" who turned out to be Fabre's mistress in male attire. On arrival at Istanbul, the Fabre mission was subject to much delay, because the Ottoman Grand Vizier failed to see how his country would benefit from an increase in trade between France and Iran. The party had to split up; Fabre and his mistress, Marie Petit, went on ahead with some servants, and reached Erīvān, then in Safavid hands, in 1707. The subsequent history of the Fabre mission is pure farce interspersed with tragedy. Marie Petit seems rapidly to have won the heart of the Iranian Governor-General, who, when one of Fabre's French servants attempted to murder Marie because she had thrown an orange at him, had the man arrested at her request. Père Mosnier, a Jesuit living at Erīvān, whom Fabre had appointed his almoner, was scandalised by the affair, and sent word of what had happened to the rest of the mission, then nearing the Iranian frontier. When the remaining members arrived, they marched to the jail and released the prisoner, two Iranians being killed and several wounded in the incident. The Governor-General then arrested all the members of the mission, including Père Mosnier, whom he proposed to put to death, but all were released from imprisonment on the intercession of Marie Petit. The Governor-General then received instructions from the Shāh to send the Fabre mission on to Iṣfahān. Before it left, he invited everyone to a farewell hunting-party; Fabre fell ill of a fever and died a few days later. The Governor-General was naturally suspected of having murdered him because of his infatuation with Marie Petit.

Differences of opinion at once arose as to who should succeed Fabre as head of mission. Père Mosnier wrote off to the Bishop of Babylon, then resident at Hamadān, to invite him to come and take charge, but the Governor-General intercepted his letter. Finally, with the support of the Governor-General, Marie Petit declared herself the head of the mission, took charge of Fabre's papers and the gifts for the Shāh, and set off for the Safavid court, then in camp near Tehran. The French ambassador at Istanbul, horrified by these events, sent one of his secretaries, Pierre Victor Michel, post-haste to Iran to try and intercept Marie Petit's party. He overtook them at Nakhchivān but, because he had no proper credentials, was unable to prevent them from proceeding. On arrival at the royal camp, Marie Petit was courteously received by the *vazīr*, who conducted her to the royal *ḥaram*, where she received all possible attention. On her return journey, Marie Petit got both Michel and the Bishop of Babylon, who had joined Michel, thrown into prison for a short period. Michel then gained the upper hand, and ordered Marie Petit to return to France; he gave her a small amount of cash, and a bond drawn on Aleppo which proved to be worthless. When she arrived in France, Marie Petit was tried and imprisoned; when she emerged from jail her health was broken and she was penniless.[17] With Marie Petit out of the way, and belatedly equipped with letters of credence, Michel was able to negotiate, despite strong opposition from the English and Dutch, the first official treaty between France and Iran (September 1708). In addition to granting certain trade privileges, the treaty gave protection to the Christian religious orders in Iran.

Shāh Sulṭān Ḥusayn decided to send a return embassy, and he selected the *kalāntar* (mayor) of Erīvān, Muḥammad Riżā Beg, as his ambassador: this was almost as odd a choice as that of Fabre. Muḥammad Riżā Beg experienced the usual difficulties of anyone trying to cross Ottoman territory, from east or west, and spent some time in a Turkish jail. He left Erīvān in May 1714, and reached Paris in February 1715. The ambassador's eccentric behaviour – he was given to sudden and unaccountable fits of rage – together with the mediocre value of the gifts he brought, caused many highly placed Frenchmen, including Montesquieu, to suspect he was an impostor. In view of the fact that Louis XIV's envoys to the Shāh in 1665 had borne no gifts at all, the latter ground for suspicion seems unreasonable. However, Marie Petit, interrogated in jail, confirmed the *bona fides* of Muḥammad Riżā Beg. Louis XIV nominated three negotiators of the highest rank to confer with Muḥammad Riżā Beg: the Secretary of State for

8. Muḥammad Riżā Beg, ambassador to Louis XIV

Foreign Affairs; the Secretary of State for the Marine; and the Comptroller-General of Finance. The Iranian ambassador was enjoying his luxurious life in Paris, spiced as it was by a number of amatory adventures, and he protracted the negotiations until 13 August 1715, when a new treaty was signed. It was extremely favourable to France: import and export duties in Iran were waived, and all limitations on French trade with Iran were removed; the French ambassador was to take precedence over all others. (Despite the promise of preferential treatment, French trade with Iran did not flourish; the Safavid dynasty fell in 1722, and the 1708 and 1715 agreements were not binding on later rulers.)

It is impossible to escape the conclusion that Iran's diplomatic and commercial relations with France during the seventeenth and eighteenth centuries were on a quite different basis from its relations with the Dutch and the English; once more the elements of farce and tragedy enter into the story, in roughly equal proportions. Muḥammad Riżā Beg embarked at Le Havre, on the first stage of his journey back to Iran. In Muḥammad Riżā Beg's cabin was placed a large box with holes in it, which was said to contain his devotional books; in fact, it contained the Marquise d'Épinay, who had arranged to elope with the ambassador. Unfortunately, Muḥammad Riżā Beg realised belatedly that he had far exceeded his mandate in negotiating the 1715 Treaty, and decided to anticipate his possible fate on his return to Iran by committing suicide. The Marquise d'Épinay went on to Iran, became a Muslim, and married Muḥammad Riżā Beg's brother.[18] In 1717, the Chevalier Ange de Gardane, Seigneur de Sainte-Croix, travelled to Iran with his brother François and took up his duties as French consul at Iṣfahān. The two brothers were still in Iṣfahān at the time of the siege and capture of the Safavid capital by the Afghāns in 1722.

The English East India Company, in order to maintain its position in face of this strong Dutch and French competition, found itself gradually forced to assume a more political role. For a time, the multiplicity of merchant companies threatened the ruin of all, but in 1708 they sank their differences and amalgamated into "The United Company of the Merchants of England trading to the East Indies". The presidents of this Company were invested with consular powers and rank. The English East India Company succeeded in maintaining its favoured position in Iran until the end of the Safavid period. In 1699, Shāh Sulaymān visited the Company's factory at Iṣfahān, accompanied by his harem. The Company's Agent spent £12,000 on the reception of his royal visitors; in return, the Shāh paid one year's arrears of the Bandar

'Abbās customs dues, and conferred other marks of royal favour on the Company. As the political power of the Safavids declined, so did the internal security on which the foreign trading companies so much depended. In 1721, a force of 4,000 Balūchī tribesmen attacked the English and Dutch factories at Bandar 'Abbās; they were beaten off, but the Dutch warehouse was plundered and goods valued at £20,000 were stolen. From the beginning of the eighteenth century, piracy in the Persian Gulf made commercial enterprises increasingly hazardous for the foreign companies. Piracy in the area was nothing new; it is mentioned by the classical writers, such as Pliny and Ptolemy, and in mediaeval times by Marco Polo. Toward the end of the seventeenth century, however, attacks on the English East India Company's merchantmen increased. The pirates were not all Arabs, though the Omanis were probably the worst offenders, but included Englishmen and Americans; even the celebrated Captain Kidd is said to have operated in Indian waters. The menance to merchantmen became so serious that the three rivals, England, France and Holland, were forced to co-ordinate their counter-measures against the pirates about the year 1700, and France was given the primary responsibility for the security of the Persian Gulf. Toward the end of the Safavid period, the Dutch began to lose ground to the English in the Persian Gulf, and in the nineteenth century the English suppressed piracy and established that *pax Britannica* so eloquently lauded by Lord Curzon: "between all parties intervenes the sworded figure of Great Britain, with firm and just hand holding the scales".[19]

Although Dutch influence in the Persian Gulf and Indian Ocean declined during the last quarter of the seventeenth century, the Dutch East India Company had not given up all hope of retaining its privileged trading position in Iran, and in 1717 it sent a mission there led by Joan Josua Ketelaar, one of its high-ranking officials. At the end of May 1717, Ketelaar's mission arrived at Iṣfahān with the six elephants which were gifts to the Shāh. After protracted negotiations with Shāh Sulṭān Ḥusayn's *vazīr*, Fatḥ 'Alī Khān Dāghistānī, Ketelaar managed to secure the renewal of most of the Dutch trading privileges, but his difficulties were not over. The *vazīr*, no doubt harking back to Shāh 'Abbās I's success in enlisting English assistance against the Portuguese at Hurmūz in 1622, demanded Dutch naval help against the Arabs from Muscat who had seized the Bahrein islands and were threatening Bandar 'Abbās. Similar requests already made by the Shāh to the English and French had been refused. Ketelaar evaded the issue, and tried to board a Dutch vessel at Bandar 'Abbās in January 1718, but the local Safavid commander tried to commandeer the ship for action against the Arabs. When Ketelaar refused to allow this, the Iranians surrounded the Dutch factory and cut off all its supplies. Ketelaar became seriously ill with a high fever, and died.

The Russian ambassador Volynksy was at Iṣfahān at the same time as Ketelaar. The intervention of the Russians in Iranian affairs portended a new era in Iran's relations with the West. By the end of the eighteenth century, Russia and Britain had emerged as the most powerful Western nations in the area, and there began the period of a century and a half during which they struggled for political and commercial supremacy in Iran, with Iran trying to preserve its existence as an independent nation by playing the two rivals off against each other. It was undoubtedly Volynsky's report to Tsar Peter the Great which encouraged the latter to adopt an expansionist policy in regard to Iran; Volynsky described the extreme weakness of Iran, and prophesied that, unless Shāh Sulṭān Ḥusayn were replaced by a strong and capable ruler, the Safavid dynasty would fall. His prophecy was fulfilled only a few years later. One of Peter the Great's principal objectives had been to give his landlocked country access to the oceans of the world; he had already, by making war on the Swedes, acquired access to the Baltic, and by attacking the Turks he hoped to obtain access to the Black Sea also. Volynsky's report encouraged him to dream of control over a warm-water port on the Persian Gulf. The fall of the Safavid dynasty in 1722, the capture of Iṣfahān by the Afghāns and the appeal for assistance against the latter from the *roi-fainéant* Ṭahmāsp II, gave Peter the Great the opportunity in 1723 to acquire possession of Darband and Bākū on the west coast of the Caspian Sea. The death of Peter the Great in 1725, and the rise of Nādir Qulī Afshār (from 1736, Nādir Shāh) in Iran, postponed but by no means terminated Russian pressure for expansion to the south at the expense of Iran.

The Afghān occupation of Iṣfahān and the resulting breakdown of law and order throughout Iran naturally posed almost insuperable difficulties for the agents and staffs of the English, Dutch and French East India Companies, some of whom lost their lives either during the six-month siege of Iṣfahān, during which many people perished from famine and disease, or at the hands of the Afghāns after the occupation of the city on 12 October 1722. Some managed to save their lives by bribing the Afghān authorities. As Owen Phillips, the English Agent, wrote to London on 30 November 1722: "Thank God, we have escaped by a timely Precaution, but by a vast Expence of Cash for which we cannot tax our Conduct with Prudence...We hope no one who hears our Conduct will want humanity enough to approve the Purchase of our Lives on the Terms we have submitted to."[20]

6

The flowering of the arts under the Safavids

Some of the architectural achievements of the Safavids are described in Chapter 7. In this chapter an attempt will be made to give an idea of their achievements in the fine and applied arts. In Iran, art has always been aristocratic art, "in the sense that it was royalty and the upper classes of society which created the demand for works of art and thus stimulated the activity of artists and craftsmen, and also in the sense that these aristocratic patrons frequently dictated what kind of art and what type of objects should be produced".[1]

PAINTING AND THE "ART OF THE BOOK"

In many respects, the Safavids were the heirs of the brilliant artistic traditions of the Timurid court at Harāt in Khurāsān. The Timurid ruler Shāhrukh (1405–47) and his son Bāysunqur were patrons of the arts and bibliophiles, and some of the finest Islamic manuscripts in existence were commissioned by them. Sulṭān Ḥusayn Bāyqarā (1470–1505) was the patron of the outstanding Harāt school of painting of which Bihzād was the leading member. In 1507, two years after the death of Sulṭān Ḥusayn Bāyqarā, the Özbegs swept across Khurāsān and entered Harāt unopposed. Three years later, in 1510, the Özbeg army was annihilated at the battle of Marv by Shāh Ismāʿīl I, who annexed Khurāsān to the Safavid empire. Although Shāh Ismāʿīl's capital was at Tabrīz, in north-western Iran, he made Harāt the second city of his empire and the seat of the heir-apparent. He thus inherited the artistic traditions of the city which has been dubbed the "Athens" of Iran.[2] One of his first moves was to take the artist Bihzād back with him to Tabrīz; Bihzād took charge of a group of artists who had fled from Harāt a few years previously, and established the Tabrīz school of painting. Shāh Ismā'īl was apparently so solicitous for Bihzād's safety that, at the time of the battle of Chāldirān in 1514 against the Ottomans, he concealed Bihzād and his favourite calligrapher, Shāh Maḥmūd, in a cave out of harm's way.[3] In 1522, Bihzād was appointed by Shāh Ismā'īl director of the royal library. His letter of appointment was penned by the eminent historian Ghiyāth al-Dīn Khvāndamīr, a personal friend of the artist and author of the *Ḥabīb al-Siyar*, one of the best histories of the reign of Ismā'īl I. In Safavid times, the royal library was not so much a library as we understand the word as a workshop under royal patronage in which a variety of craftsmen laboured to produce superb manuscripts characterised by the excellence of their calligraphy, illumination, illustration and book binding – the principal skills which together constituted the "art of the book".[4]

During the long reign of Shāh Ṭahmāsp (1524–76), the various skills which constituted the "art of the book" were brought to the ultimate pitch of perfection. This was in large part due to the fact that Ṭahmāsp was not only a keen patron of the arts but had himself devoted a lot of time in his youth to the study of painting. Several of the leading artists of the time had been his intimate companions, and he had acquired proficiency in illuminating *sarlawḥas*, or the decoration on the title-pages of manuscripts.[5] Shāh Ṭasmāsp was a "gifted, exacting patron who followed his artists' work as closely as if it were his own".[6] Given the degree of interest in the "art of the book" exhibited by both Ismā'īl I and Ṭahmāsp, it is not suprising that the nonpareil of Safavid manuscripts should be a work commissioned in 1522 by Shāh Ismā'īl for his son Ṭahmāsp but not completed until after Ismā'īl's death. This work is the *Shāhnāma-yi Shāh Ṭahmāspī*, or *King's Book of Kings*.[7] The unique nature of this work may be judged by the fact that, whereas no other extant contemporary manuscript contains more than fourteen miniature-paintings, the *King's Book of Kings* contains more than two hundred and fifty. It constitutes a "portable art gallery" since most of the most illustrious court artists of the period contributed to it.[8] The individual paintings are not necessarily all the work of one artist. "At times we find miniatures designed and largely painted by very distinguished masters, but with parts, such as distant mountain crags or an entire battalion of soldiery, executed by carefully controlled, almost miraculously discreet followers who were only slightly less senior artists themselves."[9] In other instances,

> lesser masters or assistants painted pictures either entirely alone or with some degree of aid from their betters. Sometimes a master sketched in the design and left its amplification and completion to the assistants. The master's participation varied from a scrawled hint suggesting the disposition of figures or architecture to an elaborate under-drawing requiring little beyond coloring to complete. When an assistant had done his work, a master would sometimes return to add a few improving strokes, or perhaps even a complete figure or two.[10]

Almost every characteristic of Persian painting is present in these miniatures: the reduction of the three-dimensional world to two dimensions and the use of various devices to circumvent the problems caused by this; the sure and exquisite use of harmonious colour; and the filling of every inch of the background with birds, animals, trees, vignettes depicting action subsidiary to that of the central theme of the picture. "Golden skies and silver water, black-green cypresses against white-blossoming trees, the autumn foliage of the spreading plane, dappled horses in tawny deserts, clustered figures in raiment of scarlet, crimson and azure, diaper tiles and dainty frescoes, bright gardens behind slender fences of cinnabar red: these together compose the gayest of all possible symphonies."[11]

The *King's Book of Kings* is not, however, merely a treasury of the painter's art; it is also a monument to the calligrapher's skill, since Firdawsī's *Shāhnāma*, which forms the vehicle for this wealth of illustration, consists of over 60,000 verses. In the Islamic world, of course, the dogma that the Qur'ān is the Word of God had, from the earliest days of Islam, given a theological justification for the veneration of calligraphy. This fact, together with the Islamic ban on the representation of the human form (a ban which in Iran was more often honoured in the breach), combined to give calligraphy a higher status in Muslim culture than it achieved in any other civilisation. The cult of calligraphy went far beyond the confines of the production of books and manuscripts, and the Arabic script, in a natural or stylised form, played a major role in the decoration of mosques and other religious buildings. In other words, religious feeling found an outlet both in penmanship and in the abstract illumination of manuscripts. Manuscripts were embellished by one or more whole pages of illumination, and the pages of the text were adorned with illuminated and gilded borders and other ornamentation. The chapter headings were frequently contained within panels which were little masterpieces of artistry. The skills of the miniature-painter were transferred to the tooling and embossing of leather for bookbindings, and court painters extended their technique to lacquering, which was applied not only to bookbindings but to such items as trays, dishes, pen-cases, mirror-cases and jewel- and trinket-boxes.

As Anthony Welch has pointed out, Shāh 'Abbās I (1588–1629) did not have the intense and single-minded dedication to the art of painting displayed by his grandfather Shāh Ṭahmāsp. "In general, 'Abbās would appear to have been more concerned with the arts of official conviction (architecture and city planning) and economic utility (exportable ceramics, textiles and carpets) than with the far more private and personal art of the precious book."[12] Nevertheless, 'Abbās I's patronage of artists was on an extensive scale, and he seems to have had a warm human relationship with his artists which was typical of the man. On one occasion, Rižā painted a portrait which moved the Shāh so much that he kissed the artist's hand.[13] On other occasions, the Shāh is said to have held the candle while his favourite calligrapher 'Alī Rižā was at work;[14] 'Alī Rižā's superb calligraphy adorns the entrance portal of the Masjid-i Shāh at Iṣfahān, the Masjid-i Shaykh Luṭf Allāh and the dome over the tomb in the shrine of the Imām Rižā at Mashhad.

During the reign of 'Abbās I, at least two divergent styles of painting emerged. On the one hand, Rižā 'Abbāsī crowned the achievements of his predecessors in the art of manuscript illustration, and made "a full, final statement" in this genre of paintings.[15] On the other, the aggressive and irascible genius Ṣādiqī Beg Afshār, who rose to the high position of director of the royal library, displayed in his paintings an astonishing realism which marked a new departure in Safavid art and presaged the increased realism of the late seventeenth and eighteenth centuries. His character is well told by the Safavid poet Ghurūrī and illustrated by an anecdote recorded by Anthony Welch:

I wrote a *qaṣīdah* in praise of Ṣādiqī and went to recite it in a coffee house. The *qaṣīdah* had not yet come to an end, when Ṣādiqī seized it from me and said, "I don't have the patience to listen to more than this!" Getting up after a moment, he tossed down five tomans bound in a

cloth, along with two pieces of paper on which he had executed black-line drawings. He gave them to me and said: "Merchants buy each page of my work for three tomans. They take them to Hindūstān. Don't sell them any cheaper!" Then he excused himself several times and went out.[16]

A characteristic of the great majority of paintings produced in the royal ateliers from the time of 'Abbās I onwards is that they are not designed as manuscript illustrations but are single-page paintings and drawings, intended probably for inclusion in albums belonging to members of the royal family or the nobility, or possibly for sale to persons of lower rank.[17] Another departure is that these single-page paintings and drawings are not necessarily linked to traditional literary themes. By 1596/7, when Ṣādiqī Beg Afshār was dismissed from his position of director of the royal library, Riżā 'Abbāsī had emerged as an innovative artist of genius, and he rapidly established himself as a master of the now preferred single-page painting, just as formerly he had been an acknowledged master of the miniature. "His work revolves around the idealized portrayal of beautiful people, usually unidentified and perhaps actually non-existent. The semi-canonized secular content of traditional Iranian painting – based on the great themes of the *Shāhnāmah*, the *Khamsah* of Niẓāmī, the *Haft Aurang* of Jāmī, and other works – was largely abandoned under Shāh 'Abbās."[18] Other artists, such as Mīrzā 'Alī and Shaykh Muḥammad, followed his example: "elegant youths stand in wistful awareness of nothing at all, while other beautiful people graciously hold or proffer delicate wine cups and flasks. Couples embrace each other, their feelings seemingly turned less toward each other than coyly toward admiring connoisseurs".[19] The trend toward the production of single-page paintings resulted in a relative paucity of fine Safavid manuscripts in the early seventeenth century. Anthony Welch suggests that the collectors of these single-page paintings were members of the aristocracy, both *qizilbāsh* and Tājīk, and members of the new landed and moneyed classes; he suggests further that the aesthetic taste of these new patrons of the arts was to some extent at variance with that of the artists' royal patron, Shāh 'Abbās I, and he sees this as an indication that 'Abbās I, enthusiastic promoter of the arts though he was, did not determine the course of the development of art in the way in which Shāh

9. Painting by Riżā 'Abbāsī, *ca* 1610–20

10. Riżā 'Abbāsī: portrait by Mu'īn Muṣavvir

Ṭahmāsp had determined it in the second and third quarters of the sixteenth century.[20]

As the seventeenth century wore on, the strains of sensuality and eroticism which could be clearly perceived in the later work of Riżā 'Abbāsī were blatantly displayed in the work of his successors such as Muḥammad Qāsim, Mīr Afżal and Mu'īn Muṣavvir. "Mu'īn has left a number of erotic pictures of a type unsuitable for public exhibition", state the authors of *Persian Miniature Painting* primly (writing, it should be noted, in 1933).[21] Anthony Welch is in no doubt that later Safavid painting is decadent:

> The sublety of Riżā's early work, still reminiscent of the previous generation of Safavi painters, was altered into surface values in his later pages: curves are less volumetric; pigment is less rich; expressions coarsen and become less winning. In the work of his many students and followers these trends are emphasized. There is a narrowing rather than an expansion of subject matter, which comes to rely heavily on images of external beauty – delicate young men and wistful young women who seem to assume the role of secular icons. Svelte in appearance but vapid in content, they are the evident ideals of the new social order. Where they are explicitly erotic, as they often are, their activity conveys an unreal feeling, titillating rather than passionate... It is, largely, an a-spiritual art, requiring not an eye searching for meaning but one receptive to beauty.[22]

Richard Ettinghausen argues on the other hand that

> the stylistic changes of the period of Shāh 'Abbās, and continued by his successors, were not just signs of decadence which indicated a rapid artistic and technical decay of Iranian sensibilities and capabilities. Instead it appears that the interest in reality and the life of ordinary people as well as in space and movement actually represents a revolutionary turn in the Iranian approach to the world. All of a sudden the old mold was broken and something new appeared which may have been harsh and unbeautiful, but presented the world as it was, instead of an idealized concept of the past.[23]

I suggest that both these judgements are aspects of the total picture. It seems to me undeniable that there is a *fin de siècle* quality about some of the languorous young men, languidly sniffing the perfume of a flower, about whom Welch complains. On the other hand, Ettinghausen is undoubtedly right in insisting that an artistic revolution had taken place. Instead of the conventional themes of heroes and lovers of a legendary past, we have a preoccupation with reality, with the depiction of ordinary men and women as they are. Ettinghausen lists some of them: "a kneeling cloth merchant offering his merchandise to a customer;...a middle-aged man scratching his bald pate just after having taken off his voluminous turban". Even when the theme is traditional, its treatment is now realistic. The Shīrīn discovered while bathing by Khusraw, a hackneyed theme if ever there was one, has no "delicate, ethereal body" but is an "earthy, more ordinary figure probably similar to the female persons with which the painter, Riżā-i 'Abbāsī, was familiar" from the women's quarters of his own home.[24] Similarly, Ettinghausen sees the frank treatment of sexual themes as "reflections of ordinary interhuman relationships", again representing a complete break with past tradition in which relations between the sexes were usually interpreted allegorically in terms of the mystical longing of the lover for the divine Beloved.[25] As for the foppish young men, they may well have been, he suggests, "pin-up boys" for homosexuals.[26]

CARPETS

When the exquisite sense of colour and design which had been developed by the various categories of artists involved with the art of the book was transferred to the realm of the applied arts, to the weaving of textiles and the making of carpets, the results were breathtaking. Although the making of carpets is of ancient provenance in Iran, it was the Safavids who elevated a cottage-industry to an activity on a national scale and one which formed an important part of the economy. The first actual carpet-factory was probably constructed at Iṣfahān during the reign of Shāh 'Abbās the Great (1588–1629).

The origin of the Persian carpet industry as we know it today is the tribal rug, woven by the women and children of the semi-nomadic tribes, using the wool from their own flocks and natural dyes. The tribal rugs were usually in bright, gay colours, with bold, fairly simple designs. They were (and are) highly individualistic, frequently irregular in shape, and characterised by colour changes in the wool caused by the use of different dye batches. Shāh Ṭahmāsp was keenly interested in the carpet industry, and raised it to the status of an art. It is well known that he had special carpets made and donated to the Süleymāniyye Mosque in Istanbul, and he is said to have designed some carpets himself; this would indeed not be surprising in view of his early artistic training noted above. A. Upham Pope has pointed out the close identification in Safavid times of artists and rug designers, and has mentioned the names of three of the most eminent in this connection: Bihzād (died *ca* 1535/6), Sulṭān Muḥammad (died *ca* 1543) and Sayyid 'Alī.

The continuing prestige of Persian carpets derives in part from their superior quality and in part from their perfection of colour and design. The predominant colours are blues (indigo and azure), reds (crimson and rust) and yellows; browns and greens are less commonly used. The pile is of wool, and both wool and cotton are used for the warp and weft. In the finest antique carpets, the pile is of silk, sometimes with a gold or silver thread interwoven, and occasionally the warp and weft are of silk also. Designs are predominantly floral or geometrical, although human and animal figures appear in some carpets, especially in the type known as "hunting carpets". A large central medallion appears in many designs, and all Persian carpets have a border, which may consist of a number of parallel bands; often these bands contain a motif of leaves or blossoms, in many cases in a conventionalised and virtually geometric form. Persian carpets were in great demand in Europe, and their presence in the homes of wealthy seventeenth-century burghers is faithfully recorded in the paintings of Rubens, Van Dyck, Breughel and others.

Since carpets, unlike metalwork and ceramics, are by their very nature perishable, the museums of the world have no examples of Persian carpets dating from before the sixteenth century. Among the earliest extant examples are the famous Ardabīl carpet, one of the greatest treasures of the Victoria and Albert Museum in London, dated 942 (1535/6), that is, twelve years after the accession of Shāh Ṭahmāsp, and the even earlier Milan Hunting Carpet dated 929 (1522/3), in the closing years of the reign of Ṭahmāsp's father, Ismā'īl I. The Ardabīl carpet presently in the Victoria and Albert Museum in London is one of a pair of carpets woven in Kāshān and commissioned by Shāh Ṭahmāsp as a gift to the shrine of his ancestors at Ardabīl. Every feature of the Ardabīl carpet is a masterpiece of the carpet-weaver's art. It belongs to the traditional category of medallion carpets, and in the medallion

three successive orders of pattern, three different characters of movement and colour are carried out with perfect consistency and appropriateness. In the centre is a little green flower-enwreathed pool on which float lotus blossoms. Paired arabesques formed in a pattern of great quatrefoils extend this central motif into what is in essence a shadowed quatrefoil medallion, which fits into the outer lobes of the medallion. In counter movement playing over the same space are formal cloudbands, similarly arranged on the same axes. These cloudbands are in a lighter blue and white, and so much nearer in value to the ground that they are far less conspicuous than the arabesques and quietly take their place in the second order. The third pattern consists of delicate little vines and blossoms. The patterning of the field is beyond praise and beyond analysis. The ground is a rich lustrous indigo blue with a slightly fluctuating tonality that sheds an elusive glow over the whole composition. A number of vine systems, each following its own principles, cross and recross, interweaving and colliding. Owing to the complexity and mutual interdependence of the multiple stem systems, the blossoms seem strewn with a random and lavish hand, giving rise to the happiest effect of profusion; yet actually there is a surprisingly limited number, and the control of their positions by logical stem arrangements prevents any disorder.[27]

The equally famous Milan carpet is a magnificent example of another major category of Persian carpets, the hunting carpet. The *nisba*[28] of the master weaver, Ghiyāth al-Dīn Jāmī, indicates that he came from Jām in Khurāsān. Since there are virtually no Khurāsānī features in the carpet, A. Upham Pope surmises, no doubt correctly, that Ghiyāth al-Dīn or his father "was probably one of the group of superior artists who left Khurāsān at the beginning of the sixteenth century to profit by the new and exciting opportunities opened up by the Safavid renaissance, just beginning at the court of Shāh Ismā'īl" at Tabrīz.[29] "The carpet makes an immediate impression of grandeur and beauty."[30] The central medallion, scarlet in colour, is covered with intricate designs of lotus buds, blossoms, leaves and pale blue Chinese clouds. "The ground of the main field is a very deep lustrous indigo blue," and is covered with a number of exceptionally rich flower designs. Against this variegated background, "huntsmen on red or white horses dash furiously about, hotly engaged in the final kill of a great hunt, while most of the common animals of Northern Persia, vividly and naturalistically drawn, in number and variety not equalled in any other carpet, scurry hither and thither in confused alarms of struggle and of flight".[31] The number of different colours used in the Milan carpet, approximately twenty, is greater than is used in any other early Oriental rug.[32]

As noted earlier, it was Shāh 'Abbās I who raised carpet-weaving to the status of a national industry by establishing carpet-factories at Iṣfahān, Kāshān and elsewhere. Rugs woven with silk and gold were woven at Kāshān, and at Iṣfahān were made not only the sumptuous carpets commissioned by the shahs, but carpets woven to the order of private persons by the master weavers of the royal workshops. Many of these carpets were made for export, and we are fortunate in having specific details of one such export order placed by the King of Poland, Sigismund III Vasa (1587–1632), whose reign coincided almost exactly with that of Shāh 'Abbās I. In 1601, Sigismund sent his "trusted court purveyor, the Armenian merchant Sefer Muratowicz, from Warsaw to Persia, with instructions to order several rugs for the king and to superintend their weaving personally. The Armenian family of Muratowicz had, two generations previously, obtained Polish citizenship for the purpose of transacting such business."[33] Muratowicz went to Kāshān and placed his order, and was received in audience by 'Abbās I, to whom he explained that he was not an ambassador, but only "a trading man". Subsequently, King Sigismund gave some of the Persian carpets to his daughter as part of her dowry when she married the Elector Palatine of the Rhine in 1642. Perhaps King Sigismund had not been amused by the liberties taken by the Persian weavers with the Polish royal coat of arms, which he wished to have woven into the design:

> the crown above the cartouche has been enriched by details unknown in the West, so that the leaves and balls on its circlet remind us of Eastern vessels. The heraldic eagle itself has its head turned to the right instead of to the left, the feathers of its wings and tail, which ought to be pure white, are mixed with black and yellow, the feet are blue instead of red, while the heraldic "sheaf" of the Vasas has assumed the form of a bluish flower resembling a stylized lily.[34]

TEXTILES

Like carpet-making, the weaving of textiles is of ancient origin in Iran. We possess specimens of Sasanid weaving which show that the work of that period was brilliant both in design and workmanship. Silks and brocades were common, and the elaborate animal motifs developed by the Sasanids were later copied by the Byzantines and in countries as far afield as China and

Germany. New designs, making use of arabesques and floral motifs and in many cases showing traces of Chinese influence, reached Iran in the wake of the Mongol invasions of the thirteenth century. As in carpet-making, however, the Safavid period represents the high-point in textiles also. The prosperity of Iran under the Safavids stimulated internal demand, and

> the sumptuous apparel and elaborate pavilions with rich hangings excited the admiration of travellers who visited the Persian court, and a taste for Persian luxury articles arose in Renaissance Europe and in Russia. The skilful use of complicated weaves, the combination of brilliant colours in variegated designs, and an apparently unfailing inventiveness in the use of arabesque and floral ornament, enabled the Persian to produce textiles of a unique richness and variety.[35]

As in the case of carpets, it was Shāh 'Abbās I, with his overriding interest in trade, who developed the textile industry to an astonishing degree. Krusinski, in his account entitled "Concerning the raiment and wardrobe of the royal Persian court," says that

11. Length of woven polychrome velvet, early 17th century

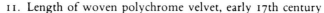

the foresight of Shāh 'Abbās the Great caused numerous and manifold factories to be established in the provinces of Shīrvān, Qarā-bāgh, Gīlān, Kāshān, Mashhad, Astarābād, as well as in the capital Iṣfahān itself, in which, under a strict supervision of overseers, silk textiles and sashes [turbans], as well for common use as royal ones...are woven in a magnificent and wonderful way, while rugs and all kinds of woven fabrics are constantly made for the royal court.

In this account, Krusinski does not mention one of the principal textile centres, Yazd; there were also other subsidiary centres of the industry at Rasht, Ardistān, Sāva and Kirmān. Krusinski adds that, in order to preserve the "specific characteristics of artistic weaving of each locality", the Shāh gave orders that each factory should "weave in its own manner".[36] A significant proportion of textile production was for export:

those factories not only produce what is necessary for the court and the courtiers with small expense to the Treasury, beyond the cost of the silver thread, but they also enrich not a little the royal Treasury, for the more precious silk weavings and the textiles that are enriched with gold and silver threads are sent with government salesmen for sale to Europe and even more to India by whole shiploads.[37]

In addition to producing woven fabrics, brocades and velvets of the finest quality, Safavid craftsmen also excelled in embroidery and printed cottons (*qalam-kār*) which were block printed in an infinite variety of designs. At Iṣfahān, the textile industry was on a huge scale. In the bazaars, there are said to have been stalls for 25,000 workers, and "the chief of the textile guild was one of the most powerful men in the country. Even the governor feared him." The court looms are said to have covered the whole distance between the Maydān and the Chihil Sutūn, a distance of about a quarter of a mile.[38] As in the earlier Safavid period, leading artists such as Rizā 'Abbāsi placed their designs at the disposal of the textile-weavers. "The increasing anthropocentric interest of the time which saw the beginning of individual portraiture"[39] meant that, instead of the small and rather incidental figures on earlier textiles, more and more one found hangings on which the design of a human figure would take up a whole panel.

Although some experts consider that the velvets and other textiles of the period of 'Abbās I do not quite measure up in quality to the productions of the earlier Safavid period, there is no doubt that the range of designs and colours of the textiles of 'Abbās I's period is infinitely greater. In addition to all the usual

12. Kāshān

colours, there is "a wide gamut of delicate greys, mauves, violets, and aubergine [*sic*] so numerous that the very inventory of names is exhausted. The colour compositions are proportionately varied and ingenious, and the pattern makers had at their command the limitless resources of the gardens of Iṣfahān and her wide, flower-spangled meadows."[40] Indeed, motifs from the animal and floral world are common: leopards, gazelles and hares abound, and the parrot is the commonest bird; of flowers, the tulip, rose, hyacinth and iris appear most frequently, but many other varieties were used by the weavers – "a more extensive array than has ever been depicted in any other textile art".[41] It is not surprising that there was a brisk market in Europe for Persian velvets, silks, damasks, satins, taffetas. The Yazd brocades in particular made use of the ubiquitous *buta* (the so-called pear or palm-leaf design). When one adds to this bewildering array of textiles the many types of embroidered fabrics, one can assert positively that textiles of the Safavid period have never been surpassed in design and technique.

CERAMICS

Persian pottery has strongly influenced pottery in both East and West and, in the general history of ceramics, stands second only to the pottery of China. While Persian pottery reached its peak during the Seljuq and Mongol periods (twelfth to fourteenth centuries), the work of Safavid potters was of high standard, and their ceramic tiles are unsurpassed. The Persian word for faience tile, *kāshī*, is derived from the name of the city of Kāshān, which since early Islamic times was renowned as a centre of the ceramics industry. By Safavid times, Iṣfahān and Mashhad had also become major centres of the industry, and a renaissance of the ceramic art was under way. Safavid potters did not slavishly copy the patterns and styles of earlier periods, but developed new types of ceramics and displayed both imagination and invention. "Perhaps the most distinguished of the new potteries" was

> a group of vessels of a particularly beautiful shade of blue, with designs of great elegance and simplicity reserved in a perfect milk white. The ornaments of arabesques of purest type of stellate medallions are drawn with remarkable precision and elegance. The mildness of the tones, the simplicity of colour and drawing and the quiet glaze give them a high quality of dignity.[42]

There was also "an interesting development of certain highly-glazed green wares, principally bottles and flasks, with relief figures, frequently in European costume". "Another large class of wares of which only a few examples have survived in good condition has a rich foliage decoration in light blue and rose on a white ground. This style was carried into a great variety of wares, plates, bowls, flasks, pitchers."[43] Safavid potters achieved striking effects with quiet colours and pastel shades: light slate colour; greens, modulated through a wide variety of shades to a yellowish cast, or from deep emerald to pale whitish green; blues, in addition to the traditional deeper shades of lapis lazuli, cobalt and turquoise, a whole range of pastel shades such as powder blues, sky blue, light grey blues and lavender. The potters of Iṣfahān were especially fond of yellow, and the flasks and jars which they produced ranged in colour from deep saffron to a light lemon yellow.[44]

The most significant fact about the history of ceramics during the Safavid period is the large-scale interchange of techniques and designs between Iran and China which took place at that time. Prior to the fifteenth century at the earliest, "the Iranian potters apparently remained unaffected by the Chinese imports of blue and white".[45] Shāh 'Abbās I, who adopted a pragmatic approach to the ceramics industry as to everything else to which he set his hand,

> could see no reason why Europeans should buy all of their porcelain in China when it could with a little effort be supplied from Persia, and thousands of miles of transit and time thereby saved. To assist the development of a ceramic style which could take advantage of the Chinese vogue in Europe, he had three hundred Chinese potters and their families brought to Persia and settled there. They seem to have been established principally at Iṣfahān. Some of the characteristic Chinese formulae were maintained for a long time, but the Persians, as usual, soon contributed some of their own stock of decorative ideas, and little by little these porcelains took on more and more a Persian character.[46]

The product of this Irano-Chinese co-operation was a distinctive blue underglaze-painted white ware, of a pseudo-porcellanous quality, imitating the Chinese blue-and-white of the Ming period.[47] Genuine Chinese porcelain had been highly prized in Iran for centuries, and had been assiduously collected by rulers in Central and Western Asia. The famous collection donated to

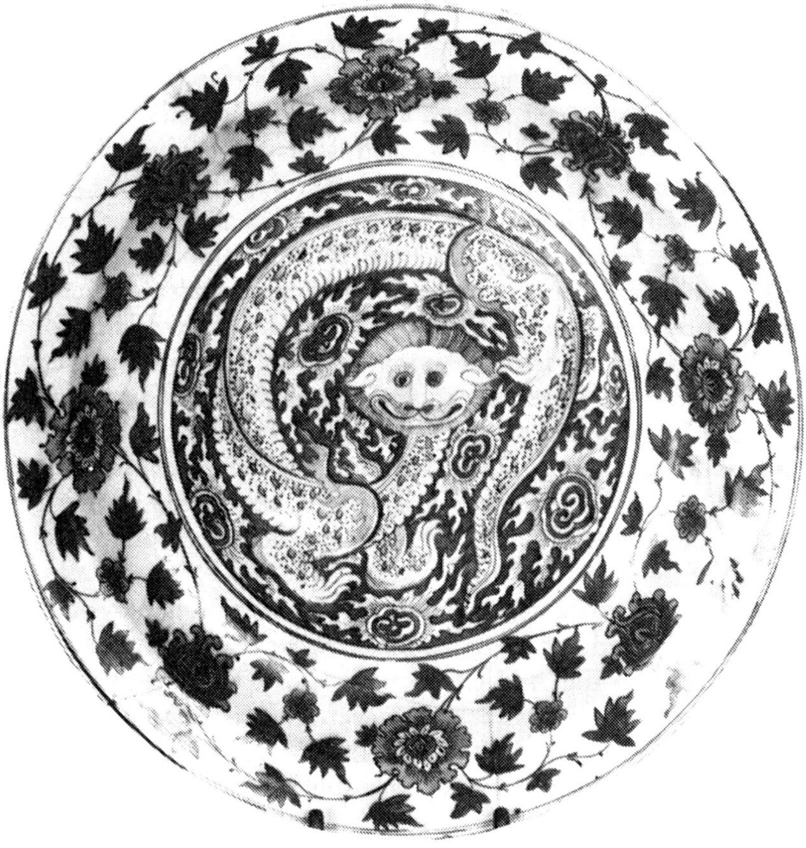

13. Blue-and-white porcelain plate, Iran, 16th century

the Safavid shrine at Ardabīl by Shāh 'Abbās I in 1611 consisted of over 1,000 pieces, which had probably found their way to Iran over a period of two and a half centuries.[48]

The manufacture of Chinese porcelain in Iran itself was well established by the early sixteenth century. Olearius reports that two Chinese merchants had a shop for selling porcelains at Ardabīl at that period, and many Persian potters tried to imitate it, but with indifferent success until 'Abbās I imported the Chinese experts mentioned above. Under their tutelage, the Persian blue-and-white ware was accepted on something like equality in Europe with the Chinese originals, which they greatly resembled. "The blue of the Persian blue-and-white is often of fine quality, and even on the common specimens it is in no way inferior to the Chinese. It is slightly purplish in tone, resembling in this quality the Mohammedan blue of the Ming period".[49] Sometimes the Persian and Chinese styles were blended in the Persian blue-and-white ware; Pope mentions a plate at the Victoria and Albert Museum on which "a typical Chinese landscape is embellished with exaggerated leopards in the Persian manner". This ware was made in many parts of the country: Shīrāz, Mashhad, Yazd, Kirmān and Zarand, and the earliest piece recorded by Pope is dated 1616.[50] In 1682, the English East India Company regarded Mashhad and Kirmān as the two places in Iran where really good imitations of Chinese porcelain could be obtained.[51]

Although the blue-and-white ware is the most famous type of Safavid pottery, there were many others equally fine. Examples of several types were found by the Russians in the late nineteenth century at the remote mountain village of Kubachi in Dāghistān. Since the Dāghistānī tribesmen, like many other montagnards, made a living by raiding caravans, and never had been potters, scholars for long speculated how such a large collection of fine pottery came to be there. The answer seems to be that the pottery was used as a barter commodity by the Safavids in return for the

14. City gate of Shīrāz

superior quality knives and daggers made at Kubachi. The main types of pottery found at Kubachi, described in detail by Pope, are a black-painted ware with either a turquoise or green glaze, and a polychrome underglaze-painted ware. The origin of the former type is a mystery, since nothing like it has been found in central Iran, yet the designs are unmistakably Safavid; Pope suggests Tabrīz as a possibility. The latter type may have been manufactured at Sāva, since the wares discovered there, though of inferior quality, strongly resemble it.[52] Underglaze-painted ware was, of course, manufactured in many places in Iran during the Safavid period, as was lustre-painted ware; there was also a revival in Safavid times of the celebrated celadon ware, again originally a copy of the Chinese ware which had been known in the West since the ninth century. Monochrome relief ware, often of superb quality; monochrome incised ware, making use of monochrome glazes in colours such as melon green, lavender and powder blue, which were developed in Iran under the tutelage of the Chinese masters imported by Shāh 'Abbās I; the white pseudo-porcelain known as "Gombroon ware" but probably manufactured at Nā'īn; and a large range of local wares such as the sixteenth-century turquoise and cobalt Varāmīn ware, all contributed to the almost infinite variety of Safavid pottery.[53]

If the wares of Safavid potters, despite their great variety and beauty, are held to fall just short of the finest products of the Seljuq and Mongol periods, in the other major branch of the potter's art, the manufacture of faience tiles, Safavid potters were unsurpassed. These tiles were of two main types: polychrome (*haft-rang*) whole tiles used in the wall revetments of mosques, *madrasas* and other buildings; and mosaic (*mu'arraq*) tiles in which the design was painstakingly assembled from individually fashioned pieces cut from whole tiles of the required colour; mosaic tile was used particularly in calligraphic decoration, the interior of domes, and so on.

The *haft-rang* tiles measure approximately 16.51 centimetres square, and consisted of pure clay with a small admixture of sand. The tiles were glazed with a mixture of pulverised white stones and sodium carbonate, fired, and trimmed at the edges to ensure a perfect joint. The design was then stencilled on to the tile, and the master potter applied the pigments. According to one tradition the "seven colours" from which the *haft-rang* tiles derived their name were black, brown, red, yellow, white, cobalt blue and turquoise; another tradition gives yellow, blue, orange, red, violet, green and indigo. The fact that the colours of Persian ceramic tiles have resisted the fierce Persian sun for centuries without fading is due in part to the skill used in the glazing and firing processes, but also to the use of only mineral pigments. Various blues were obtained from cobalt oxide; black from manganese and brown from manganese mixed with lead oxide; turquoise and green from copper oxide; yellow from lead oxide. Mosaic work was built up in frames of the required shape (flat, concave, convex), with the glazed surface face downwards; when the panel was complete, liquid plaster was poured over the back to bond all the individual pieces.[54]

METALWORK

In the realm of intellectual activity, the whole field of Safavid literature, including poetry and historiography, and the rich and important output of the Iṣfahān school of philosophy, for a variety of reasons which do not redound to the credit of either Iranian or Western scholarship, has been ignored until very recent times. Safavid arts and crafts and architecture have fared better, but even here there is a glaring omission – metalwork – and this despite the fact there were significant innovations in Safavid metalwork. "The history of Iranian metalwork has yet to be written...but no period has been so blatantly neglected as the Safavid period and the half century of Timurid rule during which the foundations of much of Safavid art were laid."[55] A. S. Melikian-Shirvani, from whose work this quotation was taken, is the first person either to attempt a comprehensive study of Safavid metalwork or to relate it to the tradition of the preceding period.

It was not until 1939, when A. Upham Pope published the monumental *Survey of Persian Art*, that any substantial body of Safavid metalwork had appeared in any publication. There was then a gap of over forty years before another group of bronze and tinned copper vessels appeared in A. S. Melikian-Shirvani's *Le Bronze iranien* (1973). K. A. C. Creswell, in his *A Bibliography of the Architecture, Arts and Crafts of Islam*, published in 1961, listed only one article on a specifically Safavid subject.[56] In the course of his research to date, A. S. Melikian-Shirvani has reached three

15. Bronze candlestick, late 16th century

main conclusions regarding Safavid metalwork: first, it represents a continuation of the Timurid, and especially Khurāsāni, tradition; second, in the time of Shāh 'Abbās I, there were two distinct schools of metalwork in Iran – one in Khurāsān, and the other in Āẕarbāyjān; third, both Ṣūfī and Shī'ī tendencies can be detected in Safavid production, and the Khurāsānī school had a "tremendous and unsuspected impact on the classical school of western Iran".[57] In this connection, it is possible that metalworkers from Khurāsān migrated westwards to the Safavid capital at Tabrīz just as did artists and other craftsmen skilled in various aspects of the art of the book.

Safavid innovations in metalwork included

> a type of tall octagonal torch-holder on a circular plinth, a new type of ewer of Chinese inspiration, and the almost total disappearance of Arabic inscriptions in favour of Persian poetry. Dense arabesques and floral designs were more to contemporary taste than figure motifs, perhaps because they provided a more low-key background for inscriptions, which were allotted a greater surface area than ever before, in bold zigzags and cartouches as well as the more conventional encircling bands. A few pieces commissioned by Armenian patrons juxtapose lines from Persian mystical poets with Armenian inscriptions. Brass was apparently often tinned to simulate silver, though the most luxurious metalwork...was inlaid with gold incrusted with jewels.[58]

In regard to the inscriptions on Safavid metal vessels, mystical themes from the great classical poets such as Ḥāfiẓ and Sa'dī were naturally favourites for wine bowls and other drinking vessels. Mystical verses were also an obvious choice for torch-stands and the like, since the metaphor of the moth hovering round the candle, willing to achieve union with it at the cost of being consumed in its flame, had long since become part of the stereotyped and hackneyed imagery of mystical poets. The "revolutionary" trend in Safavid metalwork detected by A. S. Melikian-Shirvani was the use of inscriptions of a Shī'ī nature:

> with the emergence of Safavid power, inscriptions of a militantly Shi'ite content appeared on metalwork, for which I know no precedent. These were of three categories: litanies calling God's blessing on the names of the twelve imams, or more often on the fourteen pure ones;[59] a prayer naming 'Alī; and, less often, poems celebrating 'Alī sometimes with burning extremist accents.[60]

Some of these poems come perilously close to identifying 'Alī with God, and appear on vessels not only of the revolutionary period of the establishment of the Safavid state, but even on a bowl dated 1620/1, during the reign of Shāh 'Abbās I.[61]

A major branch of Safavid metalwork, of course, was the production of arms and armour. Unfortunately, no detailed study of Safavid arms and armour has yet been made, but we do know that both were of a high standard. The finest steel for the making of swords was imported from India, and Safavid swordsmiths were particularly skilled in the art of damascening. Chardin

16. Helmet of Shāh ʻAbbās I, 1625/6

comments that "Their Cimiters are very well Damask'd, and exceed all that the Europeans can do."[62] In the seventeenth century, the finest blades were made at Qum, but by the eighteenth century those of Khurāsān took pride of place. Few of the names of the swordsmiths are known to us; Asad Allāh Iṣfahānī, who made several swords for Shāh 'Abbās I, is an exception. The sheaths and pommels of both swords and daggers were highly decorated; some were enamelled, others (especially ceremonial weapons and those designed as gifts) were jewelled.

In the sixteenth century, a new type of armour called *chahār ā'īna* (four mirrors) appeared. It consisted of four iron plates joined by hinges or straps with removable pins; two plates covered the chest and back, and the other two were worn on either side with an armhole cut out. Such armour was usually worn over a mail shirt. The other components in a complete set of armour were a pair of vambraces (*bāzūband*), a circular steel shield (*sipar*), and a helmet (*khūd*). Safavid helmets were usually conical pointed casques. The helmet and vambrace of Shāh 'Abbās I are in the British Museum; the helmet is dated 1035 (1625/6), and is decorated with verses from the *Būstān* of Sa'dī. "The surface of the bowl is yellow watered steel with burnished frames to the diamond-shaped cartouche on four sides, each containing an inscription in gold."[63] The central point of the helmet was usually forged in one piece with the bowl, and into it was screwed a long quadrangular spike. To the lower edge of the helmet was attached the aventail or mail curtain, which sometimes reached to the wearer's shoulders. Double plume tubes were a characteristic feature of Safavid helmets. The steel shields, which gradually replaced the older cane shields as the use of firearms became more common, naturally gave the metalworker great scope for decoration. "Real and false damascene in gold and silver, chiselling, engraving, and piercing, and a wide variety of contrasting colours were employed – ranging from straw to black – for the watered surface of the steel."[64] In general, armour was light and designed not to impede the movements of its mounted wearer; the heavy armour of mediaeval European knights was unknown in Iran. During the sixteenth century, horse armour also seems to have been used.

7

"Iṣfahān is half the world" – Shāh 'Abbās's Iṣfahān

Unlike Shīrāz, Iṣfahān has had no Ḥāfiẓ to sing its praises, and the people of Iṣfahān have an unenviable reputation among their fellow-countrymen for stinginess and a lack of what Sir Winston Churchill used to call "intestinal fortitude". Laurence Lockhart pointed out that jealousy lay at the root of many of the satires and attacks on Iṣfahānīs, and drew attention to the fact that the fourteenth-century Muslim traveller Ibn Baṭṭūṭa, who was a Moor and therefore presumably impartial, gave quite a different picture:[1] "their dominant qualities are bravery and pugnacity, together with generosity".[2] At all events, Iṣfahānīs must be well satisfied with the accolade bestowed by history on their city, for nearly everyone who knows anything at all about Iran has heard the jingle *Iṣfahān niṣf-i jahān*: "Iṣfahān is half the world" – the poet wishing us to understand that paradise constitutes the other half. This proud boast derives from the achievements of one man, Shāh 'Abbās the Great. As Wilfrid Blunt truly says: "Iṣfahān is Shāh 'Abbās's memorial: *Si monumentum requiris, circumspice.*"[3]

Rarely in the course of history has an entire city been planned or replanned at one time by a master mind. In recent times, Paris was doubled in size by Baron Haussmann in the time of Napoleon III; the Washington of L'Enfant is another example which springs to mind; the Iṣfahān of Shāh 'Abbās I is a much earlier example. "In a real sense Safavid architecture begins in the reign of Shāh 'Abbās."[4]

There were few novel elements in the architecture itself. The originality of the urban planning of Shāh 'Abbās lay in the boldness of its conception and in the colossal scope of the programme, embracing the building of a great capital city "with avenues, palaces, public offices, mosques and madrasas, bazaars, baths, forts and gardens".[5] The Shāh's right-hand man in the work of planning this ambitious ensemble was that truly remarkable man Shaykh Bahā al-Dīn Muḥammad 'Āmilī, known as Shaykh Bahā'ī: eminent theologian, philosopher, Qur'ān-commentator, jurisprudent, astronomer, teacher, poet and engineer, he was the very epitome of Safavid society of the time of Shāh 'Abbās the Great: urbane, sophisticated, learned and pious. On his death on 30 August 1621, those nobles who were in the capital

took up their station around the bier, and men of all classes vied with one another for the honour of acting as pall-bearers. The throng in the Maydān-i Naqsh-i Jahān was so great that, despite the size of the square, men were pressed tightly against one another, and the pall-bearers could only with difficulty make progress through the crowd.[6]

One of the chronograms devised to commemorate the date of his death was particularly appropriate: "Alas for the Exemplar of the Age!"

Iṣfahān is, of course, a city of ancient origin, but its greatness dates from the year 1597/8, when Shāh 'Abbās made it the capital of the Safavid empire in place of Qazvīn. Iṣfahān lay at the natural geographical centre of an empire which now stretched from Georgia to Afghānistān. Shāh 'Abbās I, by choosing Iṣfahān as his new capital, at once made it easier to conduct operations against the Özbegs on the north-east frontier and at the same time demonstrated his confidence that that frontier would ultimately be made secure. In addition, the more central location of Iṣfahān enabled him to exert greater control over affairs in the Persian Gulf, an important consideration in view of the great increase in commercial and diplomatic activity in that area during his reign.

Iṣfahān, lying at an altitude of about 1,585 metres, is an oasis of intense cultivation in the midst of a vast plain of almost unrelieved aridity. Shāh 'Abbās and his master planner, Shaykh Bahā'ī, provided a sound agricultural basis for the new capital city by laying out comprehensive systems of irrigation and communication, and by founding the thriving market town of Najafābād, 15 miles west of Iṣfahān, to supply the city with food. The water for irrigation was and still is supplied by the river aptly named the Zāyanda-rūd, the "river which gives life", which rises in the Zagros mountains and flows west-north-west to Iṣfahān. After passing through the city, the river follows an easterly course until it loses itself in the Gāvkhāna swamp on the edge of the Great Desert. Even in Safavid times, the flow of the Zāyanda-rūd was not adequate to meet the needs of the new capital, and Shāh 'Abbās attempted to divert some of the waters of the Kūhrang river in order to increase the flow of the Zāyanda-rūd. This necessitated cutting through the mountainside separating the headwaters of these two rivers, which rise on opposite sides of the Zagros watershed at one of the highest points in that range, near the Zarda-Kūh (4,548 metres). This grandiose scheme, first conceived by Shāh Ṭahmāsp, begun by 'Abbās I and continued by his great-grandson 'Abbās II, was completed in 1953 by Sir Alexander Gibb and Partners, who discovered that the alignment of the trench dug by Shāh 'Abbās's engineers was only slightly off true.

The two key features of Shāh 'Abbās's master plan for Iṣfahān were the Chahār Bāgh and the Maydān-i Naqsh-i Jahān. The former, said to have taken its name from four vineyards which the Shāh had to purchase in order to secure the right-of-way, was an avenue of majestic proportions. Starting from a point near the Chihil Sutūn palace, the Chahār Bāgh ran south for about a mile, crossed the Zāyanda-rūd by the Allāhverdī Khān bridge, and continued south for another mile and a quarter to the huge expanse of pleasure gardens known as Hazārjarīb, where many notables at court had their residences. Although on crown land, these pleasure gardens were open to the public. The total length of the Chahār Bāgh was thus about 2½ miles, and its width in its northern section was 48 metres to the flanking walls.

The second key feature of Shāh 'Abbās's Iṣfahān was the huge Maydān, approximately 507 metres in length and 158 metres in width, which lay to the east of the northern end of the Chahār Bāgh and at a slight angle to it. Donald Wilber does not see anything peculiar in the fact that the axis of the Chahār Bāgh is not parallel with that of the Maydān. "With the concentration of architectural details and interest upon the interiors of mosques and shrines which, in most cases, could not be circumambulated, such devices as the opening of vistas, the climactic arrangement of successive structures, and a studied relationship between important structures located in the same general area were rarely practiced."[7] This great Maydān, known as the Maydān-i Naqsh-i Jahān (Exemplar of the World), was the place where monarch and

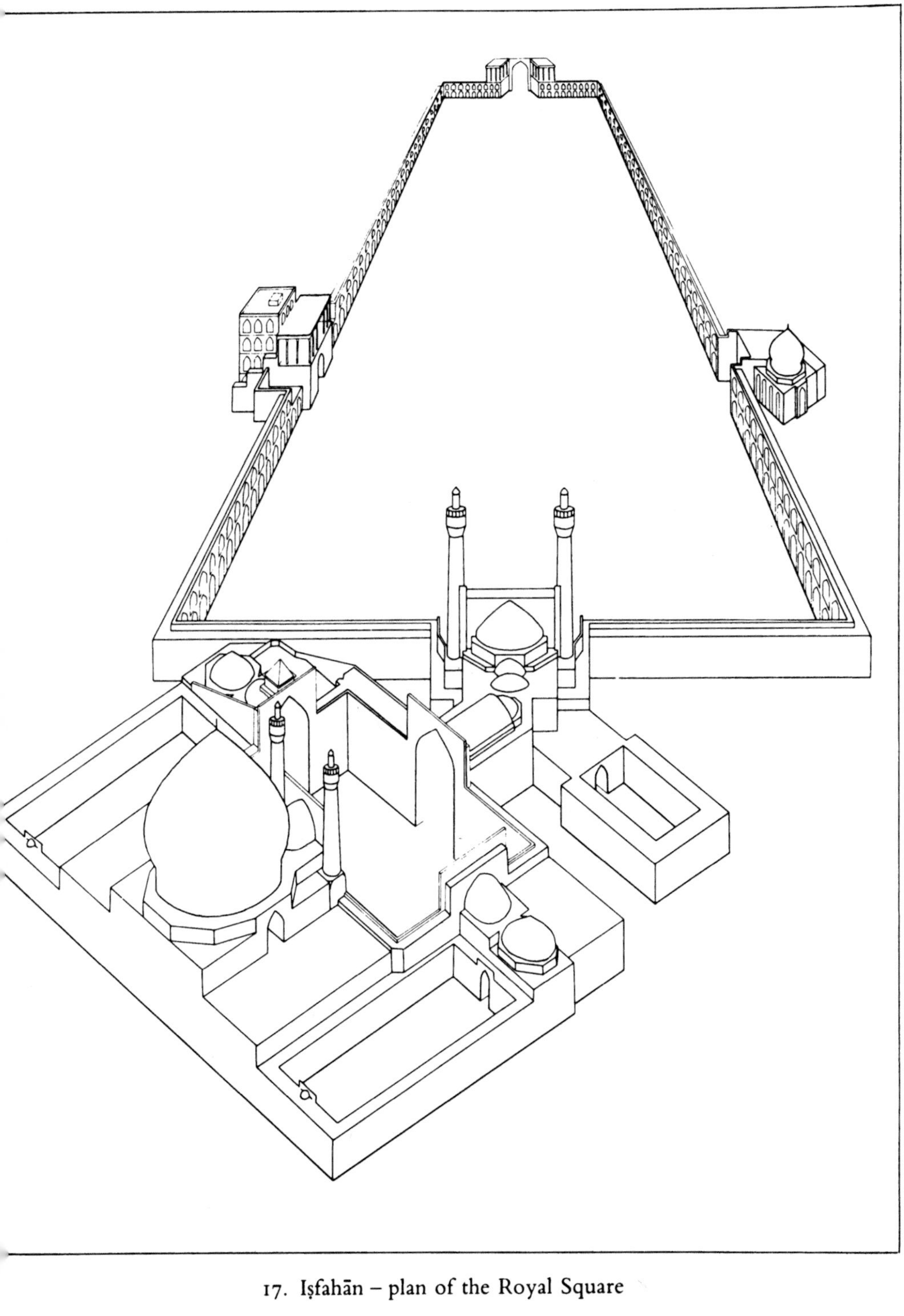

17. Iṣfahān – plan of the Royal Square

18. Iṣfahān – the Maydān

citizen met.[8] All around the edge of the Maydān ran a water-channel, $3\frac{1}{2}$ metres wide and 2 metres deep. Along the channel, a row of plane trees afforded shade for strollers. By day, the piazza was often covered with hucksters' booths, and the merchants' warehouses surrounding the Maydān were "stored with all Merchandizes, chiefly drugs, and to the place daily resort most Nations, as English, Dutch, Portugals, Arabians, Turkes, Jewes, Armenians, Muscovians, and Indians".[9] At night, the Maydān was frequented by a teeming throng of mummers, jugglers,

puppet-players, acrobats, storytellers, dervishes and prostitutes. From time to time, and especially during the great Iranian national festival celebrating the New Year (Nawrūz), the gardens flanking the Maydān were the site of the New Year's levees held by the Shāh. A contemporary chronicler describes such an occasion in 1611:

The Shah then ordered a great feast to be prepared in the Bāgh-i Naqsh-i Jahān to which all classes of society were invited: emirs, viziers, *moqarrabs* of the court; people from various parts of the Shāh's

19A. Iṣfahān – the Royal Mosque, main courtyard looking north

dominions who happened to be at court, merchants, and members of craft guilds. Each group was allotted its own particular place in the park, and gold tents and canopies of silk and Chinese brocade were set up. Booths, embellished in various remarkable ways and illuminated with lamps, were erected in front of each group. Pages plied the assembled gathering with cheering draughts, and the merrymaking went on for several days.[10]

The Maydān was also a polo ground (the marble goal-posts erected by Shāh 'Abbās I still stand at either end of the Maydān), and was used for other forms of sport as well, including the archery competitions known as *qabaq-andāzī*, in which horsemen at full gallop shot arrows at a gold cup (or a less valuable target) placed at the top of a high wooden pole.

19B. Iṣfahān – the Royal Mosque, minarets and dome

An important feature of Shāh 'Abbās's urban planning was that it did not involve the demolition of the old city; the new city simply started where old Iṣfahān ended. "The new plan was realized on open ground (the royal garden and public lands) away from the limitations and problems of the old city."[11] It was thus possible for this royal exercise in town-planning to become a reality in less than half a century. The magnificent old Masjid-i Jum'a, dating from Seljuq times, and the prosperous bazaars on which the eleventh-century traveller and Ismā'īlī missionary, Nāṣir-i Khusraw, had commented so approvingly, were not only left standing but were closely linked with the new city by the Great Maydān, which stretched away directly from the main entrance of the Qayṣariyya, or Royal Bazaar. The theme of commerce was carried into the Great Maydān itself by a two-storey row of shops which surrounded the entire Maydān, the row being broken only by the principal buildings fronting on the Maydān: the Masjid-i Shaykh Luṭf Allāh, the Masjid-i Shāh, or Royal Mosque, and the 'Ālī Qāpū palace.

Two of the greatest masterpieces of Safavid architecture were built during the reign of Shāh 'Abbās: the Masjid-i Shaykh Luṭf Allāh, situated on the east side of the Maydān, was begun in 1603 and completed in 1618. It was dedicated to the Shāh's father-in-law, who was reputed to be one of the most famous preachers of his day. The Masjid-i Shāh, located at the south end of the Maydān, is the second architectural masterpiece commissioned by Shāh 'Abbās; it was begun in 1611, but not completed until after the death of Shāh 'Abbās in 1629. The two buildings differ both in conception and in function. The Masjid-i Shāh was designed as a public building, and as the Shāh's "affirmation of the dynasty's adherence to Shi'ism".[12] Because of the Shāh's desire to have the building completed during his lifetime, short-cuts were taken in the construction; for example, painted *haft-rangī* (polychrome) tiles were largely used in place of the more time-consuming mosaic tiles. The Shāh had also ignored the warnings of the architect Abu'l-Qāsim regarding the danger of subsidence in the foundations, and pressed ahead with the construction; the architect subsequently proved to have been justified.[13] Nevertheless, the mosque complex, when completed, was spectacular in its impact. The entrance *ayvān* (portal) is almost 27 metres high, the arch framed by turquoise triple cable ornament and decorated with rich stalactite tilework and the superb calligraphy of 'Alī Riżā 'Abbāsī. Pope considered this portal "one of the most beautiful and imposing ever erected in Persia, indeed one of the most dramatic and satisfying anywhere".[14]

The shift and interplay between the sanctuary portal screen and the dome endow it with a curious living quality and enhance the contrast, which is such a necessary element in architecture. The rectangular screen contradicts the hemisphere of the dome. The tall thin minarets cut vertically across them both. Yet the contour of the arch answers to the contour of the dome, and the half-dome of the portal repeats its spherical shape.[15]

Passing through the entrance portal, one makes, almost without realising it, the half-right turn which enables the main court within, and hence the *miḥrāb*, or prayer-niche, to be aligned in the direction of Mecca. L. V. Golombek has been disturbed by what she calls "this peculiar, apparently baseless, orientation", and has concluded that it was "the pre-existing patterns of the city that determined this choice".[16] Donald Wilber, however, after pointing out that no pre-Safavid structures of any kind are mentioned by Chardin within the entire area covered by royal ensemble, suggests a reason for the "apparently baseless" divergence between the long axis of the Maydān and the Mecca-orientation of the *miḥrāb*. "Had these axes coincided," he declares, "the dome over the sanctuary of the Masjid-i Shāh would have been concealed from view by the towering entrance portal of the mosque, except from a considerable distance to the north on the maydān. The axial divergence results in the dome and its own minarets being visible from anywhere in the maydān."[17]

By contrast, the Masjid-i Shaykh Luṭf Allāh was an oratory designed for the Shāh's private worship, and it was virtually ignored by the European travellers who visited Iṣfahān during the seventeenth century because they were unable to gain access to the interior. Compared with the Masjid-i Shāh, its design is simple, and consists only of a flattened dome resting on a square dome chamber. There is no courtyard, there are no interior *ayvāns*. Yet in its construction the finest materials were used, and the most talented craftsmen employed, and I know of no finer example of the Persian Islamic genius than the interior of the dome:

20. Iṣfahān – the Shaykh Luṭf Allāh Mosque

The dome is inset with a network of lemon-shaped compartments, which increase in size as they descend from a formalised peacock at the apex and are surrounded by plain bricks; each is filled with a foliage pattern inlaid on plain stucco. The walls, bordered by broad white inscriptions on dark blue, are similarly inlaid with twirling arabesques or baroque squares on deep ochre stucco. The colours of all this inlay are dark blue, light greenish-blue, and a tint of indefinite wealth like wine. Each arch is framed in turquoise corkscrews. The *miḥrāb* in the west wall is enamelled with tiny flowers on a deep blue meadow.

Each part of the design, each plane, each repetition, each separate branch or blossom has its own sombre beauty. But the beauty of the whole comes as you move. Again, the highlights are broken by the play of glazed and unglazed surfaces; so that with every step they rearrange themselves in countless shining patterns; while even the pattern of light through the thick window traceries is inconstant, owing to outer traceries which are several feet away and double the variety of each varying silhouette.

I have never encountered splendour of this kind before.[18]

The third of the principal buildings fronting on the Maydān was the 'Alī Qāpū, or Sublime Porte, which was "at once a lodging, a grandstand, and audience chamber, and a state gateway leading to the Palace grounds".[19] Shāh 'Abbās developed and extended an existing Timurid building and added to it three additional storeys. The beauty of the 'Alī Qāpū, dismissed contemptuously by Robert Byron as "that brick boot-box",[20] lies not so much in its exterior architecture, which is undistinguished, as in its interior, in the charm of the small rooms designed for informal gatherings, in the exquisite design and colour of the frescoes etched in the stucco walls and ceilings and in the effects of light and shade created by the delicate tracery of the windows. The main feature of the 'Alī Qāpū is the *tālār*, or covered balcony, from which 'Abbās I and his successors used to watch games of polo and other forms of entertainment in the Maydān.

At the north end of the Maydān, linking the new capital with the old city, lay the Qayṣariyya, or Royal Bazaar, of Iṣfahān. Over the main entrance was located the *naqqāra-khāna*, or musicians' gallery, where music was played at sunrise and sunset whenever the Shāh was in residence at Iṣfahān. To the right of the main gate lay the Royal Mint. The bazaar itself consisted of endlessly repeated groupings of *ḥammāms* (public baths), caravanserais, mosques and *madrasas* (theological seminaries). The caravanserais were the areas in which goods were received, weighed, assessed and stored; adjacent to them were the *tīmchas*, or shopping arcades, where goods were on display. In general each section of the bazaar was devoted to a single trade, and each section was virtually self-contained, having its own gates, its own security arrangements and fire guards, and its own trade guild which administered its own section of the bazaar and arbitrated in disputes. Some of the bazaar mosques were simple and functional; others were exquisitely decorated masterpieces. The *madrasas* usually followed the same *chahār-ayvān* (four-portal) plan as the mosques and caravanserais; the arcaded sides of the *madrasas* afforded shade, and pools of water in the central courtyard kept the air cool. The bazaar covered a total area of about $11\frac{1}{2}$ square miles.[21] Fryer, who visited Iṣfahān in 1677, was tremendously impressed by the whole scene in the Royal Bazaar, which he termed "the surprizingest piece of Greatness in Honour of Commerce the whole world can boast of, our *Burses* being but Snaps of Buildings to these famous *Buzzars*."[22] Linking the Great Maydān and the Chahār Bāgh avenue were extensive gardens at the west end of which stood the Chihil Sutūn palace, constructed by Shāh 'Abbās I and completed in 1648 by his great-grandson 'Abbās II. Like the 'Ālī Qāpū, the Chihil Sutūn has been disparaged by both contemporary and recent European writers and travellers. Stevens refers to the "ungainly bulk of the Ali Kapu" and to "the quaint absurdity of the Chehel Situn". "It seems almost incredible," he says, "that buildings on the one hand so perfectly proportioned [as the two great mosques] and on the other hand so primitive should have been built at the same time under the inspiration of the same monarch."[23]

Such criticisms, it seems to me, in the first place fail to take sufficient account of the appalling defacement and destruction of Safavid monuments perpetrated during the Qājār period, particularly during the governorship of the infamous Ẓill al-Sulṭān, the son of Nāṣir al-Dīn Shāh. For example, the twenty wooden columns supporting the verandah were originally covered with delicate faceted *ā'īna-kārī*, or mirror-work. Again, the beautiful Safavid murals in the great hall and other parts of the building were obliterated by a layer of plaster on which Qājār artists superimposed their own inferior paintings. Curzon, who did appreciate the extent of the damage done to the Chihil Sutūn during the Qājār period, was not able to suppress his indignation. Referring to the obliteration of the marble wainscoting and mirror-work panels above it by a wash of pink paint, he exclaims "Had I caught the pagan, I would gladly have suffocated him in a barrel of his own paint!"[24]

21. Iṣfahān – the Chihil Sutūn palace

Secondly, criticisms of these two buildings are frequently based on a misunderstanding of their function and also of the life-style of Shāh 'Abbās I. Both buildings, for want of a better word, are often referred to in English as "palaces", but this term automatically conjures up something much more splendid and grandiose. Neither building was the official residence of the king in the European sense. The varied functions of the 'Alī Qāpū have already been mentioned; the Chihil Sutūn was the building where the king gave formal audience to ambassadors, held levees and gave state banquets. Both buildings are, in fact, not so much palaces as kiosks or pavilions, and, in summer, they served as "open banqueting houses".[25] Compared to the massive palaces of the Mogul emperors in India, they are insignificant, but Shāh 'Abbās I did not want buildings the mere size and magnificence of which would overawe the people and cut him off from them. His personal style of dress was simple and his style informal; he eschewed excessive ceremony, but he appreciated the pleasures of life: good food, good wine, good company, and he appreciated them all the more in beautiful surroundings. The 'Ālī Qāpū and the Chihil Sutūn reflect these tastes. Building on the grand scale was restricted to the glory of God, as is exemplified by the Masjid-i Shāh, and his successors followed the pattern he had established.

22. Iṣfahān – the Madrasa-yi Mādar-i Shāh

The most imposing building erected in Iṣfahān by any of his successors is the Madrasa-yi Mādar-i Shāh (Theological Seminary of the Mother of the Shāh), built between the years 1706 and 1714 by Shāh Sulṭān Ḥusayn.

Moving west from the Chihil Sutūn, one reaches the northern end of the Chahār Bāgh. In Safavid times, both sides of the avenue as far as the river, a distance of almost a mile, were lined with gardens; on the east side lay the Nightingale Garden, the Mulberry Garden and Garden of the Dervishes; on the west, the Vineyard, the Throne Garden and the Octagonal Garden.

23. Iṣfahān – the Chahār Bāgh

The lattice work walls of the gardens which bordered on the Chahār Bāgh gave views of the animated scene in the avenue to those within the gardens, and glimpses of the gardens to those promenading in the avenue. As Wilber observes, such a feature was "surely a far cry from the traditional house of the country which presented a blank wall to the world and featured an enclosed court".[26]

In the gardens were situated residences for members of the court and the *ḥaram*, and pavilions which were sometimes placed at the disposal of foreign ambassadors and other dignitaries. Some of these pavilions were constructed during the time of Shāh 'Abbās, others such as the famous Hasht Bihisht (Eight Paradises), at a later date. Describing it, the usually sober Chardin indulges in flights of fancy:

When one walks in this place expressly made for the delights of love, and when one passes through all these cabinets and niches, one's heart is melted to such an extent that, to speak candidly, one always leaves with a very ill grace. The climate without doubt contributes much towards exciting this amorous disposition; but assuredly these places, although in some respects little more than cardboard castles, are nevertheless more smiling and agreeable than our most sumptuous palaces.[27]

During the nineteenth century the philistine Ẓill al-Sulṭān stabled his horses in the Hasht Bihisht and all but destroyed it, but it is now being restored along with many other Safavid buildings in Iṣfahān.

The Chahār Bāgh, like the Great Maydān, was a meeting-place and a centre of commercial and social life. Four parallel rows of plane trees extended the whole length of the Chahār Bāgh, both north and south of the river, a distance of 2½ miles.

Water, conducted in stone channels, ran down the centre, falling in miniature cascades from terrace to terrace, and was occasionally collected in great square or octagonal basins, where cross roads cut the avenue. On either side of the central channel was a row of *chenārs* [plane-trees] and a paved pathway for pedestrians. Then occurred a succession of open parterres, usually planted or sown. Next on either side was a second row of *chenārs*, between which and the flanking walls was a raised causeway for horsemen.[28]

Some of the pavilions flanking the avenue "were places of public resort and were used as coffee-houses, where, when the business of the day was over, the good burghers of Iṣfahān assembled to sip that beverage and to inhale their *kalians* [hookahs]".[29] The nobility would sally forth in the evening to take the air. As Fryer puts it: "Night drawing on, all the Pride of Spahaun was met in the Chaurbaug, and the Grandees were Airing themselves, prancing about with their numerous Trains, striving to outvie each other in Pomp and Generosity."[30]

As one neared the river bank, one could see the quays lining the banks, and further mansions belonging to the nobility, and then one crossed the Zāyanda-rūd by the magnificent bridge which bore the name of Allāhverdī Khān, the Georgian *ghulām* who was appointed commander-in-chief of the Safavid armed forces in 1598 and retained that post until his death in 1613. The paved roadway of the bridge is 9 metres wide, and the length of the bridge with its approaches is almost a quarter of a mile. On either side of the bridge there is a covered arcade, 76 centimetres wide; the inner wall of this arcade is pierced by frequent arches

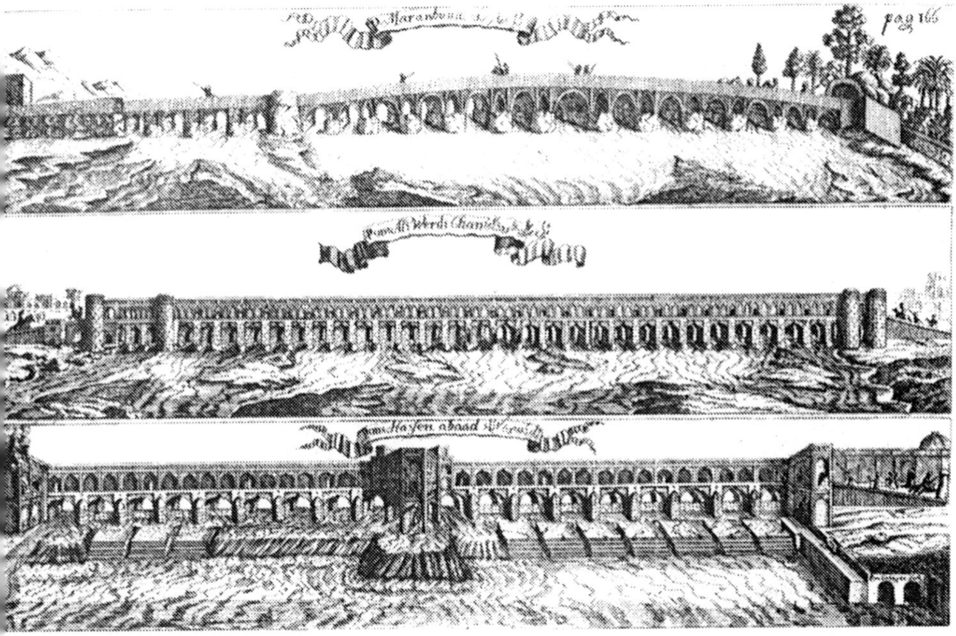

24. Iṣfahān – the Marnān, Allāhverdī Khān and Ḥasanābād (Khvājū) bridges

giving access to the roadway, while the outer wall has some ninety arches which give views of the river. The bridge has also an upper and a lower promenade; the upper is reached by staircases in the round towers at the corners of the bridge; the lower by other staircases in the basements of the towers and in the main piers. This lower promenade is a vaulted passage cut through the central piers of the bridge and raised only slightly above the bed of the river, which is crossed by stepping-stones set in the river-bed between the piers. This bridge, constructed about 1620, is popularly known as the Pul-i Sī-u-Sih, because the main arches are thirty-three in number. "One would hardly expect," says Curzon, "to have to travel to Persia to see what may, in all probability, be termed the stateliest bridge in the world."[31]

Other travellers, however, have preferred the Khvājū bridge, built half a mile downstream by Shāh 'Abbās II in 1660. The Khvājū bridge, 140 metres long, is built on a dam of stone blocks. Its construction follows the general pattern of the Allāhverdī Khān bridge, but "its peculiar charm depends upon the six semi-octagonal pavilions".[32] These pavilions were originally decorated with uplifting texts in prose and verse, and later with erotic

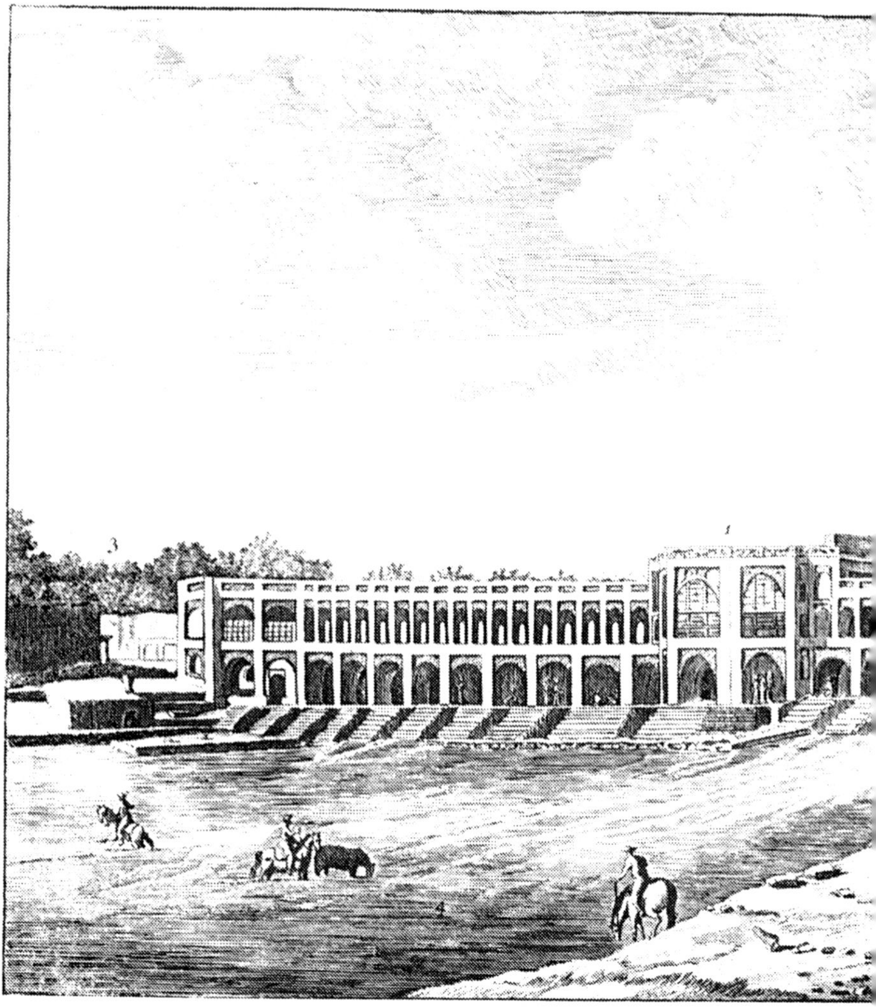

25. Iṣfahān – the Haṣanābād bridge

paintings which scandalised Sir William Ouseley when he visited Iṣfahān early in the nineteenth century. Whichever bridge appeals more to one's particular aesthetic taste, it is undeniable that both are masterpieces of the bridge-building skill of Safavid engineers. South of the Zāyanda-rūd the Chahār Bāgh avenue, as mentioned earlier, continued for another mile and a half to the royal gardens of Hazārjarīb.[33] Like the upper Chahār Bāgh, the lower avenue was "planted with rows of trees and adorned by channels filled with water, that fell from tier to tier and at regular intervals

expanded into larger basins or pools. On either side were situated the palaces and mansions of the princes or grandees."[34] The Hazārjarīb gardens at the end of the avenue were terraced, and provided the two essential ingredients of a Persian garden: shade and water. Tavernier, failing to understand the appeal of such simple gardens to the traveller bemused by the heat, glare and dust of the Persian plains, commented sourly on Hazārjarīb as he did on everything else in Iṣfahān: "Si un Persan avoit veu ceux de Versailles et d'autres maisons Royales, il ne seroit plus d'estime de ce jardin de Hezardgerib."[35] But Herbert, though he must have been equally familiar with European gardens, held a different opinion:

> The garden is called Nazar-jereeb [*sic*], 'tis a thousand paces from North to South, and seven hundred broad. It hath varieties of fruites and pleasant trees, and is watered with a streme cut through the Coronian Mountaine, and is forceably brought hither, the first walke is set with pipes of Lead and Brasse, through which the water is urged, and gives varietie of pleasure.
>
> From the entrance to the further end, is one continued open ally, divided into nine ascents, each mounting higher by a foot then [*sic*] other, the space twixt each ascent, is smooth and pleasant. In the midst is a faire Tancke or pond of water, of twelve equall angles and rowes set with pipes to spout the water.
>
> At the entrance is a little (but wel-built) house of pleasure, the lower rooms adorned with Chrystall water, immured with Tancks of rich white Marble.
>
> The Chambers above, are enricht with pictures, representing sports, hawking, fishing, archery, wrastling, etc., other places in use very richly ore-laid with Gold and Azure.
>
> But that which is of most commendation is the prospect it enjoyes, for by being seated so high, it ore-tops and gives the excellent view of a great part of the Citie, which cannot be obtained elsewhere.[36]

South of the river, too, were situated various suburbs inhabited mainly by non-Muslims. The most important of these was Julfā, which lay immediately west of the Chahār Bāgh along the southern bank of the Zāyanda-rūd. Here, in 1604, Shāh 'Abbās I settled several thousand Armenian families which he had forcibly transferred from Julfā on the river Aras in Āẕarbāyjān. His purpose was to enlist the industrious and thrifty nature and the commercial expertise of the Armenian merchants in the service of the Safavid state. To compensate them for being uprooted from their homes, Shāh 'Abbās granted the Armenians special privileges. They were allowed to practise their Christian religion without let or hindrance, and the Shāh even donated funds for the decoration of St Joseph's Cathedral, which was constructed in 1605. By granting the Armenians the right to be represented by a *kalāntar* (mayor) of their own nationality, the Shāh made them virtually a self-governing community. Having thus made provision for their spiritual and psychological well-being, Shāh 'Abbās ensured the success of his principal objective, that they should contribute significantly to the material prosperity of the realm, by making interest-free loans to the Armenian merchants. In such a favourable climate, it is not surprising that the Armenians flourished. Their merchants ranged the length and breadth of Europe, bringing back to Iran such commodities as items of haberdashery and hardware, small mirrors, enamelled rings, artificial pearls, cochineal, watches and cloth from Holland and England. Many merchants became extremely wealthy, and the office of *kalāntar* of the Armenians was clearly a lucrative one, for Tavernier mentions that the estate of one Khvāja Petrus, who held that office, included 40,000 *tumāns* in silver, not to mention houses and country properties, jewels, gold and silver plate and furniture.[37] The Armenians were not confined to Julfā, but lived also in other suburbs and in the city itself.

The principal other non-Muslim minorities in Safavid Iṣfahān were the Indians, Jews and Zoroastrians. The last named lived in a suburb south of the river known as Gabristān, or Place of the Gabrs,[38] situated downstream from Julfā. The great-grandson of 'Abbās the Great, 'Abbās II, cleared this quarter and constructed there a *ḥaram* complex which he named appropriately Sa'ādatābād, or Abode of Bliss. The Indians were not very numerous at Iṣfahān during the time of 'Abbās I, but their numbers increased subsequently. Known as "Banians", the Indians acted as brokers for foreign traders and as moneylenders, and they were notorious for charging exorbitant rates of interest. According to Tavernier, 'Abbās I did not allow Indian moneylenders to obtain a foothold in Iran, and they took up residence in Iran only under his successors Ṣafī and 'Abbās II. Herbert, however, who was in Iṣfahān in 1628, the year before the death of 'Abbās I, refers to "Bannyans, or Indyan Merchants" who, he says, "are tawny in complexion, are craftie, faire spoken, exquisite Merchants and superstitious".[39] Like the members of the other religious minorities resident at Iṣfahān, the Hindu Banians were granted freedom of worship, though officials often took advantage of Hindu sensibilities to extort sums of money in return for permitting practices, such as suttee,[40] which were repugnant to Muslims. Like the Indians, the Jews acted as brokers, dealing particularly in drugs and jewelry. They lived in their own separate quarter, but were not very numerous.

Considerable numbers of Europeans also resided in Iṣfahān:

factors of the rival English and Dutch East India Companies; religious of the various Catholic orders which were encouraged by Shāh 'Abbās to open convents in Iṣfahān and minister to the spiritual needs of Christian residents; craftsmen and artisans from both Europe and Asia, including Swiss watchmakers and Chinese potters.[41] The Augustinians, Carmelites and Capuchins resided in the city itself; the Jesuits and Dominicans in the suburb of Julfā.

Such was the Iṣfahān of Shāh the Great: a thriving and strikingly beautiful metropolis, its streets and markets thronged with Muslims, Christians, Zoroastrians and Hindus. It is no easy task to try and form an accurate picture of the size of Iṣfahān or estimate of its population. Chardin, on the whole the most judicious observer, states that the circumference of the city was 24 miles, whereas Kaempfer and Struys both estimate it at 16 *farsakhs*, or approximately 60 miles. Chardin says that the city had 12 gates, 162 mosques, 48 *madrasas*, or theological seminaries, 1,802 caravanserais, 273 public baths and 12 cemeteries, and declares that within 10 leagues (30 miles) of the city there were 1,500 villages; he estimates the population to be between 600,000 and 1,100,000. Chardin's figures are probably more reliable than those given by other European visitors, but, as Curzon justly observes,

> Nowhere have I been so bewildered at the confusing and contradictory accounts of previous travellers as in their descriptions of the sights of Isfahan. They differ irreconcilably in their orientation of buildings, in their figures of dimensions, in the number of avenues, pillars, bridges, arches etc. To correct or even to notice these countless inaccuracies would be a futile task.[42]

With the exception of the dyspeptic Tavernier, however, most European visitors found something to praise in Isfahan. Let Chardin sum it all up: "The beauty of Isfahan consists particularly of a great number of magnificent palaces, gay and smiling houses, spacious caravanserais, very fine bazaars and canals and streets lined with plane trees... from whatever direction one looks at the city it looks like a wood."[43]

8

The social and economic structure of the Safavid state

I: THE STRUCTURE OF SAFAVID SOCIETY

Safavid society was pyramidal in shape. At the apex of the pyramid was the shah, the just ruler surrounded by an aura of beneficence which sheltered his subjects. The term *dawlat*, meaning "bliss", "felicity", an abstract term just beginning in the seventeenth century to be used in the concrete sense of "the state", reflected this view of the ruler. Pursuing the same idea, the principal officers of the Safavid state were called *arkān-i dawlat*, or the pillars which supported this regal canopy, and the *vazīr*, the head of the bureaucracy, was given the title of *i'timād al-dawla*, the trusty support or prop of the state. The base of the pyamid was the common people, the peasants in the rual areas, and the artisans, shopkeepers and small merchants in the cities. Between the shah and the common people stood the aristocracy, both military and civil, and the multitude of religious officials of differing status and function. Some of the latter, administering large estates which had been bequeathed or donated for pious purposes, made common cause with the lay landowning aristocracy; others, mindful of the historic role of the religious classes as a buffer between the arbitrary power of the ruler and his subjects, did their best to shield the ordinary people from oppressive government on the part of both civil and military officials. The degree of oppression and arbitrariness experienced by the lower and middle classes was in inverse ratio to the strength of the shah. As Sir John Malcolm saw clearly, "No small proportion of that security which the rest of the community enjoy, may be referred to the danger in which those near to the king continually stand; for, unless he be very weak or very unjust, it is hazardous for any of his ministers, or courtiers, to commit violence or injustice in his name."[1]

26. Dress of the natives of Iṣfahān

The subject's traditional right of the "appeal to Caesar" was an important safeguard for the people against bureaucratic oppression. This right, according to Malcolm, still obtained in the nineteenth century: "The principal check upon the conduct of subordinate governors is an appeal to the throne, which those whom they oppress can always make, as no person can prevent an individual in Persia from seeking that relief; and when he reaches court, he is certain of attention";[2] and Malcolm tells the story of a British sergeant, in the employ of the Persian government, whose pay was withheld by a certain official. Failing to obtain satisfaction from the official concerned, the sergeant appealed direct to the Shāh. The Shāh's ministers, comments Malcolm, considered this to be a perfectly normal and proper procedure. This system resulted in an intensely personal style of government, with all the obvious merits and faults which such a style entailed; but who is to say that the lot of the average man was significantly unhappier than that of the citizen of today who tries to obtain satisfaction from a faceless bureaucracy or a computer?

In ancient Iran, the Shah had never been a remote figure like a pharaoh or an emperor of Japan. On the contrary, as I once heard Peter Brown shrewdly observe, the Sasanian shahs took care to keep their faces before the public by having their features engraved inside the base of drinking-cups. Their name and appearance were thus known to the common man, and formed part of his everyday life. In more recent times, European observers were frequently struck by the accessibility of the shahs to their people, by the informal way in which they mixed with courtiers and officials and by the seriousness with which they applied themselves to the business of government. Thévenot noted that "They show great familiarity to strangers, and even to their own subjects, eating and drinking with them pretty freely."[3] Malcolm was able to assert from personal observation that

> There is no country in which the monarch has more personal duties than in Persia... When in camp, his habits of occupation are the same as in the capital: and we may pronounce, that he is from six to seven hours every day in public, during which time he is not only seen by, but accessible to, a great number of persons of all ranks. It is impossible that a monarch, whom custom requires to mix so much with his subjects, can be ignorant of their condition: and this knowledge must, unless his character be very perverse, tend to promote their happiness.[4]

Certainly Shāh ʻAbbās I was not ignorant of the condition of his subjects, for he used to frequent incognito the coffee-houses, the tea-houses and even the brothels of Iṣfahān, and mingle with the dense crowds in the Maydān in a manner which would cause acute anxiety to modern security police. He would take the opportunity of checking the honesty of officials and tradesmen. Tavernier reports that one night the Shāh left his palace disguised as a peasant and bought a *man* (900 drachmas) of bread and the same weight of meat, no doubt from the booths set up in the Maydān. Taking his purchases back to the palace, ʻAbbās had them weighed by the *vazīr* in the presence of the principal officers of state. The bread weighed 843 drachmas and the meat 857. The Shāh was with difficulty restrained from executing on the spot the chief of police and the Governor of Iṣfahān, but contented himself with having the baker baked in his oven and the butcher roasted on a spit.[5]

It has often been observed that one major difference between Islamic society and Western society is the absence in the former of those powerful municipal institutions, enjoying a large measure

27A. Court dress, male

27B. Court dress, female

of self-government, which evolved in the West. Within Islamic society, however, there existed a considerable number of local democratic institutions which together constituted the "social cement" of that society. Examples of such institutions are the trade and artisan guilds, and socio-religious organisations such as the *futuvva* groups. The members of the *futuvva* groups were often dervishes and poor people, and their associations had a moral and religious basis. They subjected themselves to the spiritual guidance of a Ṣūfī shaykh, and followed rules of ethical conduct which were laid down in manuals called *futuvvat-nāmas*. Merchants and artisans had a formal channel of communication with government. In Malcolm's words:

In every city or town of any consequence, the merchants, tradesmen, mechanics and labourers, have each a head, or rather a representative, who...is chosen by the community to which he belongs, and is appointed by the king. He is seldom removed from his situation, except on the complaint of those whose representative he is deemed; and even they must bring forward and substantiate charges of neglect or criminal conduct, before he is degraded from the elevation to which their respect had raised him.[6]

Another official selected by the consensus of the community was the *kadkhudā*. In the cities, the *kadkhudā* functioned as an official of the *'urf*, or common law administration, and specifically as a ward magistrate subordinate to the *kalāntar*, or mayor. In rural areas, the *kadkhudā*'s position was usually that of the head-man of a village. Malcolm underlines the democratic function of the *kadkhudā*, who is not formally elected, but

the voice of the people always points them out...If the king should appoint a magistrate disagreeable to the citizens, he [i.e., the magistrate] could not perform his duties, which require that all the weight he derives from personal consideration should aid the authority of office. In small towns or villages the voice of the inhabitants in the nomination of their *kut-khodah*, or head, is still more decided; and if one is named whom they do not approve, their incessant clamour produces either his voluntary resignation or removal. These facts are important; for there cannot be a privilege more essential to the welfare of a people, than that of choosing or even influencing the choice of their magistrates.[7]

Tavernier states specifically that the king appointed a *kalāntar* in every town, that the *kalāntar* was answerable only to the king, and that his function was to protect the people against injustices and harassment on the part of the governors.[8]

Safavid society was what we would call today a "meritocracy"; it was certainly not an aristocratic system of government, although there were, of course, powerful aristocratic elements in it; still less could it be considered an oligarchy. Olearius draws attention to this aspect of the Safavid society. Officials, he says, were appointed on the basis of worth and merit, not on the basis of birth. For this reason, he says, they risked their lives gaily, for they knew that this was the only way to gain advancement to the highest offices. These offices, he says, were not hereditary or venal in Iran. It was true that the sons of nobles, when their fathers died, were considered for their fathers' offices as a mark of respect for the meritorious service of the latter to the Safavid state, but they were appointed to succeed them in office only on the basis of their own merit and service.[9] The operation of this general principle clearly militated against the establishment of an entrenched aristocracy. So, too, did the high degree of risk which went with the holding of high office. The possibility of rising from obscurity to the highest office was fact and not fiction. Manwaring records the case of a man who sold milk at Iṣfahān who attracted Shāh 'Abbās's attention and eventually became the captain of his guard in command of a thousand men.[10] The *nāẓir* Muḥammad 'Alī Beg, described by Tavernier as "the most honest man Persia has had for centuries", was spotted by Shāh 'Abbās I when the latter was out hunting; the young Muḥammad 'Alī, then a shepherd boy, was sitting playing his flute when the Shāh passed by. When the Shāh put some questions to him, the boy's answers so impressed the Shāh that he took him to court for education and training. Subsequently, he rose to the high office of *nāẓir* (superintendent of the royal workshops), and was entrusted by the Shāh with the conduct of diplomatic relations with the Mogul court.[11] Tavernier also reports that Muḥammad 'Alī Beg's successor, a certain Muḥammad Beg, was also of humble origin, having risen rapidly from being a tailor at Tabrīz to the office of *mu'ayyir-bāshī* (controller of assay).[12] Eventually, Muḥammad Beg rose to the highest bureaucratic post, that of *vazīr*, but one doubts whether he had the necessary qualifications for the job, because he was hoodwinked by a rascally Frenchman named Chapelle de Han, who claimed expertise in the mining of silver, gold, copper and other minerals. All that Chapelle de Han discovered, however, was a deposit of lead near Iṣfahān, and some talc and alum. The wood for smelting the lead had to be brought a distance of fifteen to twenty days' journey by camel, and the cost of transporting it alone absorbed any profit from the sale of the lead.[13]

It should not be forgotten that the policy of the Safavid shahs of creating a "third force" in the state which was neither of Turkish nor of Iranian ethnic origin (see Chapter 4), strongly reinforced this tendency of the Safavid society to be a meritocracy. It is true that some of the Georgians who voluntarily entered Safavid service were members of the Georgian nobility, but the vast majority of the Armenians, Georgians and Circassians who were taken prisoner during Safavid campaigns in the Caucasus from the time of Shāh Ṭahmāsp onwards and impressed into Safavid service, must have been of humble origin. The fact that they were known technically as *ghulāmān-i khāṣṣa-yi sharīfa*, or the personal "slaves" of the shah, should not blind one to the fact that many men rose from the ranks of the *ghulāms* to positions of the highest authority.

Even the *qizilbāsh*, the original military aristocracy of the Safavid state, found their dominant position in society steadily eroded as time went on, and particularly as a result of the reshaping of society by 'Abbās I described in Chapter 4. Within the ranks of the *qizilbāsh*, there were frequent shifts of power. No one tribe held the same fief for any considerable period of time, and this prevented the growth of a landed aristocracy in the Western sense. There was no continuity of power in the hands of one tribe or group of tribes; those tribes which were prominent during the later Safavid period are hardly mentioned earlier. For example, the Afshārs came to the fore from the middle of the sixteenth century onwards, and the Qājārs later still; no member of either tribe held any important office during the first half century of Safavid rule. There is no parallel, therefore, with the position of the French aristocracy in the eighteenth century, or with that of the Russian aristocracy in the nineteenth century, when each could point to several centuries of uninterrupted enjoyment of their estates.

If the Safavid administrative system was divided "vertically" into *khāṣṣa* ("crown") and *'āmma* or *mamālik* ("state") branches, Safavid society, until Georgian, Armenian and Circassian elements were introduced into it in the second half of the sixteenth century, was divided "horizontally" along ethnic lines between the two "founding" races, the *qizilbāsh* Turks and the Persians. The tension between these two important elements of Safavid society, if controlled, could be creative and a source of strength to the state; if not controlled, it could set up a centrifugal force which threatened to tear society apart. Reference was made in Chapter 2 to the stereotyped view which each of these "founding races" had of the other's role in society. From the time of Shāh Ṭahmāsp onwards, the Safavid rulers sought to blur the formerly clearly defined lines between Turk and Tājīk ("non-Turk") by a policy of taking the sons of *qizilbāsh* officers into the royal household for their education. This education consisted not only of activities appropriate to "men of the sword", such as archery, horsemanship and swordsmanship, but of instruction in painting and penmanship, which the old-style *qizilbāsh* would have regarded with contempt. As a result of this policy, by the time of Shāh 'Abbās I there was in existence a cadre of young *qizilbāsh* officers who were better educated and more cultured than the *qizilbāsh* who had stayed close to their tribal origins, and consequently had the training and ability to take on administrative jobs in areas which had hitherto been the exclusive preserve of Iranians.

An important feature of Safavid society was the close alliance which developed between the *'ulamā*, or religious classes, and the other groups which made up the bazaar community; merchants, members of the *aṣnāf*, or artisan and trade guilds, and members of quasi-religious fraternities like the *futuvva*. To an increasing extent, this alliance was cemented by inter-marriage between *'ulamā* and merchant families. The fact that under the Safavids the *'ulamā* acquired the management of a vastly increased amount of *vaqf* land and property contributed to their community of interest with the merchant class. At the same time, some of the *'ulamā* entered the ranks of the landowning class. Apart from lands assigned to officials in lieu of a salary (*tiyūl*), *vaqf* lands constituted the principal category of land. In 1607, Shāh 'Abbās I constituted all his private estates and personal property into a *vaqf* for the Fourteen Immaculate Ones (the Twelve Imāms, Muḥammad and Fāṭima), and vested the *tawliyat*, the office of *mutavallī*, or administrator of these *awqāf*, in himself, and thereafter in his successors.[14] This benefaction, in the words of the contemporary historian Iskandar Beg Munshī, was on a scale unheard of unless the royal benefactor intended to live the life of a recluse.[15] In addition to the Shāh's personal estates, valued at 100,000 royal

'Irāqī *tumāns*, there were included in the *vaqf* the hostelries, the Qayṣariyya market, the stores around the Naqsh-i Jahān square in Iṣfahān and the bath-houses in that city. The disposition of the trust funds was at the discretion of the manager. After a sum had been set aside as a management-fee, the trust income was to be used as the occasion demanded for administrative expenses and subsistence allowances for the employees at each location, and for subsistence allowances for those living in the neighbourhood of these locations, for pilgrims, scholars, pious men and students of theology. Banani suggests that

> this single action not only increased directly the area of *vaqf* lands by a sizeable amount, but it also served as the cue for many private landowners to follow suit. By vesting the *towliya* in themselves and their families, they continued to have the use of the *vaqf* revenues, after making token contributions to charities. Thus, they gained a measure of immunity from confiscation, as well as from dues and taxes...Increasingly, members of the religious classes – particularly the *mujtahids* and *sayyids* – were appointed *mutawallīs*...They began as *mutawallīs* of *awqāf* endowed by others, continued to amass extensive private estates of their own, and emerged as the esquires of their region with paramount local socio-economic and political powers.[16]

In addition, members of the religious classes were granted benefices or immunities from taxation of the type known as *suyūrghāls*. Since *suyūrghāls* had a perpetual or hereditary character, "the area held by the grantee formed a kind of autonomous enclave within the state territory".[17]

II: THE NATURE OF THE SAFAVID ECONOMY

I. THE DOMESTIC ECONOMY

The twin bases of the domestic economy were pastoralism and agriculture. At the beginning of this chapter, Safavid society was described as being pyramidal in shape. At the base of the pyramid were the peasants. Just as at the higher levels of government and administration there was a dichotomy between the *qizilbāsh* "men of the sword" and the Tājīk (i.e., Iranian) "men of the pen", so at the lower levels of society that was a dichotomy between the Turcoman tribes and the Persian peasants. The life-styles of these two principal elements of the early Safavid state were totally different. The Turcoman tribes "were cattle-breeders and lived apart from the surrounding population. They migrated from winter to summer quarters. They were organised in clans and obeyed their own chieftains."[18] The Iranian peasants, on the other hand, were settled agriculturalists living in villages. In the period prior to Shāh 'Abbās I, most of the land was assigned to officials, civil, military and religious, for the payment of salaries. From the time of Shāh 'Abbās I onwards, more land was brought under the direct control of the shah and administered directly by royal intendants. This change did not, however, affect the basis of land tenure, namely, the crop-sharing agreement between landlord and peasant based on the *'avāmil-i panjgāna* (five elements): land, water, plough-animals, seed and labour. If the peasant provided nothing but his labour, he would in theory receive only 20 per cent of the crop. But conditions varied in different parts of the country and with different types of crop.

In Chardin's opinion the landlord always had the worst of the bargain with the peasant in a crop-sharing agreement, and he describes the many ruses he alleged they used to obtain a larger share than was their due. He states that the peasants lived in tolerable comfort, and compares their condition favourably with that of peasants in the more fertile parts of Europe. He states that they everywhere wore silver ornaments and sometimes gold, and were well clothed and had good footwear. Their houses were well provided with utensils and furniture (? presumably carpets). On the other hand, they were exposed to rough treatment on the part of officials. Further, they were subject to heavy demands in the way of forced labour, particularly in crown lands held by great nobles.[19]

Agriculture in Iran was and is subject to the overriding constraints of climate and water-supply. Over most of the country, many crops can be grown only by means of irrigation, and in those parts where some crops, mainly cereals, can be grown relying on rainfall alone the yield is perhaps only one quarter of the yield from irrigated land. Fruits of all kinds, including grapes, were produced in abundance and were of excellent quality. The Islamic ban on wine drinking was "occasionally and capriciously enforced".[20] Wine was made principally by Jews and Armenians, and was consumed in large quantities at court and even on occasion by members of the religious classes. Tavernier records a meeting with "a rich mulla outside Kirmān who invited me to his house and gave me some excellent wine".[21] Wine was regularly drunk at state banquets, and some of the shahs had a legendary capacity for it; 'Abbās II, for example, after a whole day's debauch, was found to be as sober, and in as good a frame of mind, as if he had not drunk one drop.[22] It is clear that, in this instance as in many others, the pre-Islamic Persian tradition proved to be stronger than the later Islamic accretion.

When one turns to examine the internal money economy, it becomes clear that the Shāh was the largest capitalist and the largest employer of labour. Amin Banani has criticised 'Abbās's policies of "state capitalism" on the ground that, although the Shāh accumulated capital, "his policies inhibited the accumulation and the investment of capital on the part of others", and "his own 'capitalism' was devoid of any entrepreneurial spirit".[23] I believe Banani's strictures to be at least in part unjustified. He is certainly incorrect in stating that 'Abbās's policies inhibited others from accumulating capital; there is plenty of evidence that individual merchants, particularly Armenians, became very wealthy indeed. In support of his charge that Shāh 'Abbās's policies were devoid of any entrepreneurial spirit, Banani cites the case of the royal workshops (*buyūtāt-i khāṣṣa-yi sharīfa*), of which there were thirty-two at the time of Chardin and thirty-three at the time of the compilation of the *Tazkirat al-Mulūk* about 1726.[24]

It is true that many of the royal workshops, such as the kitchen, scullery, stables, kennels, etc., were simply what Minorsky called "domestic departments"; some, however, were "run like real state-owned manufactories",[5] and in general these workshops gave employment to some 5,000 artisans and craftsmen and contributed to the overall prosperity of the economy.

> Some workshops, as the dye-works and the silk factory, had been abolished, and replaced by a system under which linen to be dyed was sent into the town, and silk and gold thread were issued for the making of all kinds of textiles, brocades and carpets, the *buyūtāt* administration paying for the work at a fixed tariff. Carpets were also made in the country by workmen to whom the king gave lands and who paid their rent in the produce of their hands.[26]

The workmen in the royal workshops constituted a privileged class of artisans. In addition to their wages, the amount of which was stated in the artisan's letter of appointment and which was raised every three years, each workman received *jīra*, or rations, in the form of a quarter-plate, a half-plate or a plate. A "plate" consisted of "everything necessary for subsistence and could feed 6–7 persons".[27] If he wished, the workman could take cash in lieu of the *jīra*. Its cash value was about 20 *tumāns*. When this is compared with the wage scale, which ranged from 2 *tumāns* to 55 *tumāns* a year, it is clear that the *jīra* constituted a very substantial fringe benefit. In addition, workmen who did particularly good work were given presents, and in some cases, workmen received a gift amounting to a whole year's salary in lieu of the triennial wage increase. Workmen employed in the royal workshops had total job security: they were "kept for life and never dismissed; in case of illness or diminished capacity for work their salary was not reduced, and they received free treatment from the Court doctors and chemists". Not only did they receive their pay whether they had received any commissions from the king or not, but there was no restriction on the amount of work they performed on the side for their private profit.

The workmen who had to follow the Court on its travels were given camels and horses, but they easily obtained permission to stay at home, or, alternately, were granted leave after 6–12 months' absence. The children of the workmen were taken into service at the age of 12–15 years, and after their father's death received their salaries.[28]

The *aṣnāf*, or artisan guilds, were subject to *corvées* and also to a tax called *bunīcha*, and the task of apportioning the lump sum of the *bunīcha* among the members of the guild was one of the tasks of the *kalāntar*.

Shāh 'Abbās I took as keen an interest in the internal workings of the bazaar as he did in foreign trade. Manwaring records that in the bazaar at Qazvīn, which was three times as big as the Exchange in London, "though not so beautiful", there were shops of all manner of trades, and the king had a special throne there:

In the middle of that place standeth a round thing made with a seat, set up with six pillars...on which place they used to sell apparel and other commodities; that being bravely trimmed with rich carpets, both of gold and silver and silk, and the King's chair of estate placed in the middle, the chair being of silver plate set with turkies [turquoises] and rubies very thick, and six great diamonds, which did show like stars, the seat being of rich scarlet embroidered with pearl, and the multitude of lamps hanging about it were innumerable.[29]

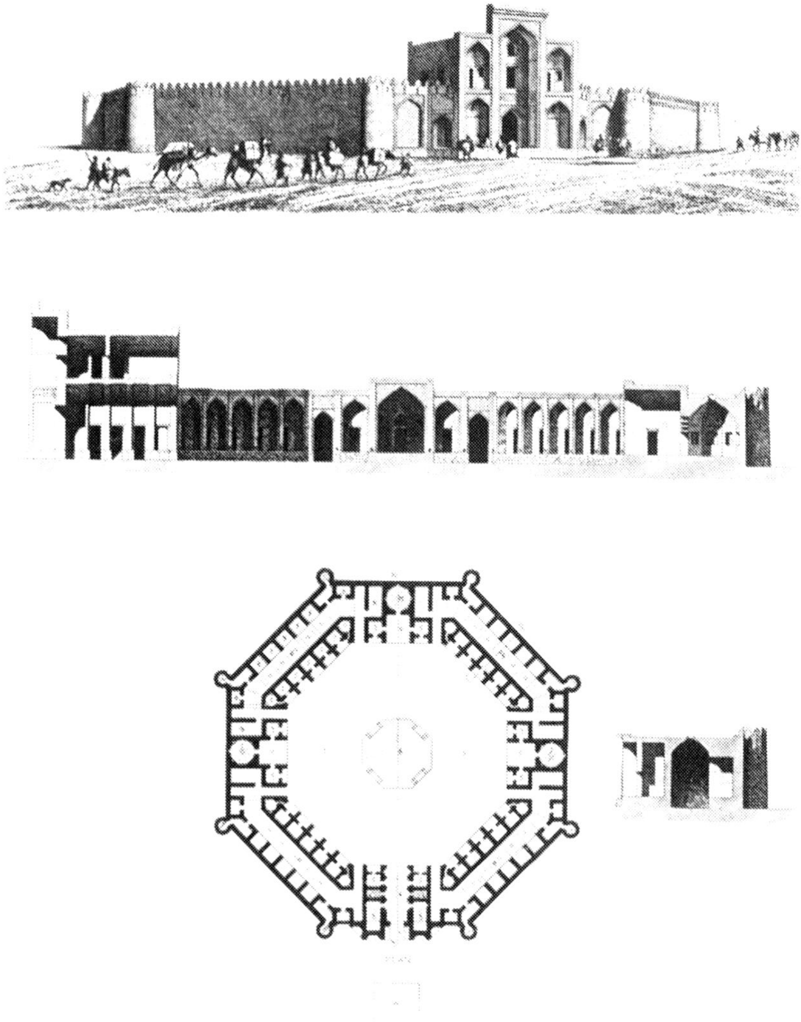

28. Octagonal caravanserai at Amīnābād

Although roads throughout Iran were poor (if one excepts Shāh 'Abbās's famous causeway in Māzandarān), and communications were slow, the network of caravanserais which covered the country along the main trade routes at least provided the merchant with protection for his goods and pack-animals, and also with facilities for displaying his wares and engaging in a little business at overnight stops. Both Thévenot and Tavernier comment that the Persian caravanserais were better built and cleaner than their Turkish counterparts. Caravanserais were designed especially to benefit poorer travellers; travellers could stay as long as they liked, without making any payment for lodging. 'Abbās I was an indefatigable builder of caravanserais, which were another essential part of his policy of promoting the commercial prosperity of the Safavid empire, and his example was followed by his relatives, by wealthy merchants and by provincial governors.[30] Caravanserais had to be provided at frequent intervals on the main highways, for caravans were slow. A horse caravan took twice as long to cover a given distance as a man on horseback, and camel caravans four times as long.[31] The caravanserais varied greatly in size. "On some of the major routes the caravanserais were huge and splendid constructions"; a caravanserai on the Bandar Rīg route, on the other hand, had only three rooms.[32]

Another source of revenue to the state was the road tolls levied on caravans. These were collected by the *rāhdārs*, or road guards, who stationed themselves at points such as river-crossings so that not even the wily merchant could avoid them. In return for the tolls, the road guards were responsible for the safety of the travellers and their belongings, and they were answerable to the local governor. The system seems to have worked effectively. Many European travellers commented favourably on the degree of security on the highways obtaining in Iran compared with that in the Ottoman empire. Tavernier, for example, stresses the fact that, beyond Erīvān, it was "perfectly safe to leave the caravan or not to travel in a caravan at all". Thévenot's caravan ceased to set a nightly guard once they were in Persia. Others contrasted the behaviour of the road guards with similar officials under other jurisdictions: Olearius was impressed with the contrast between Russian coarseness and boorishness and Persian courtesy and refinement, and Fryer by the contrast in appearance and behaviour of the Indians and Persians.[33] The road guards "were instructed to stop anyone travelling alone, by an unusual route, or who was completely unknown to them in case he might be wanted for robbery".[34] Other travellers record the speedy recovery of items stolen from their baggage in caravanserais. The usual punishment for apprehended thieves was death. Under the weak rule of the last two Safavid kings, Shāh Sulaymān and Shāh Sulṭān Ḥusayn, the system became less efficient and the road guards prone to commit abuses.[35] In times of political disturbances or war, naturally the degree of security afforded on the roads decreased,

29. Kāshān – the great inn

and on occasion provincial officials were not averse from turning a dishonest penny in a variety of ways, such as refusing to supply a caravan with fresh camels without a douceur.[36] In general, however, it is clear that the system provided merchants with a large measure of security both for their persons and for their property.

II. INTERNATIONAL TRADE

The Safavid state, though not as wealthy as the Mogul state in India (a circumstance which caused many Safavid poets to emigrate to the Mogul court: see Chapter 9), was more prosperous than any administrative entity had been which had governed Iran since Mongol times, and was probably richer than any of its successors until very recent times. It achieved this unparalleled prosperity in the main by making astute use of a major shift in

the balance of world trade which occurred at the end of the fifteenth century.

For some two and a half centuries prior to the beginning of the sixteenth century, Venice had been the supreme trading power in the Levant, but two events in the fifteenth century dealt a death blow to this supremacy. The first of these was the capture of Constantinople by the Turks in 1453; the second was the discovery by the Portuguese of the sea-route to the Indies round the Cape of Good Hope in 1487. The Venetians had done all in their power to try and hamper Portuguese trade with India via the Cape, but they had failed. The establishment of the Portuguese hegemony in the Persian Gulf and the Indian Ocean totally changed the traditional patterns of trade in the area. For centuries before the coming of the Portuguese, the Persian Gulf had been one of the great highways of East–West trade. Westward flowed the products of China, the Malay Archipelago and India; eastward, the merchandise of Iran, the Arab countries and Europe. Mercantile city-states, all without exception located in the Persian Gulf, had arisen and fallen, but no one state had ever succeeded in imposing its hegemony over the whole area.

The Portuguese, however, came not merely as traders, but as conquerors. Their aim was to establish a Portuguese *imperium* extending over the whole of Asia. The brilliant Portuguese Captain General Afonso de Albuquerque correctly identified the three key points, control of which would give their possessor mastery in Asia: Aden, Hurmūz and the Straits of Malacca. Until the advent of the nuclear age, nothing occurred to invalidate Albuquerque's analysis, and even today it is still valid in terms of warfare with conventional weapons. The grand design of the Portuguese was to force all trade between Europe and the Indies to go round the Cape of Good Hope, by blocking its traditional outlets: the Red Sea, the Persian Gulf and the Straits of Malacca. All cargoes would have to be carried in Portuguese bottoms. By seizing and fortifying ports on the coasts of Arabia, the Persian Gulf and the Indian Ocean, the Portuguese were in a position to harass the shipping of European rivals and to levy lucrative customs and port dues on foreign ships.

The Portuguese *imperium* not only sounded the death-knell of Venice as a trading nation, but it also seriously affected the commercial prosperity of the Muslim states along the shores of the Persian Gulf. The merchants of these states had handled the forwarding to destinations further east of shipments originating in Europe, and the purchase at emporia such as Ceylon, Calicut on the Malabar coast and Kalah Bar on the west coast of Malaya, of commodities destined for eventual sale in Europe. The Safavid state was one of the states affected by this Portuguese control of the coastal trade.

Hurmūz was not *prima facie* an attractive site for a base. Master Ralph Fitch, an English merchant who visited the island in 1583, declared: "It is the dryest island in the world, for there is nothing growing in it but only salt."[37] Nevertheless, Hurmūz was the key to Portuguese commercial dominance of the region, and for more than a century the Safavid shahs could do nothing to wrest it from them. The Portuguese rapidly converted Hurmūz from a protectorate to the status of a Portuguese colony. Portuguese officials were placed in charge of the Hurmūz customs in 1522, and all Portuguese ships calling at Hurmūz were exempt from customs duty. The maritime trade to Gujerat, and the caravan trade between Hurmūz and the cities of the Iranian hinterland, which were the bases of the prosperity of Hurmūz, were seriously affected by the actions of the Portuguese. When in addition the Portuguese levied taxes on the people of Hurmūz on an ever heavier scale, the fortunes of Hurmūz, not surprisingly, declined. Hurmūz fell behind in the payment of tribute to the Portuguese, and in 1542 the Portuguese Viceroy was obliged to waive the arrears due. It was not until 1581 that the arrival of the English merchant John Newberie at Hurmūz heralded the increased interest of the English in the trade possibilities in the area and the subsequent founding of the English East India Company in 1600. In 1602, Shāh ʻAbbās I drove the Portuguese out of Bahrein, but he realised that he could not hope to expel them from their far stronger base at Hurmūz without naval assistance. With his usual astuteness, Shāh ʻAbbās manoeuvred the English into helping him to achieve this objective.

In 1615, Shāh ʻAbbās I granted to two factors of the English East India Company a *farmān* which conferred on the Company's agents various trading privileges and authorised them to establish factories in Iran. After the Company had opened factories at Jāsk, Shīrāz and Iṣfahān, Shāh ʻAbbās was in a position to exert pressure on the Company, and enlist its co-operation in a joint Anglo-Iranian attack on Hurmūz (see Chapter 5).

The fall of Hurmūz portended the end of the Portuguese *imperium* in the Persian Gulf; their successors, the English, Dutch and French, came as merchant adventurers and not as colonisers. The terms of trade were not imposed on the Safavid shahs by the agents of these European powers, but were negotiated freely with them, and the Safavid state consequently shared the profits deriving from this trade. The English East India Company tried to bring pressure to bear on Shāh ʻAbbās I with a view to extracting from him terms of trade more favourable to themselves, but the capture of Baghdād by the Safavids in 1623 deprived the Company's factors of any leverage they might have exerted as a result of the Shāh's anxieties in regard to the Ottomans. After the fall of Hurmūz, it would have been to the English East India Company's advantage, since it was then in a dominant position in the Persian Gulf, to try and divert Safavid international trade away from the traditional routes and transfer it to the sea-route from the Persian Gulf, thus increasing the Shāh's dependence on the Company. However, the Company was in this strong bargaining position for only about a year. The first Dutch trading expedition arrived in the Persian Gulf in June 1623, and established a factory, and the English had thus lost their opportunity to achieve the sort of hegemony which the Portuguese had enjoyed before them.

The Portuguese stranglehold on trade from the Persian Gulf was broken by their loss of Hurmūz. In the long term, however, this trade was of less importance to the overall prosperity of the Safavid state than was the trade by the traditional routes to Europe, and Shāh 'Abbās I was determined to expand this trade to the maximum degree possible. One consideration which led him to make this policy decision was undoubtedly his desire to avoid undue dependence on any of the European East India Companies. But there were serious problems connected with the use of the traditional routes. The Venetian trade hegemony in the Levant had been terminated, but one of the forces which had helped to overthrow it, the Ottoman empire, now stood astride the most important of these traditional trade routes: the route across Iraq and Syria to the Mediterranean ports, and the route across Anatolia to Istanbul. The Ottoman empire was an arch-enemy of the Safavid state, and the two empires were at war, at first almost continuously, later intermittently, throughout the sixteenth century and well on into the seventeenth century.

A route was therefore devised which circumvented Ottoman territory: by sea from Gīlān across the Caspian Sea to Astrakhan, up the Volga and thence by land across the Ukraine. A fourth route, by sea round the north of Scandinavia to the White Sea ports, and thence overland across Russia, which had been pioneered by the merchants of the Muscovy Company, had been abandoned by the latter in 1581 as being too hazardous. The Gīlān–Astrakhan–southern Russia route assumed paramount importance when, as was often the case, the Ottomans and the Safavids were at war. The international trade which followed this route was on a large scale and of a very varied character. Brocades, taffeta, shagreen, moroccan leather, velours and, above all, silk, were exported via Gīlān to Muscovy and thence to Poland and

Europe generally. In the sixteenth and seventeenth centuries, Iran was pre-eminent in the silk trade, which Shāh 'Abbās I made a royal monopoly, and an extremely effective one. In 1619/20, when the English factors "declared a buyers' strike in order to force down the Shāh's price", they "found it impossible to procure silk for export on the free market".[38]

> The organisation of the silk trade in the 1620s must be regarded as one of 'Abbās's great organizational achievements. He did not succeed in putting into effect the intended ban on export through Turkey, and the export merchants still made direct purchases in the production areas. When purchases other than from the Royal treasury were made, however, 12 tomans per load had to be paid in duty on the silk bought for export and 4 tomans per load on the silk bought for processing in Persia.[39]

Iranian ambassadors to European rulers were regularly expected as part of their duties to sell some bales of silk while they were abroad and to remit the proceeds to their royal master. In the 1660s, according to Chardin, the annual production of silk in Iran was 1,672,000 pounds, a considerable proportion of which was exported.

One of the privileges granted by Shāh 'Abbās I to the employees of the English East India Company was freedom of worship, and this privilege lay at the root of Shāh 'Abbās's policy of expanding overseas trade. Without it, no such expansion would have been possible. Whereas internal trade was largely in the hands of Persian and Jewish merchants, foreign trade was almost exclusively in the hands of Armenians.[40] The commercial and financial expertise of the Armenians, and their European contacts, were essential to Shāh 'Abbās's purpose. At the same time, he wanted European merchants to think that the climate in Iran was favourable to the prosecution of trade; he therefore encouraged various Catholic orders to found convents in Iran. This policy was completely successful. "The Persians give full liberty of conscience to all Strangers of whatsoever Religion they be"; so wrote Thévenot, who was in Iran in 1664.[41] This had by no means been true of the predecessors of 'Abbās I, and it was not entirely true of his successors, including Shāh 'Abbās II during whose reign Thévenot visited Iran. 'Abbās II, for instance, condoned the attempt by the vizier forcibly to convert the Jews of Iṣfahān to Islam. Nevertheless, the degree of religious tolerance induced by the policies of 'Abbās I, and maintained in large measure by his successors until the accession of Shāh Sulṭān Ḥusayn (1694), was in striking contrast to the religious climate prevailing in most of Europe at the same period.

The Armenians in particular made full use of their opportunities. The largest single source of cash for the royal treasury was the silk trade, and the silk trade was handled by Armenian merchants.[42] The Armenians in their suburb of New Julfā on the south bank of the Zāyanda-rūd at Iṣfahān "constituted a separate group, a commercial élite with their own distinctive cultural traditions and religion, residing in their own community physically and nationally apart from the Persians. It was a subtle, brittle relationship of mutual interest, trust, dependence, and toleration."[43] Armenian merchants not only carried on the Shāh's trade but competed with European merchants, including the various East India Companies. Among these, the Dutch showed more adaptability than the English and displayed a greater willingness to meet the conditions set by Shāh 'Abbās I. In April 1626, only three years after the establishment of the first Dutch factory in Iran, the Dutch concluded a three-year contract with Shāh 'Abbās which regulated both prices and quantities of goods. The Dutch were to import into Iran goods to the value of 40,000 *tumāns* or 1,600,000 Dutch florins. Of the commodities imported, pepper constituted some 40 per cent of the total, and most of the remainder originated in the East Indies; only slightly over 8 per cent was of European origin. These goods were to be paid for in silk. The English factors assured the Company Court that the terms obtained by the Dutch were not as good as the ones they themselves had obtained in 1624, but the fact that, as soon as the conditions of the Dutch contract leaked out, the English immediately sent agents to the Shāh to try and obtain similar ones, shows clearly that the English had been outmanoeuvred; in any case, their attempt was unsuccessful.[44] In the event, the contract with the Dutch proved unsatisfactory from the Iranian point of view; not only was the market saturated with pepper, the price of which in the Iranian bazaars consequently dropped, but the Dutch did not fulfil the clause in the contract which stipulated that 10,000 *tumāns* of the total contract should be delivered in the form of ready cash. Disillusioned, the royal agent resumed negotiations with the English East India Company. The latter fulfilled the terms of the resulting contract signed in 1628, but the English imports of cloth and tin similarly glutted the Iranian market and caused a slump in the price of these commodities. The quality of the English cloth, too, was not all that it might have been, and Safavid soldiers who had received consignments of it in lieu of pay ran after English merchants in the street and cursed them for its poor quality. Despite these gross misjudgements of the market situation, the royal agent was not dismissed from office until 1632, after the death of Shāh 'Abbās I.[45]

With the accession of Shāh Ṣafī in 1629, royal control of trade diminished. Whereas under Shāh 'Abbās I the silk trade had been a royal monopoly, Shāh Ṣafī, influenced by substantial bribes from the Armenian community, gave licences to buy silk to all and sundry. Once again, the Dutch East India Company outmanoeuvred the English and succeeded in exploiting this new situation by trading both with the king and with local merchants, including Armenians, who were busy strengthening their connections with Italy and extending their commercial network to France, England, Holland and Russia.[46] To begin with, the English East India Company's factors declined to co-operate with the Armenians. Their agent, William Gibson, sent to London a testy report in which he described the Armenians as "soe griping and deceitful in their dealings and so slowe in performing of their promises"; he strongly advocated that the Company not cooperate with them, and concluded rhetorically, "knowing them to be as aforesaid how think your worships 'tis to be imbraced".[47]

During the reign of Shāh Ṣafī (1629–42), the Dutch continued to purchase large quantities of Iranian silk, mainly from private sources. Government officials tried to offset the resultant loss of revenue to the state by imposing heavy customs duty on silk bought privately. This in turn led the Dutch authorities in Batavia to order their factors in Iran to stop buying silk from private sources. The Dutch merchants were by no means totally dependent on the silk trade; after the foundation of their factory at Bandar 'Abbās, which rapidly replaced Hurmūz as the principal Iranian port-of-entry in the Persian Gulf, they soon established a monopoly of the spice trade between the East Indies and Iran. The rivalry between the Dutch and English East India Companies prevented either from achieving a dominant position, and both were able to derive profit from the transit trade between Bandar

'Abbās and the Indian Ocean ports. Ships of both Companies carried goods for both Iranian and Indian merchants, who were able to obtain attractive freight rates and reliable service by playing off one Company against the other. The pressure these merchants were able to exert caused Jan Smidt, the Dutch ambassador to Iran in 1629, to exclaim indignantly: "they do not at all realise what profit and advancement their country and its inhabitants achieve with our extensive trade, on the contrary they brazenly assert that it is *us* who are quite dependent upon their trade and cannot manage without it".[48] Clearly, the age of imperialism had not yet dawned!

By the second half of the seventeenth century, the Dutch had outstripped both its English rivals and also the French, whose Compagnie Française des Indes was founded in 1664; Thévenot, Fryer and Chardin all testify to the supremacy of Dutch trade in the Persian Gulf at that period. The Dutch success was achieved primarily by their quickness in adapting to changing circumstances. They abandoned the concept of bilateral trade which had been the basis of the operations of both the early Dutch and English traders, in favour of multilateral, co-ordinated trade throughout Asia based on Batavia. Capital invested by Dutch merchants was not to return to source immediately, but was to circulate permanently in Asia, Dutch merchants taking a profit from each successive stage. This policy received its classic formulation by Coen in 1619:

Piece goods from Gujarat we can barter for pepper and gold on the coast of Sumatra, rials and cottons from the coast for pepper in Bantam, sandalwood, pepper and rials we can barter for Chinese goods and Chinese gold; we can extract silver from Japan with Chinese goods, piece goods from the Coromandel coast in exchange for spices, other goods and gold from China, piece goods from Surat for spices, other goods and rials, rials from Arabia for spices and various other trifles – one thing leads to the other. And all of it can be done without any money from the Netherlands and with ships alone.[49]

The English East India Company was constrained to acknowledge that desperate measures were needed if the Company was not to be forced out of business altogether, and in 1688 the Company took the unprecedented step of conferring on Armenians equal status with Englishmen in the conduct of commercial operations – a step which would have been unthinkable a hundred years later. Under the terms of the 1688 Agreement, Armenians were to have "the liberty to live in any of the Company's cities Garrisons or Towns in India and to buy, sell and purchase Land or Houses and be capable of all Civil Offices and preferments in the same manner as if they were Englishmen born".[50] The hopes of the English East India Company were not fulfilled. For one thing, competition with the Levant Company was at its most bitter and militated against the East India Company's improving its trading position in Iran; for another, the Armenians, despite their having signed the 1688 Agreement, were far from convinced of the advantage to themselves of giving the English East India Company preferential status. As they said vividly in 1697: "As for bringing Silk to Iṣfahān, it is but wind."[51] The profits to be made on the Aleppo route, through close co-operation with the Levant Company, continued to be more tempting than the uncertain prospects of the sea-route via the Persian Gulf. Even the Russian route, despite its unpromising beginnings, appeared more attractive to the Armenians at the turn of the eighteenth century. In the words of R. W. Ferrier, "the experience of the East India Company in Persia in the seventeenth century underlines the importance of ready money to the European trade in the East, the tenacity of the traditional trading patterns, the crucial parts played by the local merchants and brokers, and, for Persia in particular, the close interdependence of the cloth and silk trades".[52] The English merchants frequently found themselves embarrassed by the lack both of capital and of ready cash, which the Armenians could supply in abundance. "Although merchants traded exclusively for cash, money was scarce. Most of it found its way into the Treasury, where it was hoarded."[53] According to Banani, "the silver coins of the Safavids were worth less by weight than their face value indicated; they found few takers. Gold coins were struck only for special and infrequent occasions, and then only in small quantities. Naturally, they were hoarded. The most desirable was the Venetian gold ducat."[54] "The Armenians not only had supplies of ready money but they had also a well-organized system of credit facilities along the routes in the towns where they traded."[55] The Armenians were also adepts at avoiding currency and exchange regulations, and regularly carried ready money into and out of Iran "by avoiding the royal mints and not complying with royal instructions against exporting it to India and elsewhere".[56]

In the long term, the alternative trade routes which had been developed in response to political exigencies, namely, the sea–land-route via the Caspian Sea and Russia, and the sea-route via the Persian Gulf, did not prove to be satisfactory substitutes for the traditional routes through Anatolia and across Iraq and Syria to the Levant ports, and this despite the fact that the alternative routes, by by-passing the Ottoman empire, enabled Safavid merchants to avoid Ottoman transit dues and customs, and reduced the inflationary pressure on Iran from Turkey.[57] After the conclusion of the Treaty of Ẕuhāb between the Ottomans and the Safavids in 1639, which ushered in a prolonged period of peace between the two antagonists, much of the Iranian export trade reverted to the traditional routes.[58] One major export item which reverted to the Anatolian route was mutton "on the hoof". Tavernier reports that there was a large-scale traffic in sheep from the Tabrīz and Hamadān areas to the markets in Istanbul and Adrianople, and that the greater part of the mutton consumed in Anatolia and Rumania emanated from Iran. In the months of March, April and May, he says, the roads were packed with flocks of sheep a thousand strong.[59] The fact that Middle Eastern merchants survived the challenge of the European East India Companies during the seventeenth century, and continued to contrive to make an adequate profit, is probably due to two things: first, the Armenian, Jewish, Persian and Indian merchants almost certainly were capable of striking harder bargains and buying their goods at lower prices than their European rivals; second, because of their expensive overheads, European merchants needed to make a gross profit of 60 or 70 per cent in order to show a reasonable net profit, whereas the local traders of the region were satisfied with much lower profit margins.

9

Intellectual life under the Safavids

LITERATURE

Until recently, the accepted view among scholars was that no poetry of note was composed in the Safavid period. The person most responsible for enunciating and giving currency to this view was E. G. Browne:

One of the most curious and, at first sight, inexplicable phenomena of the Ṣafawí period is the extraordinary dearth of notable poets in Persia during the two centuries of its duration...though poets innumerable are mentioned in the *Tuḥfa-i Sámí* and other contemporary biographies and histories, there is hardly one (if we exclude Jámí, Hátifí, Hilálí and other poets of Khurásán, who were really survivors of the school of Herát) worthy to be placed in the first class. During the seventy stormy years of Tímúr's life there were at least eight or ten poets besides the great Ḥáfiẓ, who outshone them all, whose names no writer on Persian literature could ignore; while during the two hundred and twenty years of Safawi rule there was in Persia, so far as I have been able to ascertain, hardly one of conspicuous merit or originality. I say "in Persia" advisedly, for a brilliant group of poets from Persia, of whom 'Urfí of Shíráz (d. A.D. 1590) and Ṣá'ib of Isfahan (d. A.D. 1670) are perhaps the most notable, adorned the court of the "Great Moghuls" in India, and these were in many cases not settlers of the sons of emigrants, but men who went from Persia to India to make their fortunes and returned home when their fortunes were made. This shows that it was not so much lack of talent as lack of patronage which makes the list of distinctively Ṣafawí poets so meagre.

E. G. Browne considered it so remarkable that "no great poet should have arisen in Persia in days otherwise so spacious and so splendid as those of the Ṣafawís" that he wrote to the Iranian scholar Mīrzā Muḥammad Khān Qazvīnī to ask whether he agreed.

Qazvīnī replied: "There is at any rate no doubt that during the

Ṣafawí period literature and poetry in Persia had sunk to a very low ebb, and that not one single poet of the first rank can be reckoned as representing this epoch." Qazvīnī gave various reasons for this phenomenon. First, the religious unification of Iran effected by the Safavids and the propagation of the Ithnā 'Asharī Shī'ī doctrine which, he said, was inimical to literature, poetry, Sufism and mysticism. Pointing to the persecution of Ṣūfīs by the religious classes, he observed: "the close connection between poetry and Belles Lettres on the one hand, and Ṣufíism and Mysticism on the other, at any rate in Persia, is obvious, so that the extinction of one necessarily involves the extinction and destruction of the other. Hence it was that under this dynasty learning, culture, poetry and mysticism completely deserted Persia", and he went on to accuse the Safavids of utterly destroying the cloisters, monasteries, retreats and rest-houses of the Ṣūfīs throughout Iran. "In place of great poets and philosophers there arose theologians, great indeed but harsh, dry, fanatical and formal, like the Majlisís, the Muḥaqqiq-i thání, Shaykh Ḥurr-i-Ámulí and Shaykh-i-Bahá'í, etc." One may ask in passing, if the atmosphere at the Safavid court was *per se* unconducive to the composition of poetry, how was it that many Safavid poets flourished at the three Shī'ī courts in India: Aḥmadnagar, Golconda and Bījāpūr?

The second reason adduced by Qazvīnī to account for the dearth of first-rate poets is the lack of royal patronage and encouragement. Both Shāh Ṭahmāsp and 'Abbās I are alleged to have expressed the wish that panegyrics, on which court poets to a considerable extent relied for a living, should be addressed to the Imāms rather than to themselves. Since royal patrons paid better than the Imāms, the argument goes, many Safavid poets moved to the Mogul court at Delhi where the financial rewards were greater. So many poets emigrated in this way that a whole genre of Persian poetry, known as the *sabk-i hindī*, or "Indian genre", was established by these Persian poets in self-imposed exile.[1]

Browne's generalisations on poetry under the Safavids were sweeping enough, but Mīrzā Muḥammad Khān Qazvīnī extended them to a blanket condemnation of the entire Safavid period as a cultural desert in which learning, poetry, mysticism and even philosophy were non-existent. It is a curious and, at first sight, inexplicable phenomenon, as Browne might have said, that these views were accepted uncritically for several decades after Browne's death, as was his equally sweeping condemnation of Safavid historiography, on which I shall comment later. Jan Rypka, in his chapter on Safavid literature, opens with the words: "The literature of the Safavid period is usually regarded as a literature of decline",[2] and he makes the sweeping generalisation that there was a "palpable lack of interest in the poets, their works and their burial-places".[3] This was the view not only of Western scholars but of most Iranians too, including the nineteenth-century critic Riżā Qulī Hidāyat and the poet-laureate Bahār, who died in 1951.[4] It was not until Ehsan Yar-Shater's seminal paper, "Safavid Literature: Progress or Decline", was published in 1974 that the harsh views expressed by Browne, Mīrzā Muḥammad Khān Qazvīnī, Rypka and others were subjected to any critical analysis at all.[5]

Qazvīnī's second reason for the lack of great poetry in Safavid Iran, namely, that the best poets had been attracted to the Mogul court by the greater financial rewards to be obtained there, has considerable validity. Under the Great Moguls, Delhi was unquestionably the Mecca of poets. The Muslim courts of India had for centuries given generous support to Persian poets, some of whom, such as Mas'ūd-i Sa'd-i Salmān (d. 1131) and Amīr Khusraw of Delhi (d. 1325), were of the highest class. With the establishment of the Mogul empire by Bābur in 1526, it was only natural that this support should be on a much larger scale, because Bābur, though descended from Tīmūr on his father's side and claiming descent from Chingiz Khān on his mother's, had been born and raised in the Persian cultural milieu of Transoxania. Persian was the language in use at the Mogul court, and many of the Mogul princes composed poetry in Persian themselves. Their example of generous patronage of Persian poets was followed by their viziers and other members of the nobility. The Mogul emperors Akbar (1556–1605), Jahāngīr (1605–27) and Shāh Jahān (1628–58), assembled brilliant gatherings of Persian poets at their courts. "No wonder, then, that anyone in Persia who aspired to the writing of poetry conceived the desire of travelling to India and trying his fortune there."[6]

> Great is India, the Mecca for all in need,
> Particularly for those who seek safety.
> A journey to India is incumbent upon any man
> Who has acquired adequate knowledge and skill.

So wrote the son-in-law of the celebrated Safavid philosopher Mullā Ṣadrā Shīrāzī.[7] It is no wonder, then, that the bulk of the poetry composed in Persia by Persian poets during the Safavid period was written in India. Aziz Ahmad considers that if the patronage of the Safavid shahs made less impact on Safavid poets, and the latter migrated to India, "the probable reason is the greater wealth and richer economic resources of India at that stage of history".[8]

When full allowance has been made for the fact that the grass for poets appeared greener on the Mogul side of the hill, it must be firmly stated that the view expounded by Qazvīnī and many others, namely, that the Safavid shahs did not encourage poets, is a fallacy. Apart from the fact that several of the shahs themselves composed poetry, they and other members of the royal family were patrons of poets and bibliophiles, calligraphers and musicians. Shāh Ismā'īl I composed poetry of no mean merit in Āẕarī Turkish under the pen-name of Khaṭā'ī. Sulṭān Muḥammad Shāh composed poetry under the pen-name of Fahmī. The concomitant fallacy, that all Safavid shahs directed that panegyrics be written in praise of the Imāms rather than of themselves seems to have its origin in the following extract from the chronicle of Iskandar Beg Munshī about Shāh Ṭahmāsp:

List of poets who were still in full spate at the death of Shāh Ṭahmāsp.

The number of poets who were still flourishing at that time, either at court or in the provinces, was legion. Early in his reign, Shāh Ṭahmāsp gave special consideration to the class of poets, and for a time Mīrzā Sharaf Jahān and Mawlānā Ḥayratī were companions at the Shāh's table and other social gatherings. During the latter part of his life, however, when the Shāh took more seriously the Qur'anic prescription to "do what is right and eschew evil", he no longer accounted poets pious and upright men, because of the known addiction of many of them to the bottle, and he ceased to regard them with favour, and refused to allow them to present to him occasional pieces and eulogistic odes. On one occasion, Mawlānā Muḥtasham Kāshī had written an ode in praise of the Shāh, and another eulogising Parī Khān Khanum, and had sent them from Kāshān. Parī Khān Khānum had presented the former to Ṭahmāsp, who remarked: "I am not willing to allow poets to pollute their tongues with praises of me; let them write eulogies of 'Alī and the other infallible Imāms. Tell him to look first for his reward to the holy spirits of the Imāms, and after that to hope for a reward from me. He has used far-fetched metaphors and profound images, and attributed them, most inappropriately, to kings; whereas, had he applied these metaphors and images to the holy Imāms, it would have been impossible to use expressions too extravagant to describe their exalted rank." In short, Mawlānā Muḥtasham did not receive any reward for his ode. When the Mawlānā received the Shāh's reply, he despatched to him a work by the late Mawlānā Ḥasan Kāshī on the Imām 'Alī, which he had put into verse in the form of a *haft-band*[9] – a really inspired piece of work – and in reward for this he received a fitting present. At once all the poets at court set to work, madly writing *haft-bands*, and fifty or sixty poems rained down on the Shāh, and their authors were all rewarded.[10]

This account by Iskandar Beg Munshī, enlivened by the usual touches of the author's delightful humour, makes it clear that Qazvīnī's strictures are entirely without foundation. In the first place, during the earlier part of his reign, Ṭahmāsp not only acted as a patron of poets but made them his intimates. Later in his life, when he became more puritanical and unwilling to condone the convivial habits of some poets, he directed that eulogies of him be redirected to the Imāms. Not only did the poets not go unrewarded, however, but it appears that the rewards were sufficiently generous to stimulate greater poetic output and to persuade the poets of the advantages of remaining at the Safavid court.

Similarly, Shāh 'Abbās I valued and encouraged poets. He appointed poets to the position of poet-laureate, and "at least once he paid a poet (Shāmī) the equivalent of his weight in gold as a mark of his appreciation".[11] On his visits to coffee-houses, 'Abbās I used to listen to poets reciting verses, and sometimes encouraged them to try their hand at extempore versification.[12] With the exception of the emperor Jahāngīr, the Mogul emperors on the whole did not appreciate poetry themselves; the poets who thronged their court were there for decorative purposes, to enhance the prestige of their court. The Safavid shahs, on the other hand, not only personally appreciated poetry, but their relations with poets were often of a much more intimate nature than were those between the Mogul court poets and the Mogul emperors.[13]

Until recently, it did not occur to anyone that the poetry written by Persian poets at the Mogul court might be called "Safavid". Many Iranian critics asserted that it was not even written in good Persian. The term "the Indian genre" was used as a pejorative term, denoting poetry written in Persian but of an inferior kind. Shāh Ṭahmāsp's brother, Sām Mīrzā, in his contemporary notices on these poets, considered them to be superior to the poets of the past, but the critics of subsequent centuries became more and more censorious: "The substance is wrong, the meaning is wrong, and the style is wrong; all is wrong" (Ḥazīn, d. 1766); "After Ṣā'ib, who was the instigator of this new distasteful style, the level of poetry continued daily in decline, until this time of ours, when, thanks be to God, their fabrications have completely fallen into disuse and the rule of the old masters revived" (Luṭf 'Alī Āẕar Begdīlī, 1711–81); "Under the Turcomans and the Safavids, reprehensible styles appeared...and since there were no binding rules for lyrics, the poets, following their sick natures and distorted tastes, began to write confused, vain and nonsensical poems" (Hidāyat, 1800–72); and finally Bahār (d. 1951):

> The Indian style possessed novelty,
> But had very many failings,
> It was infirm and spineless,
> Its ideas were feeble, its imagery odd.
> The poems were crowded with ideas, but unattractive;
> They were wanting in eloquence.[14]

Confronted with such a chorus of disapproval, it may seem foolhardy to question this apparently unanimous opinion. On closer examination, however, we find that some of our worthy critics discredit themselves. Ḥazīn, we discover, not only "considered his contemporary poets important enough to compile a laudatory biography of them", but composed no less than five *dīvāns* (collections) of poetry in the despised "Indian" style![15] Hidāyat, too, discredits himself totally as a critic by purporting to see no virtue in any Persian poetry after the Seljuq period with the exception of the poetry of Ḥāfiẓ, "whose *ghazals* have been well appreciated by the admirers of form and substance" (but not, apparently, by Hidāyat?); and one cannot but have doubts about the literary judgement of even the celebrated Bahār when he claims that the period of Fatḥ 'Alī Shāh (1797–1834) was "a brilliant period of poetry, similar to that of Sulṭān Maḥmūd of Ghazna".[16] Perhaps the criticisms of Luṭf 'Alī Āẕar Begdīlī and Bahār, however, contain clues which may account for this barrage of vituperation from the literary critics. Āẕar refers to "this new distasteful style", and sighs with relief when poets return to writing in the old, approved way; and Bahār refers to the "novelty" of the "Indian genre", and admits that the poetry of the "Indian" school was "crowded with ideas", although he found the ideas unattractive. Could the disapproval of the Safavid poets on the part of the literary establishment be rooted mainly in a dislike of their use of new themes expressed in a new style? If so, the breaking of new ground by the Safavid poets would be exactly analogous to the introduction of new themes by Safavid artists and their use of a more realistic style of painting which represented a definite departure from the accepted style (see Chapter 6).

Before discussing this idea, let us return to the question as to whether the "Indian genre" of Persian poetry can be considered "Safavid" poetry. Interestingly enough, some Iranian critics are now asserting that it can. Some even wish to call it the "Iṣfahānī" school, "on the grounds that it was largely fostered in Iṣfahān at the time of the Safavids".[17] It looks as though at least some Iranians are now ready to reclaim this part of their literary heritage. Perhaps it is time to drop the term "Indian genre", with its automatic implication that here is something alien to the Persian literary tradition, and substitute "Safavid genre". This would enable these novel ideas which so upset the critics to be viewed within the Persian literary tradition rather than as something external to it, as an aberration. For it is essential not to lose sight of the fact that not only the contemporary Persian critics, but also the contemporary Ottoman and Indian critics, who were far more numerous, were in agreement that the Safavid period was one of great literary merit. Indeed, outside Iran itself, in India, Afghānistān, Transoxania and Turkey, where the Persian cultural tradition continued to reign supreme during the nineteenth century, the "Safavid genre" continued to flourish until literary trends from the West began to make their impact.[18] I regard it as highly significant that Shiblī Nu'mānī (d. 1914) devoted the whole of one volume of his five-volume work *Shi'r al-'Ajam* to a study of seven major poets of the Safavid period. Of these seven poets – 'Urfī, Ṣā'ib, Faghānī, Fayżī, Naẓīrī, Ṭālib-i Āmulī and Abū Ṭālib Kalīm – only one, Fayżī, was born in India. For Shiblī Nu'mānī, the decline of Persian poetry occurred not in the Safavid period, but in the eighteenth century, after the fall of the Safavid empire and the decline of the Mogul empire,[19] and I agree entirely with Ehsan Yar-Shater that Nu‘mānī's work is still the best history of Persian literature from early times to the end of the seventeenth century.

If one accepts the argument that a just assessment of Safavid poetry cannot be made without including within one's purview the works of the so-called "Indian genre" school, what are the distinguishing characteristics of Safavid poetry, and what were the literary canons of the Safavid period? In the first place, the Safavid poets did not consider their poetry to be part of a "literature of decline". On the contrary, the major poets of the period considered themselves to be poets of a very high order, and they "also considered their period one of literary prosperity and fertile imagination. In their estimation, this age had given birth to thousands of fresh poetic ideas and had excelled other periods by the subtlety of its thought, the richness of its substance and the novelty of its imagery." The Safavid poets looked less to the models of the past, and had sufficient confidence in themselves and their contemporaries to adopt the metres and rhymes of their contemporaries, rather than those of the great masters of the past, and incorporate them in their own work.[20]

What were the "fresh poetic ideas" on which Safavid poets prided themselves? Ehsan Yar-Shater, in his important article on Safavid literature from which I have quoted frequently in this chapter, lists a number of them and gives examples of each. They include: the use of a novel simile or metaphor; variations on older themes and imagery; the unusually subtle expression of an emotion such as jealousy; and the use of novel verbal witticisms and conceits and rhetorical devices. The use of such devices is not considered a defect in Persian poetry; quite the contrary. The mere expression of an idea will win a Persian poet little applause from his compatriots; what matters is the apt and above all ingenious and sophisticated expression of the idea. As a result, what may appear to the Western reader over-elaborated or even artificial verse will not seem so to an Iranian. "To call rhetorical devices 'embellishing' devices, as they have often been called, is misleading. Persian poetry is *essentially* rhetorical."[21] In the course of "striving for novelty and for exploring subtle and ingenious ideas", Safavid poets succeeded "in producting terse, pithy epigrammatic lines or clusters of lines, which are not to be found in the poetry of other periods". It is this feature, says Yar-Shater, and this feature alone, which is the unique characteristic of Safavid poetry and represents progress from the poetry of earlier periods, and it is the "intensity of this quality which has bestowed on Safavid poetry the title of a new style".[22] Of this new Safavid style, Ṣā'ib was the supreme exponent. E. G. Browne, though he thinks that "Rieu goes too far when he describes Ṣā'ib as 'by common consent the creator of a new style of poetry, and the greatest of modern Persian poets'," is prepared to assert that Ṣā'ib "is without doubt the greatest of those who flourished in the seventeenth century of our era, and, I think, the only one deserving a detailed notice in this volume".[23] In his younger days, Browne rated Ṣā'ib among the greatest Persian poets of all ages, for, he tells us,

> Nearly forty years ago (in 1885) I read through the Persian portion of that volume of the great trilingual anthology entitled *Kharābāt* which deals with the lyrical verse of the Arabs, Turks and Persians, both odes and isolated verses, and copied into a note-book which now lies before me those which pleased me most, irrespective of authorship; and, though many of the 443 fragments and isolated verses which I selected are anonymous, more than one-tenth of the total (45) are by Ṣā'ib.[24]

Yar-Shater comments ironically that "Browne need not have felt ashamed of his choice."[25] Ṣā'ib, at any rate, was not altogether deprived of that appreciation in his own country which Browne sees as the main reason why Safavid poets emigrated to India, for, on his return to Iṣfahān, his native city, he was made poet-laureate by Shāh 'Abbās II.

Incontrovertible evidence that Safavid poetry did constitute a new style of poetry seems to me to be provided by the nature of the comments, both adverse and favourable, made on it by eighteenth- and nineteenth-century critics. For example, Ṭālib-i Āmulī is criticised because "he had a peculiar style in verse which is not sought after by elegant poets".[26] Riżā Qulī Khān Hidāyat said that Ṣā'ib "had a strange style in the poetic art which is not now admired".[27] Shiblī Nu'mānī says of Faghānī of Shīrāz (with approval) that he was "the creator of a new style of poetry".[28] E. J. W. Gibb, in his *History of Ottoman Poetry*, speaking of 'Urfī and Fayżī, two more Safavid poets composing poetry in the despised "Indian genre", says that "after Jāmī, 'Urfī and Fayżī were the chief Persian influences on Turkish poetry until they

30. The poet laureate Shifā'ī

were superseded by Ṣā'ib", and he refers to the novelty of their style and the fact that they introduced a number of fresh terms into the conventional vocabulary of poetry.[29]

Naturally, the "Safavid genre" carried within itself the germ of its own decline, and eventually over-elaboration and an excess of complex rhetorical devices led to artificiality. Sometimes, too, the quality of the vocabulary did not match the loftiness of the thought expressed. Two further novel features of Safavid poetry should be mentioned: first, the "language of the streets" crept into the poetry to a rather greater degree than was acceptable to those trained in the classical tradition; second, there was less concern for linguistic purity during the Safavid period. A. Bausani attributes these trends to the "replacement at court...of the class of secretaries and literary men by that of the Shi'ite clergy, which had little or no particular taste for classical poetry".[30] There may be some truth in this, but I do not agree that the secretarial and literary class disappeared from the Safavid court, except possibly in the final days of the decline of the Safavid state when the religious classes exerted a stranglehold on affairs. The great Safavid historiographer, Iskandar Beg Munshī, was himself not only a member of the class of high-ranking court secretaries and liked to compose verse, but he mentions many members of the bureaucratic class who were cultured men and appreciated fine literature. In any case, the most brilliant exponents of the "Safavid genre" spent most of their lives at the Mogul court and were therefore not subject to the alleged religious pressures of the Safavid court.

I suggest that the predominantly military character of the Safavid state at least up to the time of Shāh 'Abbās I may have been far more responsible for these new linguistic trends. Many *qizilbāsh amīrs* resided at court, and held high administrative office, and military men, at least since the time of Julius Caesar, have been noted for brevity and directness and earthiness of speech. Another factor which should be noted is that the *qizilbāsh* normally spoke their Āẕarī brand of Turkish at court, as did the Safavid shahs themselves; lack of familiarity with the Persian language may have contributed to a decline from the pure classical standards of former times. Furthermore, the "language of the streets" did not make its first appearance in Persian poetry in Safavid times. It had been present from at least the Mongol period, and one has only to examine the great mystical epic of Jalāl al-Dīn Rūmī (1207–73) to see this. It is no coincidence that the Persian *qaṣīda*, or formal ode, reached its peak in Seljuq times with such brilliant practitioners as Anvarī, Mu'izzī, Khāqānī and 'Unṣurī. From the Mongol period onwards, the *ghazal* (lyric) and *mathnavī* (poem, usually long, in rhymed couplets) became the most popular Persian verse-forms, and each of these verse-forms lent itself to the use of the "language of the streets" more readily than did the *qaṣīda*, with its rigid conventions.[31] R. A. Nicholson, in his translation of the *Mathnavī-yi Ma'navī* of Jalāl al-Dīn Rūmī, would not have deemed it necessary to translate so many passages into Latin rather than English had he not considered these passages too vulgar (in every sense of the work) for refined ears.

As we have seen, Qazvīnī's peremptory dismissal of Safavid poetry extended to Safavid literature as a whole and indeed to most forms of Safavid intellectual activity. The uncritical condemnation of Safavid poetry by the majority of both Western and Iranian scholars is paralleled by their extraordinary neglect of a major branch of literature in which the Safavid period is rich – historiography. H. A. R. Gibb, in his long article on Islamic historiography ("Ta'rīkh") in the Supplement to the *Encyclopaedia of Islam* (1938) appeared unaware of the existence of Safavid historiography, and offered only the mysterious comment, "Persian historiography also suffered from the sectarian isolation of Persia".[32] E. G. Browne, on the other hand, was aware that the materials were ample, but asserted that to anyone not specially interested in military matters the Safavid historical chronicles were "very dull and arduous reading"; "even from the point of view of history," he said, "they are vitiated by overwhelming masses of trivial details and absence of any breadth of view or clearness of outline".[33]

As in the case of Safavid poetry, it is only in quite recent times that scholars both in Iran and in the West have begun to reassess these judgements. It is only in the last twenty years or so that some Iranian historians have begun to see the Safavids in their proper light, as the founders of modern Iran. Prior to that, it was the fashion to blame the Safavids for the political and economic weakness of Iran at the beginning of the nineteenth century, a weakness which enabled the Great Powers progressively to interfere in and gain control of Iranian affairs. This view ignored the fact that the complex but functional centralised system developed by the Safavids was largely destroyed by the actions of Nādir Shāh and by the civil war between the Zands and the Qājārs during the second half of the eighteenth century. Others have attributed the slow progress made by Iran during the nineteenth century in the direction of social or economic reform to the entrenched power of the religious classes, and have seen this entrenched power as a direct legacy of the Safavid period. This view ignores the fact that the religious classes attained a position of dominance in the Safavid state only under the last representative of that dynasty, Shāh Sulṭān Ḥusayn, whose reign marked a rapid decline in Safavid fortunes. The gradually changing attitude in Iran toward the Safavid period has led to the publication of an increasing number of historical texts, which in turn has facilitated more detailed study of the period. The doyen of Safavid historiographers is now recognised by leading Islamic scholars to be that same Iskandar Beg Munshī whose work was so severely castigated by E. G. Browne. M. G. S. Hodgson, in his monumental work, *The Venture of Islam*, spoke of the "judicious accuracy" of Iskandar Beg's *History of Shāh 'Abbas the Great*, of "its psychological perceptiveness, and the broad interest it manifests in the ramifications of the events it traces".[34] A. K. S. Lambton has drawn attention to the unique character and the great value of the biographical material contained in Iskandar Beg's *History*,[35] and J. R. Walsh has assessed it as not only a great work of Safavid and of Iranian historiography, but as "one of the greatest of all Islamic historical works and, indeed, perfect within the limitations of its traditions".[36]

PHILOSOPHY AND METAPHYSICS

In what must by now be becoming for the reader a monotonous refrain, I am constrained to state that the Safavid contribution to Iranian and Islamic philosophy has also, until recent times, either been underestimated or held not to exist at all. It had been widely assumed, on evidence no more valid than the evidence for the "non-existence" of Safavid poetry or the "non-existence" of Safavid historiography, that Islamic philosophy came to a dead stop after the end of the classical period of Islam. Most histories of Muslim philosophy by Western scholars consider Ibn Rushd, known in the West as Averroës, who was born at Cordoba in 1126 and died in 1198, as the last Muslim philosopher; occasionally Ibn Khaldūn, who was born at Tunis in 1332 and died in Cairo in 1406, is brought within their purview.[37] But Ibn Khaldūn, one of the greatest thinkers of the Islamic Middle Ages, was a philosopher of history and of society rather than a "pure" philosopher; indeed, he has been called the "father of sociology"; in any case, de Boer considers him "a unique and isolated phenomenon, without forerunners and without successors".[38] This mistaken view of Islamic philosophy was adopted by modern Arab, Pakistani and Indian scholars, "many of whom rely primarily on works of modern orientalists for their knowledge of the history of Islamic philosophy and are unaware of the importance of the Ishrāqī school, perhaps because it was primarily in Persia that this form of wisdom found its home and where it has subsisted to the present time".[39]

The resurrection of the important Ishrāqiyya or "Illuminationist" school of Iranian philosophy, and the active study of the philosophers of the Safavid period, are largely the work of the French Iranologist Henri Corbin and the Iranian scholar Seyyed Hossein Nasr. The founder of this school of philosophy was Shihāb al-Dīn Yaḥyā Suhravardī, who was born in 1153 in the village of Suhravard near Zanjān in Āẕarbāyjān, and died in jail in Aleppo in 1191, the victim of the hostility of the *'ulamā*, or theologians. Though only thirty-eight at the time of his death, Suhravardī was the author of over fifty works, which Seyyed Hossein Nasr has classified in five categories: major didactic and doctrinal works dealing with Peripatetic philosophy as modified and interpreted by Suhravardī, and with the Ishrāqī or "Illuminationist" theosophy which he developed from this doctrinal foundation; shorter treatises dealing with the same material in simpler language; mystical narratives; translation of and commentaries on earlier philosophic works; and missals similar to the Books of the Hours familiar to Christian Europe.[40]

The basis of Suhravardī's Ishrāqī wisdom is that there is a universal and perennial wisdom which unites the rational and esoteric strands of philosophy; this universal wisdom, he says, existed among the ancient Hindus and Persians, Babylonians and Egyptians, and among the Greeks up to the time of Aristotle; Aristotle, in his view, terminated this tradition of wisdom and restricted it by confining philosophy to its rational aspect and ignoring its esoteric side. It followed logically from this view of the history of philosophy that Suhravardī considered his intellectual and spiritual forebears to be not the well-known Islamic philosophers like Avicenna (Ibn Sīnā: 980–1037), who based their work largely on Aristotle, but the early Islamic mystics and the pre-Aristotelian Greek philosophers such as Pythagoras and Plato, and, subsequently, the neo-Platonists.[41] He aimed at not only the formal training of the mind, but the purification of the soul. In other words, Suhravardī asserted the importance in philosophical thought of intellectual intuition, contemplation and ascetic practices, as well as of discursive reasoning. He used the Zoroastrian symbolism of light and darkness without subscribing to the formal dualism of that faith, although some modern scholars have accused him of harbouring anti-Islamic sentiments and of attempting to revive Zoroastrianism against Islam.[42]

Various philosophers and thinkers of the thirteenth, fourteenth and fifteenth centuries commented on Suhravardī's works, but it was in the Safavid period that his teachings came into full bloom and profoundly influenced Islamic intellectual life.[43] Suhravardī's ideas were revived and developed principally by two Safavid philosophers, Mīr Dāmād (d. 1631/2), who significantly adopted the pen-name of Ishrāq, and Mullā Ṣadrā (d. 1640/1). Mīr Dāmād was the sobriquet of Mīr Muḥammad Bāqir of Astarābād who lived most of his life at Iṣfahān and stood high in the favour of Shāh 'Abbās the Great. Despite the high regard Shāh 'Abbās had for Mīr Dāmād and for the other eminent theologians and philosophers at his court, he knew how to keep them in their place. The *mujtahids*, by and large, were content with their lot under the Safavid shahs because, although the shahs had usurped their prerogative to act as the general agency of the Hidden Imām, they still wielded much more power without this prerogative in the Shī'ī state established by the Safavids, than they had wielded when they still possessed this prerogative under a Sunnī regime. 'Abbās I used to boast that his reign was free from the quarrels between men of religion which had under his predecessors threatened the tranquillity of the state. An anecdote quoted by Browne[44] makes it clear that Mīr Dāmād knew how to make his opinions palatable to both the Shāh and to the theologians. After Mīr Dāmād's death, his pupil and son-in-law Mullā Ṣadrā saw his ghost in a dream and said, "My views do not differ from yours, yet I am denounced as an infidel and you are not. Why is this?" "Because," replied Mīr Dāmād's spirit, "I have written on Philosophy in such wise that the theologians are unable to understand my meaning, but only the philosophers; while you write about philosophical questions in such a manner that every dominie and hedge-priest who sees your book understands what you mean and dubs you an unbeliever."

Mullā Ṣadrā went further than Mīr Dāmād in attempting to synthesise the rationalist tradition of Avicenna and the intuitive tradition of Suhravardī within Shi'ite esotericism. He made

> a grand synthesis of all the major intellectual perspectives of nearly a thousand years of Islamic intellectual life before him. The teachings of the Quran, of the Holy Prophet and the Imāms, of the Peripatetic philosophers, of the Illuminationist theosophers and of the Ṣūfīs were like so many colours of the rainbow which became unified and harmonized in the transcendent theosophy (*al-ḥikmat al-muta'āliyah*) of Mullā Ṣadrā. No other figure of the Safavid period characterizes as well as Mullā Ṣadrā the special genius of this age for intellectual synthesis and the expression of unity in multiplicity, which is also so evident in the extremely rich art of the age.[45]

Ṣadr al-Dīn Shīrāzī, known as Mullā Ṣadrā (1571/2–1640/1) "is one of the greatest intellectual figures of Islam, although his doctrines have long remained in obscurity outside the group of disciples who have kept his teachings alive in Persia and in certain centers in India until the present day".[46] According to Seyyed Hossein Nasr, the reason why not only the works of Mullā Ṣadrā, but also the works of all the members of the Ishrāqī school of Iranian theosophy, have been overlooked by Western scholars until recent times, is that, unlike the works of those Islamic philosophers and theologians whose works were influential in the formation of mediaeval Western scholasticism, their works were never translated into Latin.[47] After Mullā Ṣadrā had completed his education in the transmitted and intellectual sciences, his "too carefree exposition of esoteric doctrines" and his "open defense and propagation of gnostic doctrines" incurred the wrath of the orthodox theologians.[48] Fortunately for Mullā Ṣadrā, his father, Mīr Qavām al-Dīn Shīrāzī, was the personal *vazīr* (minister) of the Queen, Mahd-i 'Ulyā, who wielded the real power in the state (see Chapter 3). But for his father's influence at court, Mullā Ṣadrā might have suffered the same fate as had been experienced by the founder of the Ishrāqī school, Shihāb al-Dīn Yaḥyā Suhravardī, in the twelfth century. As a result of the attacks of the theologians, Mullā Ṣadrā retired to a village near Qum where he spent a long period, variously given as seven and fifteen years, in meditation. At the end of that time, he returned to his native city at the invitation of the celebrated Allāhverdī Khān, then Governor-General of Fārs, and was actively engaged in teaching and writing there until his death in 1640/1. Under his direction, the school at Shīrāz become one of the principal centres of learning in Iran and drew students from many parts of the Islamic world.[49]

The cardinal point of Mullā Ṣadrā's thought is that neither rational enquiry nor intuitive speculation can *by itself* lead the enquirer to a complete vision of the truth; what is needed is a fusion of the two. Mullā Ṣadrā spent the first period of his life perfecting his formal knowledge and learning; the second period was spent in meditation and ascetic practices; during the final period of his life, at Shīrāz, he amalgamated the exoteric and the esoteric knowledge he had thus acquired and harmonised philosophy and revelation in a great outpouring of metaphysical works. One of these, the *Asfār*, is "one of the greatest monuments of metaphysics in Islam"; it "deals with the origin and end of all cosmic manifestation and in particular the human soul".[50] Mullā Ṣadrā was not, of course, the first Muslim intellectual to attempt to co-ordinate faith and reason or science and religion; but no one before him had attempted a synthesis on such a vast scale, interweaving the strands of Islamic revelation; of Aristotelian and neo-Platonic thought; of the "Illuminationist" theosophy of Suhravardī; and of the gnostic doctrines of the Andalusian intellectual Ibn 'Arabī. The way in which these various strands are united, and the manner in which the distinctive features of Mulla Ṣadrā's doctrines are "developed, harmonized, presented with demonstrative proofs and correlated with revealed truths is unmistakably his own. One can, therefore, say with every justification that not only did Mullā Ṣadrā revive the study of metaphysics in the Safavid period but also he established a new intellectual perspective and founded the last original school of wisdom in Islam".[51] Mullā Ṣadrā's thought is of especial relevance to a Western world which, as it loses faith in the ability of rationalism and scientific thought to provide the ultimate answer to the secrets of the universe, is inclined to turn in desperation to the "abysmal terrors of the irrational and the subconscious. Mullā Ṣadrā offers a world view in which reason preserves its proper role while remaining subservient to the intellect which is at once its origin and source of inspiration."[52]

SCIENCE AND MEDICINE

Ever since the Arab conquest of Iran in the seventh century A.D., Persians had excelled in those branches of science which were considered unsuitable for Arabs to study: philosophy, logic, medicine, mathematics, astronomy, astrology, music, mechanics and alchemy.[53] In the pre-Mongol period, Iran produced two outstanding mathematicians: the ninth-century al-Khvārazmī, from whose name the term "algorithm" is derived and the title of whose book, *al-jabr wa'l-muqābala*, probably gave rise to the word "algebra"; and the eleventh-century 'Umar Khayyām, who carried on al-Khvārazmī's work and gave "a complete classification of the forms of cubic equations and constructed a geometrical solution for each type".[54] In addition, Iran was the birthplace of one of the greatest geniuses of the mediaeval world, al-Bīrūnī (973–1048), a veritable polymath who wrote works not only on astronomy and mathematics but also on physics, geography, history and medicine. The outstanding Iranian scientist and thinker of the thirteenth century was Naṣīr al-Dīn Ṭūsī, mathematician, astronomer and philosopher, whose work was so prized by his patron, the Mongol Īlkhān Hülegü, that the latter in 1259 built him a new observatory at his capital, Marāgha in Āẕarbāyjān. There, Naṣīr al-Dīn Ṭūsī drew up the astronomical tables known as the "Īlkhānī" tables, and his "Treatise on the Quadrilateral" represented a considerable advance on previous work in the field of spherical trigonometry.

By the sixteenth century, Islamic science, which in large part meant Persian science, was resting on its laurels. *Al-Hāwī*, the encyclopaedic work of the Iranian physician al-Rāzī (known to the West as Rhazes), first translated into Latin in 1279 under the title *Liber Continens*, was still a standard textbook in European universities. By 1542, five editions of this "vast and costly work" had appeared.[55] The fact that this work was still in general use more than six centuries after the date of its compilation is eloquent testimony to its status in the medical world, but also suggests that not much progress had been made in the science of medicine since the time of al-Rāzī (*ca* 865–925), "the greatest physician of the Islamic world and one of the great physicians of all time".[56] Even more popular among physicians had been the work of his fellow-Iranian, Avicenna, whose massive *al-Qānūn fi'l-Ṭibb* (*Canon of Medicine*), had been translated into Latin by Gerard of Cremona in the twelfth century. Such was the demand for this work that "in the last thirty years of the fifteenth century it was issued sixteen times – fifteen editions being in Latin and one in Hebrew", and "was reissued more than twenty times during the sixteenth century"; the book "continued to be printed and read into the second half of the seventeenth century".[57]

The status of physicians during the Safavid period stood as high as ever. Whereas neither the Greeks nor the Romans accorded high social status to their doctors, Iranians had from ancient times honoured their physicians, who were often the counsellors of kings and sometimes reached the exalted rank of vizier. In Safavid times, the *ḥakīm-bāshī*, or Chief Physician, was an important official at court. But what was the state of medicine under the Safavids? Avicenna's *Canon* was still one of the two principal textbooks studied by medical students. Since the *Canon* had been written in Arabic, and medical students in Safavid times did not always possess a knowledge of that language, a large number of commentaries on the *Canon* was available in Persian.[58] Physiology was still based on the four humours of ancient and mediaeval medicine. Bleeding and purging were still the principal forms of therapeusis. Thévenot, who had personal experience of Safavid surgeons, speaks well of their ability: "There are many Physicians in Persia, and amongst them some skilful men...They let bloud too, and are very dextrous at it; I speak by experience, they tye a ligature of leather very streight about the Arm, and then without rubbing or looking much on the place, they take their Lance...and prick very skilfully."[59] A wide variety of surgical procedures was performed, but pre-operative care was unknown; indeed, greater emphasis was laid on the need for the surgeon to protect himself against infection from a suppurating wound than on the safety of the patient; a rudimentary surgical glove might be made in the bazaar from the mucous membrane covering the testicles of sheep.[60] Elective surgery was virtually unknown, and

90 per cent of surgical operations related to accidents or wounding in fights. Anaesthesia consisted of inducing unconsciousness by means of various narcotics. Of all the branches of Islamic medicine, pharmacy survived longest. Persians had always led the field in pharmacology; the ninth-century pharmacopoeia of Sābūr b. Sahl, and the twelfth-century *Antidotary* of Ibn al-Tirmiẕ, "formed the bases of all other pharmacopoeias and catalogues of simples which were subsequently written".[61] If a Safavid physician were to view the medical world today, "he would find the least change in that section which is concerned with the patient and his drugs".[62] Hospitals maintained elaborate pharmacies, and private dispensaries existed for the patients of doctors who practised outside a hospital.

It is clear that excessive reverence for the mediaeval tradition in the field of medicine persisted into Safavid times in Iran and indeed well on into the nineteenth century. The Safavid system was a long time in dying. The late E. G. Browne could write: "When I was in Tihran in 1887 Dr. Tholozon, physician to his late Majesty Nasiru'd-Din Shah, kindly enabled me to attend the meetings of the Majlis-i Sihhat, or Council of Public Health, in the Persian capital, and a majority of the physicians present at that time knew no medicine but that of Avicenna."[63] In view of this persistent attitude, can any advances in the field of medicine be perceived during the Safavid period?

In pharmacology, a science in which the Iranians had always excelled, further progress seems to have been made. A pharmacopoeia compiled in 1556 entitled *Ṭibb-i Shifā'ī* formed the basis of the *Pharmacopoea Persica* of Fr Angelus printed in France in 1681. However, despite the fact that excellent medical manuals continued to be written during the sixteenth and seventeenth centuries, one's general impression is that they constituted restatements or rearrangements of existing knowledge and did not break new ground to any significant extent.

I should not conclude this chapter without some mention of astrology, since the Safavid kings were accustomed to consult their astrologers before deciding on any major course of action. In mediaeval Europe, astronomy and astrology were synonymous terms in popular belief. In the Islamic world, the study of the heavens was eagerly pursued at least in part because of its connection with astrology, but astronomy had its serious side too,

31. Brass astrolabe engraved with the name of Shāh Sulṭān Ḥusayn, 1712

especially as it related to the art of navigation and the calculation of the calendar. The astrolabe, an astronomical instrument devised by the ancient Greeks, was substantially improved by Muslim scientists before they returned it to Europe in the tenth century. For centuries, Muslims made astrolabes which were beautiful works of art, engraved with great care and skill. Even the greatest Islamic astronomers, however, such as al-Bīrūnī, did not hesitate to write manuals on judicial astrology, and it is no accident that in the Islamic languages the word *munajjim* means both astronomer and astrologer. The casting of a horoscope required complex calculations to determine the position of the planets at a particular point in time, for example, on the birth of a royal prince, so that the astrologers could predict the influence of the planets on the prince's subsequent life and fortunes. Each year, it was important to determine accurately the moment of the spring equinox so that the astrologers could make predictions about the course of events for the coming year.

At the Safavid court, astrologers were persons of status and importance. They took themselves seriously, and expected their predictions to be believed. In 1625, when the Ottomans were making a determined effort to recapture Baghdād, Mawlānā Muḥammad Ṭāhir Yazdī, one of the astrologers of the royal household of Shāh 'Abbās, had maintained from the beginning of the siege, on the basis of the positions of the stars and other celestial signs, that the Ottomans would not succeed; when the Shāh appeared unconvinced, the astrologer demanded to be allowed to join the Safavid garrison in the beleaguered city in order to demonstrate his confidence in the accuracy of his own prognostication! An interesting rider to this story is that, although the Shāh granted the astrologer's request, the Safavid field commander refused to allow the latter to enter Baghdād;[64] this supports the contention that Shāh 'Abbās I allowed his field commanders considerable discretion in their conduct of operations. According to Thévenot, the court astrologers cost "yearly vast sums of money", and he declares that no class of society was immune from the prevalence of superstition based on astrology: "Not only the Learned and Men of Letters solicitously apply themselves to it, but even the common people and soldiers tamper with it...In conversation all their Discourse is of Spheres, Apogees, Perigees, Excentricks, Epicycles."[65]

To some, it may seem strange to discuss music under the head of the sciences, but "for Muslim theorists, as for their mediaeval counterparts in Europe, music belonged to the mathematical sciences".[66] Of course, for many centuries after the revelation of Islam, there was continuing debate as to whether the performance of music was a permissible activity for a Muslim at all. In the end, despite the frowns of the theologians, who associated music with dancing and other questionable activities, the strong and deep musical traditions, particularly of the Iranians, Turks and the Muslims of India, proved irresistible and, in the Ṣūfī Orders which spread throughout the Islamic world between the twelfth and fourteenth centuries, both music and dance formed an indispensable part of mystical ritual. Though it served religion in this and other contexts, however, music never played the important part in Islam that it did in the Christian tradition.

At the popular level, and among the tribes, music was a part of social life, and events like weddings, funerals and festivals were marked by music, in which the public could participate by singing, dancing or hand-clapping. At the highest levels of society, too, at state banquests, receptions for foreign ambassadors and court festivities in general, musicians and dancing-girls were a standard part of the entertainment. Military bands had an important public function. The musical instruments used in Safavid times did not differ markedly from those which had been in use in Iran for centuries, and the shape and appearance of instruments are well known to us from manuscript illustrations and other paintings: they included trumpets, horns, flutes, lutes and a variety of other stringed instruments, harps, numerous types of drums and other percussion instruments, including castanets and tambourines, and the unique *santūr* (a type of psaltery). In music, as in medicine, the Safavids were not innovators but merely continued the tradition of earlier centuries.

10

Decline and fall of the Safavids

"When this great prince [Shāh 'Abbās I] ceased to live, Persia ceased to prosper!" This was the considered opinion, already quoted, of the Huguenot jeweller Chardin, the most penetrating and well informed of the Europeans who visited Iran during the Safavid period. Chardin was writing during the reign of Shāh Sulaymān, at whose coronation he was present in 1666; he was looking back at the reign of Shāh 'Abbās the Great from a distance of some forty years, and already it seemed to him that 'Abbās's reign had been a golden age and that his death had marked the beginning of a decline not only in the fortunes of the Safavid dynasty but also of Iran itself. The Safavid state, as rebuilt by Shāh 'Abbās, had an imposing façade which concealed to a considerable extent the decay which spread with increasing rapidity during the second half of the seventeenth century. In Chapter 4, an account was given of the way in which 'Abbās I met and solved in the short term the grave and pressing problems which confronted him, and reference was also made to the fact that some of these solutions contained within themselves the seed of future decay. For example, the creation of a standing army of "third force" elements solved the immediate problem of how to curb the overweening power of the *qizilbāsh*, but ultimately weakened the military strength of the state. Again, the conversion of *mamālik*, or "state" provinces into *khāṣṣa*, or "crown" provinces solved the immediate problem of how to pay this new standing army, but in the long term this policy led among other things to a greater degree of tax oppression and to inferior provincial administration. Further, the policy of incarcerating the royal princes in the *ḥaram* may in the short term have relieved the ruler of the fear of plots against him, but in the not so long term it resulted in the marked degeneration of the dynasty; it also led to the undue influence of

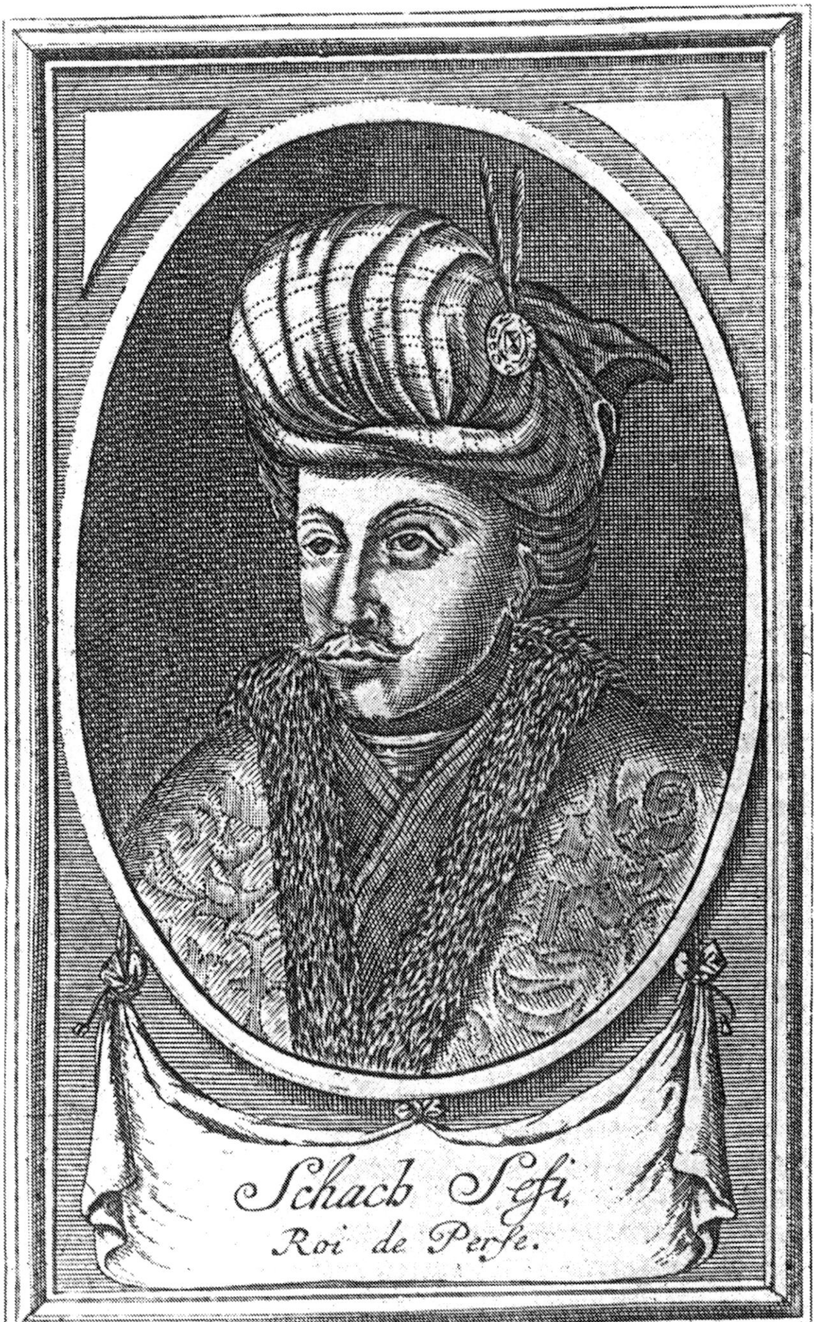
Schach Sefi,
Roi de Perse.

32. Shāh Ṣafī

the women of the *ḥaram*, and of the court eunuchs and other officials associated with the *ḥaram*, in political life and in succession problems. Had ʿAbbās I been followed by rulers of the same calibre, the decline of the Safavid dynasty might have been postponed, but his own policies had made it unlikely that his successors would be worthy of the throne, and his own actions had left him without a son who was capable of taking his place.

ʿAbbās I was succeeded by his grandson Sām Mīrzā, the son of his eldest son Muḥammad Bāqir, also known as Ṣafī, who took his father's name of Ṣafī on his accession on 17 February 1629. Under Shāh Ṣafī, one of the policies initiated by ʿAbbās I, namely, the conversion of "state" to "crown" provinces, was extended. Ṣafī's *vazīr*, Sārū Taqī, put forward an argument which the Shāh found attractive: since the Safavid state was now relatively secure from its external enemies, he said, there was no point in allowing a large part of Safavid territory to remain in the hands of *qizilbāsh* governors, who remitted little to the royal treasury. The Shāh agreed, and the rich province of Fārs which, because of its distance from Iran's eastern and western borders, was considered safe from foreign attack, was converted into a "crown" province, and was administered directly by an overseer on behalf of the Shāh. It was Ṣafī's successor, however, ʿAbbās II (1642–66), who carried this policy to dangerous lengths. Under his rule, the provinces of Qazvīn, Gīlān, Māzandarān, Yazd, Kirmān, Khurāsān and Āẕarbāyjān were all brought under the administration of the Crown except in time of war, when *qizilbāsh* governors were reappointed. This was obviously an unsatisfactory expedient, because the administrative infrastructures of the two systems of government were different, and it was not possible to switch from one to the other overnight. Apart from that, there were serious objections to the conversion of key strategic provinces like Khurāsān, Āẕarbāyjān and Kirmān to "crown" province status. It is no coincidence that it was the provinces of Kirmān and Khurāsān that were first penetrated by the Afghān usurpers, because the latter, from about the year 1705 onwards, had been able to determine at first hand the appalling state of military weakness and unpreparedness in those provinces. An early indication of the alarming extent to which Safavid military power had declined was the loss of Baghdād to the Ottomans in 1638, only fourteen years after its recapture by ʿAbbās I, and of the key city of Qandahār to the Moguls in the same year.

Shāh Ṣafī's character has been blackened by the Jesuit Fr Krusinski, who did not arrive in Iran until more than sixty years after Ṣafī's death, and by Jonas Hanway, who reached Iran a century after Ṣafī's death, and most later Western historians have accepted their judgement uncritically and unquestioningly. Krusinski always given to hyperbole, says "'tis certain there has not been in Persia a more cruel and bloody reign than his", and describes it as "one continued series of cruelties", and Hanway refers to the "frequent instances of barbarity which stained his reign with blood".[1] The authors of *A Chronicle of the Carmelites in Persia*, on the other hand, state that

> Nothing in the mass of original letters and other records left by the Carmelites confirms the way in which his reputation has been besmirched by non-contemporary writers of history; on the contrary, with the exception of the extirpation root and branch of Imām Qulī Khān and his offspring for reasons of state (which may be paralleled in European countries a century or two previously), Shāh Ṣafī appears in these archives clement and pleasant in his dealing.[2]

The Carmelite records must be used with caution, because they are apt to make a ruler's attitude toward Christians the principal criterion in judging his character, but nevertheless there is a discrepancy between the two assessments of such magnitude that it is clear that a substantial modification of the Krusinski view is required.

The "extirpation root and branch of Imām Qulī Khān and his offspring" about the year 1633, referred to in the Carmelite account, is undoubtedly the action of Shāh Ṣafī which earned him the execration of many later Western writers. The Carmelite account also hints at the motive behind the Shāh's action: "for reasons of state". Quite simply, Imām Qulī Khān is yet one more example of a royal servant become too powerful, who has thereby occasioned either the jealousy or the fear of his royal master. Imām Qulī Khān was a Georgian *ghulām*, the son of 'Abbās I's famous commander-in-chief, Allāhverdī Khān. Like his father, he had risen to high office in the service of the state. Appointed Governor-General of Fārs in 1613, he had become the virtual ruler of southern Iran, and his jurisdiction extended far beyond the borders of Fārs along the shore of the Persian Gulf to Makrān. He had been the prime mover in securing the co-operation of the English in the combined Anglo-Iranian attack on the Portuguese positions at Hurmūz in 1622. During the lifetime of 'Abbās I, his

33. Shāh ʿAbbās II

wealth and power had become a byword, and 'Abbās I said jocularly to him one day: "I request, Imām Qulī, that you will spend one dirhem less per day, that there may exist some slight difference between the disbursements of a khan and a king!"[3] Unfortunately for Imām Qulī Khān, Shāh Ṣafī was not as wise a king as Shāh 'Abbās I.

In May 1642, Shāh Ṣafī died at the early age of thirty-two, as he was making preparations for an expedition to recover Qandahār from the Moguls. There seems to be general agreement that he was addicted to opium, and, according to some, was prescribed alcoholic drinks by his physicians to counteract the evil effects of the opium. The combined effect was said to have debilitated his constitution. He was succeeded by his son, 'Abbās II, who came to the throne on 12 May 1642 at the age of eight and a half. In many ways, 'Abbās II resembled his great-grandfather and namesake, 'Abbās I. A strong and vigorous ruler, he from his accession displayed decisiveness and determination, although so young. For example, in 1645, when he was still only twelve years of age, the *vazīr* Sārū Taqī was assassinated by a group of *qizilbāsh* chiefs led by the *qūrchībāshī*, one of the most powerful officers of state; a few days later, 'Abbās II had all the assassins executed. Like his great-grandfather, he had a passion for justice, and complaints of malfeasance and oppression on the part of government officials were dealt with speedily; in fact, 'Abbās II spent three days a week presiding over an official judicial tribunal (*dīvān-i 'adālat*), which dealt with suits brought both by the military and by civilians, and two more days hearing grievances from all parts of the empire. Like his great-grandfather, too, he was in general tolerant in religious matters, and allowed the Catholic orders considerable freedom of action. A notable exception, however, was his treatment of the Jews. At the instigation of his *vazīr*, Muḥammad Beg, he decreed that not only the Jews resident at Iṣfahān but Jews throughout the Safavid empire should make public profession of their conversion to Islam, and should receive instruction in the Islamic faith. Some 100,000 Jews are said to have outwardly embraced Islam but to have continued to practise their religion in secret.

As already mentioned, the process of converting "state" to "crown" provinces was extended and carried on by 'Abbās II on a large scale, with the result that almost the whole of the country was brought under the direct administration of the crown except in time of war, when *ad hoc* military governors were appointed to strategically important frontier provinces. Despite the fact that this policy meant the weakening and virtual disappearance of those *qizilbāsh* tribes which had figured so prominently in the early Safavid period, 'Abbās II managed to preserve the frontier of the empire intact, and even recaptured Qandahār from the Moguls in 1648 and repulsed three subsequent attempts by the Emperor Awrangzīb to recover it. On the north-west frontier, 'Abbās II reversed the policy of his great-grandfather, who had created a sort of "demilitarised zone" by the wholesale removal of the population to other areas; 'Abbās II, on the contrary, attempted to stabilise the area by the resettlement there of tribes from Āẕarbāyjān.

Like his great-grandfather, 'Abbās was interested in the arts and in the erection of public buildings. He had the Chihil Sutūn palace at Iṣfahān built, and he had the Masjid-i Shāh, built by 'Abbās I, and the old Masjid-i Jum'a near the bazaar, repaired; he also constructed a dam on the Zāyanda-rūd in 1654. 'Abbās II was keenly interested in painting, both Oriental and Western, and he liked to try his hand at painting himself. His great weakness was his addiction to alcohol, and his excessive drinking terminated his life at the age of thirty-two, the same age as his father at his death.

With the accession of Ṣafī Mīrzā as Shāh Sulaymān, the Safavid dynasty and state entered upon a period of rapid decline. The new monarch's outward manner was pleasing:

> He was tall, strong and active, a little too effeminate for a monarch – with a Roman nose, very well proportioned to other parts, very large blue eyes and a middling mouth, a beard dyed black, shaved round and well turned back, even to his ears. His manner was affable but nevertheless majestic. He had a masculine and agreeable voice, a gentle way of speaking and was so very engaging that, when you had bowed to him he seemed in some measure to return it by a courteous inclination of his head, and this he always did smiling.[4]

This smiling exterior, however, concealed a weak and capricious nature. During his reign, the position of the shah as the apex of the whole administrative structure of the state, as the unquestioned and absolute ruler with supreme authority in matters temporal and spiritual, was undermined in a manner far more insidious and destructive than the open and straightforward usurpation of the royal prerogatives by the *qizilbāsh* in the time of Shāh Ṭahmāsp. It will be recalled that Shāh Ismā'īl I had given a new emphasis to the office of *ṣadr* by making the *ṣadr*, the head of the religious classes, a political appointee answerable to himself for the good behaviour of the '*ulamā* (doctors of religion) in general and of the *mujtahids*, the most eminent Shī'ī theologians and jurisprudents, in particular. This political control of the *mujtahids* and the religious classes was necessary if the position of the Safavid shah as the representative on earth of the Mahdī, the Shī'ī messiah, were not to be threatened, because that function belonged rightfully to the *mujtahids* themselves and that prerogative had been usurped by the shah. Already during the reign of Shāh Ṭahmāsp, when the influence of the *ṣadr* declined, there were indications of a desire on the part of the *mujtahids* to reassert their authority. The strong rule of 'Abbās I had militated against any attempt on the part of the '*ulamā* to challenge the authority of the Shāh, and the Shāh used to boast that his reign was free from the destructive dissensions between rival religious officials, and from their aspirations to political power.

> It is related, that when he [Shāh 'Abbās I] was one day riding with the celebrated Meer Mahomed Bauker Dâmâd[5] on his right hand, and the equally famed Shaikh Bahâudeen Aumilee[6] on his left, the king desired to discover if there lurked any secret envy, or jealousy, in the breasts of these two learned priests. Turning to Meer Mahomed Bauker, whose horse was prancing and capering, he observed, "What a dull brute Shaikh Bahâudeen is riding! He cannot make the animal keep pace with us." "The wonder is, how the horse moves at all," said the Moolah, "when he considers what a load of learning and knowledge he has upon his back." 'Abbās, after some time, turned round to Shaikh Bahâudeen, and said to him, "Did you ever see such a prancing animal as that which Meer Mahomed Bauker rides? Surely that is not the style for a horse to go in who carried a grave Moolah." "Your Majesty will, I am assured," said the Shaikh, "forgive the horse, when you reflect on the just right he has to be proud of his rider." The monarch bent his head forward on his saddle, and returned thanks to the Almighty for the singular blessing He had bestowed upon his reign, of two wise and pious men; who, though living at a court, had minds untainted by envy and hatred.[7]

It is hard to avoid the suspicion that the Shāh also bent his head forward to conceal the broad grin on his face!

If 'Abbās I was able to manage his theologians in this way, his successors were less and less able to do so. They themselves were to a large extent responsible for creating a situation in which the religious classes were able to increase their power. The all-important office of *ṣadr* was left vacant by 'Abbās II for eighteen months after his accession in 1642, and in 1666 Shāh Sulaymān divided the *ṣadārat* (the office of the *ṣadr*) into a "crown" (*khāṣṣa*) and a "state" (*mamālik*) branch. Although this was a logical step in view of the increased importance of the *khāṣṣa* branch of the administration, the division of the office necessarily meant shared and therefore weakened authority. The *ṣadr* continued to be responsible for the administration of the *awqāf* (lands, etc., held in mortmain for pious purposes), and had certain juridical functions. The political role of the *ṣadr*, however, was taken over by the *shaykh al-islām* and, during the reign of Sulaymān's successor, Shāh Sulṭān Ḥusayn, by a new religious official termed the *mullābāshī*. One of the most important features of the period from 'Abbās II onwards is the greatly enhanced influence of the religious classes as a whole, as they freed themselves progressively from political control. Powerful theologians emerged of whom a typical example is Muḥammad Bāqir Majlisī, who held the office of *shaykh al-islām* from 1687 and, after the accession of Shāh Sulṭān Ḥusayn in 1694, was appointed to the new office of *mullābāshī* and held it until his death in 1699. It is ironical that, in a state in which Ithnā 'Asharī Shi'ism had from the start been the official religion, it was only in the twilight of the Safavid regime that serious work was done in the fields of Shī'ī theology and jurisprudence, in the form of the collection and collation of Shī'ī traditions,[8] commentaries on the four Shī'ī canonical books, and so on. It is tempting to speculate whether the Safavid shahs may not have been more concerned about power than about Shi'ism. As Ithnā 'Asharī Shi'ism was codified under the later Safavids and became more uncompromisingly orthodox, there was naturally greater emphasis on the rooting out of heresy. One theologian of Rasht entitled Ḥujjat al-Islām (Proof of Islam) is said to have put to death seventy persons for various sins or heresies.[9]

A group that suffered particularly during this period of the persecution of heretics was the Ṣūfīs. The tightly knit Ṣūfī organisation of the Safavid Order had, in the days before the establishment of the Safavid state, disseminated the Safavid *da'va*, or propaganda, had guarded the person of its leader, the *murshid-i kāmil*, or perfect spiritual director, and had worked ceaselessly to promote the Safavid revolution. After the successful culmination of this revolution, Shāh Ismā'īl I had tried to incorporate this Ṣūfī organisation in the more conventional administrative system, based on the Iranian Islamic tradition, which he had inherited from the Āq Quyūnlū, the Qarā Quyūnlū and the Timurids. As we have seen, the attempt failed, and the Ṣūfī organisation remained in existence but without any organic function within the body politic. Although devoid of any real power, the head of this organisation, the *khalīfat al-khulafā*, retained considerable prestige at least up to the time of Shāh Ismā'īl II.

The reason why this Ṣūfī organisation had been allowed to continue in being long after it had ceased to serve its original purpose, was that it provided the Safavid shahs with a convenient mechanism which could be used to support their own legitimacy, and to which they could appeal in the event of any challenge to their own authority on the part of *qizilbāsh* chiefs and others. An essential part of the relationship between any Ṣūfī or *murīd* (disciple) and his spiritual director (*pīr*; *shaykh*; *murshid*) was the unquestioning obedience of the disciple to the commands of his spiritual director. The basic principles of the *pīr–murīd* relationship were: "not to leave the side of one's *murshid* in adversity or prosperity; to endure patiently all kinds of misfortune; and to put acquiescence to the will of the *murshid* before all worldly interests".[10] The Safavid shahs developed and extended this relationship in two extremely significant ways: in the first place, they transferred to the political plane what was essentially a religious and mystical relationship between a spiritual director and a traveller along the *via purgativa*. They were able to do this because they were not only the *murshid-i kāmil* but also the *pādishāh*, or temporal ruler, of their subjects. Disobedience to the orders of the *murshid-i kāmil*, which in Ṣūfī Orders would normally be punished by penance or by expulsion from the Order, thus became treason against the king and a crime against the state, and as such punishable by death. "Conduct appropriate to a Ṣūfī" (*ṣūfīgarī*) therefore acquired a new and significant connotation of "loyalty to the king"; the converse, *nā-ṣūfīgarī*, "conduct inappropriate to a Ṣūfī", became the equivalent of "disloyalty to the king" and the most serious charge that could be levelled against a person. In times of crisis, the Safavid shahs found it convenient to invoke the unquestioning devotion to their own persons of the Ṣūfīs, by appealing to those who were *shāhī-sevän* (who loved the shah), to come to their aid.

If there was the slightest doubt about the loyalty of the *khalīfat al-khulafā* himself or of the other members of the Ṣūfī organisation, the shah acted swiftly to establish his supremacy. In 1576, Ismā'īl II took severe disciplinary measures against the *khalīfat al-khulafā*, whom he had blinded, and he followed this up by massacring 1,200 Ṣūfīs who were closely associated with the *khalīfat al-khulafā*. The charge against the *khalīfat al-khulafā* stated that he had wilfully disobeyed an order from his *murshid-i kāmil*, namely, Shāh Ismā'īl II, and was therefore rejected or "beyond the pale". The rapid decline in the status of the Ṣūfīs, however, occurred after the accession of 'Abbās I. Shāh 'Abbās became suspicious of the Ṣūfīs because, at the beginning of his reign, they had conspired to put his father, Sulṭān Muḥammad Shāh, back on the throne. Sulṭān Muḥammad Shāh was persuaded to incite the Ṣūfīs to seek a meeting with Shāh 'Abbās and to put him the following question: "Who is our spiritual director?" The point of the question was that, since Sulṭān Muḥammad Shāh was still alive, he was still their spiritual director and 'Abbās a usurper. The Ṣūfīs hoped that 'Abbās would be forced to admit this, and that Sulṭān Muḥammad Shāh would be reinstated as their spiritual director and therefore as king. Shāh 'Abbās was forewarned of the intention of the Ṣūfīs. He ordered them to send three representatives to him if they had anything to discuss. When the delegation arrived, its members were executed on the spot, and the remainder of the Ṣūfīs scattered "without even stopping to put their shoes on". From that time on, 'Abbās I took every opportunity to reduce the status of the Ṣūfīs, by ignoring them and treating them with disdain. A few years later, in 1592/3, the Ṣūfīs incurred the wrath of Shāh 'Abbās again, when one of their leaders, Shāhverdī Khān, Governor of Qarājadāgh, was executed on the grounds that he had collaborated with the Ottomans during their occupation of Tabrīz. Disloyalty on the part of the Ṣūfīs from Qarājadāgh was viewed particularly seriously by the Shāh, because this group had held a position of special honour during the early Safavid period. Shāhverdī Khān's father, Khalīfa-yi Anṣār Qarājadāghlū, had been commandant of the fortress–prison of Qahqaha, a post given only to the most trustworthy officers. Shāhverdī Khān had not only defected to the Ottomans himself, but had forced his followers to take the oath of allegiance to the Ottomans. Shāh 'Abbās had a long memory in such matters; some twenty years later, in 1614/15, a number of these followers fell into his hands and were promptly executed on a charge of *nā-ṣūfīgarī* (conduct unbecoming to a Ṣūfī and disloyalty to the king).

'Abbās felt that, if he could no longer rely implicitly on the loyalty of the Ṣūfīs, there was no point in allowing them to retain their privileged status. They were no longer allowed to be in attendance on the Shāh, or to act as his personal bodyguard. Instead, they were allotted menial tasks such as sweepers of the palace buildings, gatekeepers and jailers.[11] Their outward ritual was maintained to the extent that they continued to meet every Thursday evening for *ẕikr* meetings under the leadership of their *khalīfat al-khulafā*, but the *khalīfat al-khulafā* himself was reduced to the status of a tame religious official at court. On feast days, he appeared at court with the rest of the Ṣūfīs, and approached the Shāh with a bowl of candies, and offered him the felicitations appropriate to the festival. The Shāh would then take a piece of candy from the bowl and place it in his mouth, whereupon the nobles and leaders of the realm would follow suit, first placing the candy on their eyes and their foreheads as a sign of obeisance. The *khalīfat al-khulafā* had one other function. He was able to give absolution. Nobles and others who sought absolution would kneel before the *khalīfat al-khulafā*, and the latter would strike them several times on the back and shoulders with a stick, as a sign that their sins were forgiven. This ceremony was called "confession" (*i'tirāf*).[12]

After the death of Shāh 'Abbās I, the status of the Ṣūfīs continued to decline, and in the late seventeenth century, less than two hundred years after Ṣūfī zeal and devotion had brought the Safavids to power, the *mujtahid* Muḥammad Bāqir Majlisī denounced Sufism as "this foul and hellish growth". Muḥammad Bāqir was defending his father, Muḥammad Taqī Majlisī, also a distinguished theologian, against charges of having been too tolerant of and sympathetic to Ṣūfīs. "Let none think so ill of my father," he said, "as to imagine that he was of the Ṣūfīs...My father thought ill of the Ṣūfīs, but at the beginning of his career, when they were extremely powerful and active, my father entered their ranks so that by this means he might repel, remove, eradicate and extirpate the roots of this foul and hellish growth."[13] "My father," he said, "would never have contaminated the hem of his garment with the defilement of Sufism!" In his voluminous writings, Muḥammad Bāqir Majlisī attacked the most fundamental principles of Sufism, and took the extreme position that all Ṣūfī sects were outside the pale of Islam. Both the monastic principle, and the practice of living as a hermit or in retreat, were prohibited by the Prophet, he said. Various Ṣūfī practices such as the *ẕikr-i khafī* and the *ẕikr-i jalī*[14] constituted *bid'a* (an innovation; a departure from accepted practice) and were therefore unacceptable. Regular Ṣūfī practices such as the wearing of woollen garments, and the dance (*samā'*) which often accompanied the rhythmic chanting of the name of God, were also condemned by Majlisī. Fasting was denounced because it weakened the body and hence enfeebled the mind, with the result that any statement made by the *pīr*, or spiritual director, however fantastic, found credence. Warming to his task, Majlisī thundered that all Ṣūfī sects, from the point of view of the Shī'ī faith, were to be rejected and renounced, and their *ẕikrs* and other practices were to be considered innovation and error. Finally, certain Ṣūfī doctrines regarding the mystical union of the disciple with God, and regarding incarnation (*ḥulūl*), constituted unbelief and heresy, he said. What an extraordinary reversal of fortune for the descendants of those who had formerly worn the *tāj-i ḥaydarī*, the distinctive headgear devised for his Ṣūfī followers by Ḥaydar, with such pride!

Under weak and ineffective shahs, the *'ulamā* tended to reassert their independence of the political institution. It is no surprise, therefore, to find that they were at the height of their power during the reigns of the two weakest Safavid shahs, Sulaymān and Sulṭān Ḥusayn, who together ruled for fifty-six years, from 1666 to 1722. During this period, the *mujtahids* fully reasserted their independence of the shah, and reclaimed their prerogative to be the representatives of the Twelfth Imām and thus the only legitimate source of authority in a Shī'ī state. It should not be supposed that even a strong ruler like 'Abbās I had been able to muzzle the theologians altogether. Browne quotes a story from the *Qiṣāṣ al-'Ulamā* which must be apocryphal because its theologian–author is said to have died in 1585 while Shāh 'Abbās

I, to whom he is said to have written, did not ascend the throne until 1588.[15] However, like many apocryphal stories, it enshrines an important truth. The theologian addressed his letter to "'Abbās, the founder of a borrowed empire", which does not suggest that he felt in imminent danger of the royal wrath. 'Abbās apparently meekly swallowed this piece of impertinence and sent the theologian a mild reply, signing himself in a very favourite manner, "'Abbās, the dog of 'Alī's threshold".

The *mujtahids*, from asserting more and more their independence of the shah, moved gradually toward a position of actually controlling the shah. According to Banani, "some sources suggest a direct religious rule by means of a concourse of *mujtahids above the monarch* " (my italics).[16] In other words, the potential danger to the stability of the Safavid state, perceived as a threat by Ismā'īl I from the inception of that state, had become a reality. The *'ulamā* pressed forward to obtain a dominant position in the state, heedless of the fact that by so doing they were helping to destroy it.

Another political force which manoeuvred itself into a position of great power during the reigns of Sulaymān and Sulṭān Ḥusayn was the *ḥaram*, and, associated with the *ḥaram*, the office of *vazīr*. As already noticed, control of the princes of the blood royal in the *ḥaram* gave the *ḥaram* extraordinary political power, to which Chardin drew attention. The *ḥaram*, he said, constituted "a Privy Council, which usually prevails over everything, and lays down the law in all matters".[17] This "Privy Council" consisted of the shah's mother, the chief eunuchs and the shah's principal mistresses. The *vazīrs*, according to Chardin, ignored the wishes of the *ḥaram* at their peril. The royal princes under its control were reared in a state of unbelievable ignorance about the outside world. "The eldest son of the King," says Chardin, "is never told that he is the heir-apparent. Sometimes he is not even told that he is the King's son, but merely that he is of royal blood. The result is, he does not know for what he is destined until the sceptre is placed in his hand."[18] It is small wonder that the products of this system were weak-willed and easily manipulated by the *ḥaram* and the *vazīrs*. Another probably apocryphal, but again significant, story is told about the succession to Shāh Sulaymān. The latter did not nominate an heir, but is alleged to have said to his officers of state that, if they wanted peace and quiet, they should choose his son

34. Shāh Sulaymān

Ḥusayn, but if they wanted a strong ruler and an expanding empire, they should choose his son ʻAbbās. Given a choice in these terms, the *ḥaram* and the *vazīr* selected Ḥusayn, because they hoped to establish their ascendancy over a mild and pliant monarch. Their hopes were soon fulfilled. Shāh Sulṭān Ḥusayn soon abandoned his austere way of life and, like his father Sulaymān, took to drink and debauchery. (Another story alleges that his court officials deliberately introduced him to and encouraged him to drink in order the better to bend him to their will.) He became so uxorious that the size and magnificence of his *ḥaram* was a serious drain on the exchequer. Like Sulaymān, he had no interest in state affairs, and the *ḥaram*, the court and the *vazīr*'s office were able to dictate policy. Against this formidable alliance even the *mujtahids* could make little headway, though occasionally they had a resounding success, as when 60,000 bottles of wine were brought out of the royal cellars and publicly smashed.

The lack of interest in state affairs was a distressing and ultimately disastrous aspect of the reigns of both Sulaymān and Sulṭān Ḥusayn. Within the empire, this lack of interest signalled increasing corruption and inefficiency in provincial government. Insecurity on the highways, always a sign of the breakdown of government, was widespread. Often travellers were robbed by the very officials who were supposed to protect them. In regard to Iran's relations with foreign powers, this lack of interest meant both indifference to the activities of those powers, even when Iran's interests were immediately affected, and a lack of concern about the obvious and growing weakness of the armed forces. A Carmelite wrote in 1685: "Many ambassadors are coming here from the Christian princes to stir up the king to make war against the Turks, but in vain; for he rather shows displeasure at the defeats of the latter, besides which his object and world is nothing else than wine and women."[19] The military weakness of the country was thrown into sharp relief in 1698/9, when a band of Balūchī tribesmen raided Kirmān, nearly reached Yazd and threatened Bandar ʻAbbās. Shāh Sulṭān Ḥusayn turned to the Georgian prince Giorgi XI, who happened to be at the Safavid court, for help in repelling the Balūchīs; Giorgi was appointed Governor of Kirmān in 1699, and defeated the invaders. This story speaks for itself; that a Safavid king should have to turn for help to a visiting Georgian prince was humiliating enough, but the

inferences one may draw from this are alarming: either Shāh Sulṭān Ḥusayn did not know where else he could find a body of troops to deal with an emergency, or he had the troops but did not trust them. In any event, the Shāh did not think there was any cause for alarm, for in 1706 he left the capital and was away for nearly a year on pilgrimage to the two chief Shīʿī shrines in Iran, that of Fāṭima the daughter of the 7th Imām, at Qum, and that of her brother, the 8th Imām ʿAlī al-Rizā, at Mashhad. Shāh Sulṭān Ḥusayn took with him his *ḥaram*, his court and a retinue numbering 60,000; the cost of this expedition not only drained the exchequer but placed an intolerable burden of additional taxation on the provinces through which the royal cavalcade passed. Comparisons may be odious, but the picture of ʿAbbās I striding along on foot and covering the distance between Iṣfahān and Mashhad in twenty-eight days in 1601, when he made the pilgrimage to the shrine of the 8th Imām, provides a striking contrast. Not for nothing was Shāh Sulṭān Ḥusayn derisively dubbed "Mullā Ḥusayn"!

Ten years after the Balūchī incursion, the military feebleness of the Safavid empire and, in particular, the defenceless state of the eastern frontier, were demonstrated again, and this time with more serious consequences for the Safavid state. In 1709, the Ghilzāy Afghāns under their leader, Mīr Vays, seized Qandahār and killed Giorgi XI; Qandahār had been in Safavid hands since its recapture by ʿAbbās II in 1648. Shāh Sulṭān Ḥusayn dispatched from Iṣfahān Giorgi's nephew, Kay Khusraw, but the latter was unable to restore the situation. There seems to have been friction between him and the *qizilbāsh* troops under his command, friction of a type which recalls earlier instances of dissension between the *qizilbāsh* and Tājīk, i.e., Iranian, commanders. Although Kay Khusraw, like all Georgians in Safavid employ, was a convert to Islam, in his case, as in many others, the conversion was purely nominal, and this again occasioned friction between him and his Muslim troops. Moreover, Kay Khusraw's position seems to have been weakened by treasury officials and other bureaucrats at Iṣfahān who strongly resented the hold of this Georgian "dynasty" over Shāh Sulṭān Ḥusayn, and who withheld or greatly delayed payments to his troops. Georgi XI had been deposed by Shāh

---

35. Shāh Sulṭān Ḥusayn

Sulaymān in 1688, reinstated in 1691, had lost his throne again in 1695 as the result of intrigue, and had taken refuge at the Safavid court. With him came his brother Levan (Leon), who was appointed *dīvānbegī*[20] of Iṣfahān about the year 1700, and his nephew Kay Khusraw, who became *dārūgha*, or Governor, of Iṣfahān. Kay Khusraw decided to starve Qandahār into surrender, and at the end of two months the Afghāns offered to surrender on terms. When Kay Khusraw insisted on an unconditional surrender, Mīr Vays summoned help from the Balūchīs, who turned the tables on the besiegers by cutting their supply-lines. Kay Khusraw, forced to withdraw, was attacked by the Afghāns; his army was routed, with the loss of all its cannon and baggage, and he himself was killed. Another force was sent out from Iṣfahān under the aged *qūrchībāshī* Muḥammad Zamān Khān, who died before he reached Qandahār; as a result, his troops dispersed. After that, Mīr Vays was left in undisturbed possession of Qandahār until his own death in 1715. His son Maḥmūd assumed the leadership of the Ghilzāy Afghāns the following year.

It is doubtful whether Mīr Vays aspired to overthrow the Safavid state, although he had had ample opportunity to see for himself the weakness of that state at the centre when Giorgi had sent him a prisoner to Iṣfahān. By astutely playing on the hostility of Giorgi's enemies there, and by judicious use of bribes, Mīr Vays had succeeded in getting the ear of Shāh Sulṭān Ḥusayn, to whom he had protested his own innocence of any design against Iran, and had complained about the injustice and brutality of Giorgi's regime at Qandahār. Mīr Vays had certainly taken the opportunity to equip himself with a legal basis for any future revolt against Iran, for, on a pilgrimage to Mecca (itself part of his plan to surround himself with the odour of sanctity) he had obtained a *fatvā* (legal opinion) from the Sunnī *'ulamā* to the effect that it would be lawful for him to break his oath of allegiance to a heretical (i.e., Shī'ī) shah. Back in Iṣfahān, he found the court in a jittery state regarding the real intentions of a Russian mission headed by one Israel Ori which was on its way from Tsar Peter the Great. Rumours were soon rife to the effect that Israel Ori was descended from the ancient kings of Armenia and had announced that he intended to claim his patrimony. Foreigners resident in Iran magnified this alleged danger to the utmost: the Catholic missionaries because they thought Ori intended to get them expelled from Iran, and the European merchants because they thought that part of Ori's mission was to secure an increase in Russian trade with Iran at their expense. Michel, the French envoy who had recently concluded a treaty with Shāh Sulṭān Ḥusayn, did his utmost to warn the Shāh's ministers of Ori's reputedly sinister designs, and either he or someone else is said to have pointed out to them that the name Israel Ori was an anagram for *il sera roi*! Mīr Vays exploited this situation to the utmost, insinuating that Peter the Great was about to invade Iran and annex Georgia and Armenia, and that Giorgi intended to defect to him with all his Georgian troops. The upshot was that Mīr Vays was given a robe of honour by the Shāh, and sent back to Qandahār to keep a check on the supposedly disloyal Giorgi.

After the death of Mīr Vays in 1715, his peace-loving brother 'Abd al-'Azīz succeeded him as chief of the Ghilzāy Afghāns. In 1716, when 'Abd al-'Azīz proposed to submit to Shāh Sulṭān Ḥusayn, the tribesmen incited Mīr Vays's elder son, Maḥmūd, to murder his uncle and assume the leadership of the Ghilzāys. Whether or not Mīr Vays had dreamed of overthrowing Shāh Sulṭān Ḥusayn, it was certainly the ambition of his son Maḥmūd to do so. He was materially aided in furthering this ambition by the revolt of the other major grouping of Afghān tribes, the Abdālīs, who inhabited the region of Harāt. The Abdālīs failed to take Mashhad, but inflicted a number of humiliating defeats on various Safavid forces sent against them. A striking feature of the declining years of the Safavid dynasty is the low morale of the Safavid armies, the legacy of years of neglect of the military; coupled with this was a dearth of field commanders of ability and experience. Knowledge of the Shāh's way of life cannot have raised the morale of the troops. After the loss of the Bahrein Islands (1717), Maryam Begum, Shāh Sulaymān's aunt, upbraided Shāh Sulṭān Ḥusayn for his indolence and indifference to the fate of the state. She set an example by giving a large sum of money to raise another army against the rebels, and the Shāh was shamed into moving court to Qazvīn in order to levy some fresh troops, but once again inaction was the order of the day:

The leaders and pillars of that state, each one by reason of his vain personal interests and hypocrisy against the others, veiled his eyes to what was expedient for the state. Whenever anyone wished to move [against the enemy], each [of the others] would make an excuse and prevent anything from being done. They postponed their departure and occupied themselves with pleasure. For three years they remained in Qazvīn, practising the selling of offices and the receiving of bribes.[21]

The Afghāns were by no means the only neighbours of Iran to sense that the collapse of the Safavid empire was near and that portions of it might be annexed without the expenditure of too much effort. Peter the Great was in close touch with the Georgians and Armenians, and the regions inhabited by those peoples. In 1715, the Tsar sent the 28-year-old Artemii Petrovich Volynsky as ambassador to Shāh Sulṭān Ḥusayn; he was to conclude a commercial treaty with Iran, and in particular seek to divert the silk transit trade, then carried by Armenian merchants through Syria and Turkey, through Russian territory; he was also to collect as much military intelligence as possible, including information on Iranian resources and communications.[22] Volynsky reported that the general situation in Iran was so disturbed, and the army so demoralised and inefficient, that the country could easily be conquered by a small Russian army. Both Volynsky and John Bell, the Scottish surgeon attached to his mission, reported that Shāh Sulṭān Ḥusayn left the conduct of affairs of state wholly to his ministers.[23] On Volynsky's return journey through Shīrvān, he received a message from the Georgian prince Wakhtang, a nephew of Giorgi XI and a brother of the Kay Khusraw killed at Qandahār, offering to co-operate with Russian forces if the latter invaded Iran.[24]

It was Maḥmūd's good fortune to seize the chieftainship of the Ghilzāy Afghāns at a time when not only the Safavid state but also the Mogul empire was in decline. After the death of the Emperor Awrangzīb in 1717, the Mogul empire was torn apart by the incessant struggles of rival claimants to the throne, and Maḥmūd knew that, if he marched west into Iran, he had nothing to fear from Mogul forces in his rear, in particular any attempt on their part to recover Qandahār. Maḥmūd, having achieved what Shāh Sulṭān Ḥusayn could not, the defeat of the Abdālī Afghāns, received from the grateful Shāh the governorship of Qandahār and the title of Ḥusayn Qulī (the slave of Ḥusayn) Khān. In the late summer of 1719, Maḥmūd demonstrated the ironical nature of this title by leading a force of some 11,000 men across the Dasht-i Lūt to Kirmān, which he entered unopposed.[25]

After he had been at Kirmān for nine months, he hurriedly returned to Qandahār on hearing news of an attempted *coup* against him there. Shāh Sulṭān Ḥusayn took no advantage of this breathing-space to put his own house in order. Such action as was taken was directed against the Arabs of Muscat rather than toward strengthening the eastern defences. The Shāh continued to remain at Qazvīn, much to the indignation of the population of the capital, where in 1719 there had been a second conspiracy with the aim of replacing Shāh Sulṭān Ḥusayn by his more vigorous and competent brother ʻAbbās; this plot ended in failure, as had the earlier one in 1715. Any chance of positive action on the part of the principal officers of state was frustrated by the rivalries and dissensions among them, dissensions which the Shāh took no steps either to resolve or terminate. In the summer of 1720, the *vazīr* Fatḥ ʻAlī Khān Dāghistānī finally decided to give priority to the restoration of Safavid sovereignty in the provinces of Harāt and Qandahār. His plan was that the royal army should march by easy stages to Khurāsān, and that his nephew Luṭf ʻAlī Khān, the Governor-General of Fārs, should join forces with it en route. The plan came to nothing, apparently as a result of the opposition on the part of Muḥammad Ḥusayn the *mullābāshī*[26] and Raḥīm Khān the *ḥakīm-bāshī*, or chief physician. The Shāh refused to leave Qazvīn until October 1720, and then moved only to Tehran, 90 miles to the east. In December 1720, the *mullābāshī* and the *ḥakīm-bāshī*, by producing forged evidence, convinced the Shāh that the *vazīr* was plotting against his life. The credulous Shāh believed their story, and ordered the execution of the *vazīr*, but the conspirators, wishing to get their hands on his alleged vast wealth, merely arrested him and had him blinded. Next, the conspirators seized the *vazīr*'s nephew Luṭf ʻAlī Khān and dismissed him from his governorship and army command. Replacing him by a certain Ismāʻīl Khān, they put the latter in command of the remnants of Luṭf ʻAlī Khān's troops and dispatched him to Khurāsān, but Ismāʻīl Khān was unable even to subdue the rebellious Governor of Tūn.

The Ottoman Sulṭān had, like the Tsar, been receiving reports about the state of weakness and near collapse obtaining in Iran, and in 1720 he sent Durrī Efendi as ambassador to the Shāh's court. The Shāh's pusillanimous ministers, who had worked themselves up into a state of panic over the mission of Israel Ori, convinced themselves that Durrī Efendi had come to announce a declaration of war by the Ottoman Sulṭān. Reassured on that point, they arranged an audience for the Ottoman ambassador with Shāh Sulṭān Ḥusayn. In his subsequent report to the Sulṭān, Durrī Efendi made a number of interesting observations. Like Volynsky, he commented on the lack of intelligence of those then in charge of the affairs of the Safavid state; he also commented on the inadequacy of the numbers of those working on the land, which resulted in the price of wheat, barley and other commodities being twice as high in Iran as in Turkey. In the cities, on the other hand, there was great wealth, and prosperous merchant communities engaged in the manufacture of silks, satins and other stuffs.[27] Fortunately for Iran, the intentions of Sulṭān Aḥmed III were peaceable, since those of Tsar Peter the Great were most definitely not. Volynsky, after he had submitted his (from the Russian point of view) encouraging report on Iran in 1717, had been appointed Governor of Astrakhan with orders to hold a watching brief in regard to affairs in Iran, and a number of Russian military and naval officers were hard at work preparing detailed surveys of the Caspian coasts and reports on military routes in Gīlān. In 1719, the Tsar sent Semeon Avramov as consul in Rasht. By 1721, if not before, the Tsar had decided to invade Iran, giving as his *casus belli* two incidents involving Russian nationals in Iran; neither incident had been willed by the Iranian government; on the contrary, both incidents had occurred because of the lack of will of the government to govern. The Russian consul at Rasht, Semeon Avramov, was ordered to go to Iṣfahān to protest about these incidents, but was unable to reach the city because the siege of Iṣfahān by the Afghāns was already in progress.

In the late summer of 1721, Maḥmūd had again crossed the Dasht-i Lūt, as on the previous occasion losing men and animals in the heat and drought of the desert, and reached Kirmān in October. The city was occupied, but the Governor-General, Rustam Muḥammad Sa'dlū, repulsed an assault on the citadel with heavy losses to the Afghāns. By the end of January 1722, there were murmurings in the Afghān ranks, and some men had already deserted, when Maḥmūd had an unexpected piece of good fortune; Rustam Muḥammad Sa'dlū died, and his successor saved Maḥmūd's face by bribing him to raise the siege. Maḥmūd marched away to Yazd but, repulsed again there, he by-passed the city and marched on the Safavid capital, Iṣfahān. In the capital, there were divided counsels. The *vazīr* advised the defence of the city, on the grounds that the only forces available were no match for the Afghāns in the open field; others counselled an immediate offensive. The Shāh decided to attack; there was a hasty levy of untrained peasants and merchants, many of whom had never borne arms before, in the Iṣfahān area, and this scratch force, with only a stiffening of regular troops from the *ghulām* regiments and tribal levies, marched out to meet Maḥmūd at Gulnābād, about 18 miles from Iṣfahān. Whatever chance of victory this motley army might have had was vitiated by dissensions between the joint-commanders, the *vazīr* and the Vālī of ʻArabistān. Inept battle tactics on the part of the Safavid field commanders, and the steadiness of Maḥmūd's general Amān Allāh, converted a possible Afghān defeat into a victory. Maḥmūd could have entered Iṣfahān the same day, 8 March 1722, but he wrongly thought that there would be Safavid reserves available to be hurled against him.

Thus began the long drawn-out agony of Iṣfahān. The Afghāns, too few in numbers to risk an assault, contented themselves with blockading the city. Within the city, the Shāh was in the hands of a treacherous group of appeasers. Early in June, the troops of the Vālī of Luristān, ʻAlī Mardān Khān, reached a point only 40 miles north-west of Iṣfahān, and demanded the abdication of Shāh Sulṭān Ḥusayn in favour of his brother ʻAbbās. The Shāh refused, but his third son, Ṭahmāsp, who was weak and ineffectual like his father, was passed through the Afghān lines; instead of joining forces with ʻAlī Mardān Khān, however, Ṭahmāsp went to Qazvīn, where he proclaimed himself Shāh Ṭahmāsp II, but otherwise remained inactive. Within the capital, famine was now acute; the people ate cats, dogs, mice and even human flesh; hundreds of rotting corpses clogged the streets. Finally, after a six-month siege, Shāh Sulṭān Ḥusayn surrendered the city unconditionally to Maḥmūd on 12 October 1722. At least 80,000 people are said to have perished during the siege from starvation and disease. On 25 October, Maḥmūd entered Iṣfahān and ascended the throne. For more than half a century, the political, military and social foundations of the Safavid state had been steadily eroded; its overthrow, when it came, needed only a slight push on the part of some 20,000 Afghāns.

The Afghāns, although they were now the nominal rulers of

Iran, never succeeded in making themselves masters of the whole country, and for fourteen years representatives of the Safavid family maintained a shadowy existence in various parts of northern Iran. The *roi-fainéant* Ṭahmāsp II was driven out of Qazvīn and retreated to Tabrīz, but the Afghāns were then themselves driven out of Qazvīn by the townspeople, a clear indication of what might have been achieved under more loyal, resolute and capable leadership. Maḥmūd, fearing a similar uprising of the civilian population at Iṣfahān, slaughtered many high-ranking Iranian officials and nobles, together with about 3,000 *qizilbāsh* guards. Again, this action shows clearly the precarious nature of the Afghān hold on Iran. In February 1725, Maḥmūd, his fears again aroused by reports that Ṣafī, another of Shāh Sulṭān Ḥusayn's sons, had escaped from Iṣfahān, ordered a general massacre of all members of the Safavid royal house with the exception of Shāh Sulṭān Ḥusayn and two young princes; at least eighteen members of the royal house perished in this massacre. Two months later, Maḥmūd was overthrown by a *coup* in favour of his cousin, Ashraf, who was proclaimed shah on 26 April 1725. For some time Maḥmūd's behaviour had been unpredictable, bordering on madness. Some authorities declare that he was suffering from leprosy; others, that he was paralysed. On the basis of the description of the symptoms of Maḥmūd's illness contained in Krusinski, however, there is very little doubt that Maḥmūd, at the time of his overthrow, was in the final stages of tertiary syphilis.[28] Maḥmūd either died shortly after the *coup*, or was done away with by Ashraf, at the age of twenty-six.

While the people of Iṣfahān were enduring the hardships of the Afghān siege, the Tsar Peter the Great embarked at Astrakhan in July 1772 with a huge army of more than 100,000 men, and went ashore off Terki on the west coast of the Caspian. During the southward march along the coast, the Tsar's men suffered from the unaccustomed heat, and many died of heat-stroke. The Tsar marched as far south as Darband, some 150 miles from his point of disembarkation, but shortage of supplies, the onset of winter and the hostility of the Ottoman government toward his venture, forced him to retire. Considering that he lost about one-third of his entire force, the results of this expedition were meagre.

We have already seen that the increased militancy of the Shīʿī theologians during the reigns of Shāh Sulaymān and Shāh Sulṭān

Ḥusayn had led to the placing of greater emphasis on the rooting out of heresy. This increased militancy may have been a factor of the revolt of the Sunnī Kurds in 1704, but it was the non-Muslim religious minorities which bore the brunt of religious persecution. Shāh Sulṭān Ḥusayn was persuaded to sign a decree for the forcible conversion of the Zoroastrians, and many Jews were also forced to embrace Islam. The Christian minority groups, consisting in the main of Armenians belonging to the Gregorian Church, suffered less, but the law passed by 'Abbās I and re-enacted by 'Abbās II, entitling a Jew or Christian who became a Muslim to claim the property of his relatives, was from time to time enforced. Shāh Sulṭān Ḥusayn does not seem to have been hostile to Christians personally, but was persuaded to issue unjust and intolerant decrees by the religious leaders who had so much influence over him, in particular the *mullābāshī* Muḥammad Bāqir Majlisī and a later holder of that office, his grandson Mīr Muḥammad Ḥusayn Khātūnābādī, who died in 1739.

Serious as were the implications of this policy for the internal peace and prosperity of the Safavid state, its implications in regard to Iran's relations with foreign powers were potentially disastrous. As mentioned earlier, the Ottoman Sulṭān Aḥmed III (1703–30), was a ruler of peaceable disposition. His reign is known as the "Tulip period", and represents the last flowering of Ottoman artistic achievement in architecture, miniature-painting, ceramics and textiles. His Grand Vizier, Dāmād Ibrāhīm, was a generous patron of literature and the arts, and was responsible for the setting up of the first printing press in Istanbul. His policy toward Iran was one of non-interference and friendship, but he and the Sulṭān were under considerable pressure to go to the aid of the Sunnī populations of Shīrvān and Dāghistān who were feeling the weight of Shī'ī persecution. The signature of the Treaty of Passarovitz with Austria and Venice in 1718 freed Turkey's hands in the west, and encouraged Turkish irredentists to agitate for military action against Iran designed to regain those areas of north-western Iran which had been seized by the Ottomans during the reign of Sulṭān Muḥammad Shāh.

After the fall of Iṣfahān to the Afghāns in October 1722, Ṭahmāsp II sent an envoy to the Porte asking for assistance against the Afghān usurpers. The Grand Vizier replied that, if Ṭahmāsp would cede to the Ottoman empire all the provinces claimed by the latter, Turkey would help Ṭahmāsp to recover the rest of Iran. *Mutatis mutandis*, these were precisely the same terms as had been offered to Ṭahmāsp by Peter the Great. The Tsar's showing of the flag in the Caspian coastal provinces in 1722 had occasioned great alarm in Istanbul, and there was a flurry of diplomatic activity as the possibility of war between Russia and Turkey became stronger or receded. The outcome was the Russo-Ottoman Treaty for the partition of Iran's north-west provinces, dated 24 June 1724.[29] The dismemberment of Iran was short-lived. Six Russian battalions landed in Gīlān in 1723, and another Russian force captured Bākū, but the death of Peter the Great in 1725 meant the end for the time being of Russian expansionist policies, and Turkish encroachments on Iranian territory after 1726 were terminated by Nādir Khān (later Nādir Shāh).

Ashraf had succeeded Maḥmūd on 26 April 1725. His territory consisted of central and southern Iran, the province of Sīstān, and the western part of Khurāsān, but in reality the Afghāns controlled only the principal urban centres in those regions. Ashraf, who had throughout been on bad terms with Maḥmūd because the latter had been the murderer of his (Ashraf's) father, inaugurated his reign by executing all Maḥmūd's principal supporters; to make his position even more secure, he then put to death the Afghān officers who had placed him on the throne, and blinded his own brother. He then attempted to lure the deposed Safavid Shāh, Sulṭān Ḥusayn, to his death by offering him the crown; Sulṭān Ḥusayn wisely avoided this trap, and countered by offering his own daughter in marriage to Ashraf. Reassured that he had nothing to fear from the ex-Shāh, Ashraf next tried to lure the *soi-disant* Ṭahmāsp II into a meeting with him, but some loyal Iranian nobles, subsequently executed by Ashraf, warned Ṭahmāsp of Ashraf's intentions. Ashraf then marched against Ṭahmāsp, caught his men by surprise near Tehran and routed them; Ṭahmāsp escaped to Māzandarān, where he was eventually joined by the *qizilbāsh* chief of the Qājār tribe, Fatḥ 'Alī Khān.

In 1726, the Ottomans, taking advantage of the 1724 Treaty with Russia, marched into north-western Iran with a force of 60,000 men and 70 guns under Aḥmad Pasha. Checked between Qazvīn and Iṣfahān, the Turks were subjected to psychological warfare by Ashraf, who sent four *mollās* to Aḥmad Pasha to enquire why he was waging war on fellow-Sunnīs "who were obeying the divine precepts of the law in subverting the power of the heretical Shias"[30] Aḥmad Pasha protested that he was only carrying out the orders of the Sulṭān, but Ashraf's propaganda had the effect of causing many of the Pasha's Kurdish, and some Turkish, troops to desert. Aḥmad Pasha hastily attacked Ashraf near Hamadān before his forces became further depleted, but the desertion of a further 20,000 Kurdish cavalry, and the refusal of many of his Turkish troops to advance, led to his total rout by Ashraf on 20 November 1726. Although Ashraf's victory was one of the factors which led the Porte to recognise him as Shāh of Iran in 1727, it was a much truncated Iran, in fact, little different from the one which Ṭashmāsp II could have ruled had he been prepared to do what Ashraf did, namely, to cede to the Ottomans all Iran's Caucasian and north-western provinces.

In 1729, Ashraf resumed the offensive against Ṭahmāsp II, who had found in Nādir Khān Afshār a new champion to replace Fatḥ 'Alī Khān Qājār. Defeated in two battles by Ṭahmāsp and Nādir, Ashraf abandoned his capital, Iṣfahān, in November 1729, but was overtaken near Shīrāz and suffered a third defeat. Ashraf himself fled in the direction of Qandahār, but was killed en route, probably by a detachment of Afghān troops sent from Qandahār by his brother Ḥusayn. His death brought to an end the seven-year Afghān interregnum in Iran, during which the country had lapsed into a state of chaos. Nādir Khān entered Iṣfahān on 16 November 1729, and restored the Safavid monarchy by placing Ṭahmāsp II on the throne. (The harmless Shāh Sulṭān Ḥusayn had been murdered by Ashraf prior to the battle with Aḥmad Pasha, because the latter had announced his intention of reinstating the deposed Shāh.) Nādir Khān did not have in mind the permanent restoration of the Safavid dynasty. In August 1732, he deposed Ṭahmāsp II in favour of the latter's eight-month-old son 'Abbās, who was crowned as Shāh 'Abbās III, but even the regency was not sufficient to satisfy Nādir for long, and on 8 March 1736, he had himself crowned as Nādir Shāh, the first ruler of the Afshār dynasty. The Safavid dynasty, which had existed in name only since 1722, no longer existed even in name. The *mullābāshī* Mīrzā 'Abd al-Ḥasan lost his head on the eve of Nādir's coronation because he had been overheard to say, "Everybody is in favour of the Safavid dynasty." Though the Safavid state had been destroyed as a political reality, so strong were its institutions, and so great was its prestige, that its ghost took half a century to lay and was not finally exorcised until the death of the last Safavid puppet shah, Ismā'īl III, in 1773.[31] After a period of vicious civil war between two rival factions, the Zands in the south and the Qājārs in the north, in 1795 the Qājārs, the "last of the *qizilbāsh*", "claimed the Safavid legacy of despotic royalty under a new name".[32] Unfortunately for the Qājārs, they inherited an administrative machine the keys of which had either been thrown away or lost.

NOTES

1 The Lords of Ardabīl

1 Thus the *Ṣafvat al-Ṣafā*; the later source, *Silsilat al-Nasab-i Ṣafaviyya*, gives the name of Quṭb al-Dīn's son as Ṣāliḥ, and makes Amīn al-Dīn Jibrā'īl his grandson. The *Ṣafvat al-Ṣafā* also gives Quṭb al-Dīn's name as Abū Bakr, not Abu'l-Bāqī Aḥmad. Many Safavid sources give, without comment, conflicting evidence on this point.

2 *Awtād* (literally, "stakes", "tent-pegs"), and *abdāl* (literally, "substitutes") rank third and fifth respectively in the Ṣūfī hierarchy of saints (*rijāl al-ghayb*; literally, "men of the Unseen World") who, "unknown by the masses, participate by means of their powerful influence in the preservation of the order of the universe" (see I. Goldziher, article "Abdāl" in *Encyclopaedia of Islam*, 2nd edn, vol. I (London and Leiden 1960), pp. 94–5; hereinafter referred to as EI^2).

3 The ritual dance of the Ṣūfīs, frequently accompanied by music, designed to induce in the performer a trance-like state of ecstasy.

4 R. M. Savory, "The Development of the Early Safawid State under Ismā'īl and Ṭahmāsp", unpublished University of London Ph.D. thesis (1958), p. 13.

5 Savory, "Development", p. 14.

6 A. H. Morton, "The Ardabīl Shrine in the Reign of Shāh Ṭahmāsp I", in *Iran*, XII (1974), p. 51. See this article and its sequel, also by Morton, in *Iran*, XIII (1975), pp. 39–58, for a detailed description of the Ardabīl shrine.

7 The constant remembrance of God and repetition of His name.

8 See Savory, "Development", pp. 90–1.

9 *Suyūrghāl:* "a grant of land or its revenue in lieu of salary or by way of pension" (A. K. S. Lambton, *Landlord and Peasant in Persia* (Oxford 1953), p. 440).

10 See Savory, "Development", and Lambton, *Landlord and Peasant*, p. 104.

11 "Bāz ham Ṣafaviyya", in *Āyanda*, II (1927–8), pp. 803 ff.

12 H. Horst, *Tīmūr und Ḫoǧā 'Alī* (Wiesbaden 1958).

13 *Silsilat al-Nasab-i Ṣafaviyya*, p. 48.

14 Quoted in *Tadhkirat al-Mulūk*, translated and explained by V. Minorsky (London 1943), pp. 189–90 (hereinafter cited as *TM*). I have slightly amended Minorsky's version.

15 Asia Minor.

16 Iskandar Beg Munshī, *Tārīkh-i 'Ālam-ārā-yi 'Abbāsī*, translated by R. M. Savory, Persian Heritage Series, ed. Ehsan Yarshater, no. 28, 2 vols. (Boulder, Colorado, 1978), vol. I, p. 28 (transliteration adapted); hereinafter referred to as *Shah 'Abbas*.

17 The "infidel" in this case was the Christian populations of Circassia, Georgia and Shīrvān.

18 V. Minorsky, "Jihān-shāh Qarā-qoyūnlū and his Poetry", in *Bulletin of the School of Oriental and African Studies*, XVI (1954), p. 274.

19 *Shah 'Abbas*, p. 31.

20 *Shah 'Abbas*, p. 32.

21 John E. Woods, *The Aqquyunlu*, Bibliotheca Islamica (Minneapolis and Chicago 1976), p. 289.

22 R. M. Savory, "The Struggle for Supremacy in Persia after the Death of Tīmūr", in *Der Islam*, XL (1964), p. 58.

23 Savory, "Struggle", p. 59 (both quotations).

24 *TM*, p. 1.

25 Those wishing to pursue this idea are referred to my article, "Some Reflections on Totalitarian Tendencies in the Safavid State", in *Der Islam*, LIII (1976), pp. 226–41.

26 A perversion of the orthodox Muslim profession of faith: "There is no god but God."

27 See Michel M. Mazzaoui, *The Origin of the Ṣafawids* (Wiesbaden 1972), p. 73.

28 See V. Minorsky, "The Poetry of Shāh Ismā'īl I", in *Bulletin of the School of Oriental and African Studies*, X (1942), p. 1047a. See also various publications by T. Gandjei on the subject.

29 See A. S. Tritton, *Islam, Belief and Practice* (London 1951), p. 83; and M. G. S. Hodgson, article "G͟hulāt", in *EI²*, vol. II, pp. 1093–5.

30 See J. Spencer Trimingham, *The Sufi Orders in Islam* (Oxford 1971), p. 83; and article "Bektās͟hiyya" in *EI²*.

31 Quoted in Mazzaoui, p. 83.

32 *Ideals and Realities of Islam* (Boston 1972), p. 127.

33 *Travels of Venetians in Persia*, Hakluyt Society (London 1873), p. 206.

2 The reign of Shāh Ismā'īl I

1 Naṣr Allāh Falsafī, *Zindigānī-yi Shāh 'Abbās-i avval*, 4 vols. (Tehran 1955–61), vol. III, p. 31; also quoted in R. M. Savory, "Iran: A 2,500 year historical and cultural tradition", in *Iranian Civilization and Culture*, ed. Charles J. Adams (Montreal 1972), p. 85.

2 All quotations in this paragraph are from British Library MS. Or 3248, fols. 73b–74b. See R. M. Savory, "The Development of the Early Safawid State", unpublished University of London Ph.D. thesis (1958), pp. 90–1.

3 R. M. Savory, "Safavid Persia", in *Cambridge History of Islam*, 2 vols. (Cambridge 1970), vol. I, p. 398.

4 R. M. Savory, "Some Reflections on Totalitarian Tendencies in the Safavid State", in *Der Islam*, LIII (1976), p. 235; see also Leon Trotsky, *The History of the Russian Revolution*, 3 vols. (London 1967), vol. I, p. 212.

5 *TM*, p. 188.

6 *History of Persia*, 2 vols. (London 1815), vol. I, p. 481.
7 See my article "Ḳizil-bāsh", in *EI*[2].
8 H. A. R. Gibb and Harold Bowen, *Islamic Society and the West* (Oxford 1957), vol. I, part 2, p. 189.
9 J. Spencer Trimingham, *The Sufi Orders in Islam* (Oxford 1971), p. 83.
10 R. M. Savory, "The Consolidation of Ṣafawid Power in Persia", in *Der Islam*, XLI (1965), p. 86.
11 D. Ayalon, *Gunpowder and Firearms in the Mamlūk Kingdom* (London 1956), p. 109.
12 Gibb and Bowen, vol. I, part 2, p. 189.
13 Savory, "Consolidation", p. 88.
14 *Shah 'Abbas*, vol. I, p. 68.
15 Janissary: anglicised form of Turkish *yeñi čerī*: "new soldiery".
16 Quoted in *Travels of Venetians in Persia*, Hakluyt Society (London 1873), p. 62, n. 1.
17 Caterino Zeno, "Travels in Persia", p. 61, in *A Narrative of Italian Travels in Persia in the 15th and 16th centuries*, translated and edited by Charles Grey, in *Travels of Venetians in Persia*.
18 Ayalon, pp. 109–10.
19 R. M. Savory, article "Bārūd. v. The Ṣafawids", in *EI*[2], p. 1067.
20 Caterino Zeno, p. 61.
21 "Jang-i Chāldirān", in *Majalla-yi Dānishkada-yi Adabiyyāt-i Ṭihrān*, I (1953–4), p. 121.
22 Savory, "Consolidation", p. 93.
23 See *Shah 'Abbas*, vol. I, pp. 71–2.
24 R. M. Savory, "The Principal Offices of the Ṣafawid State during the Reign of Shāh Ismā'īl I (907–30/1501–24)", in *Bulletin of the School of Oriental and African Studies*, XXIII (1960), p. 98.

3 The Safavid state from 1524 to 1588

1 The three ranks of *qizilbāsh* officers, in ascending order, were: Beg, Sulṭān, Khān. It is interesting to note that Ḥusayn Beg Lala Shāmlū continues to be so termed in the sources, even after he was appointed to the two highest offices in the state.
2 R. M. Savory, "The Principal Offices of the Ṣafawid State during the Reign of Shāh Ṭahmāsp I (930–84/1524–76)", in *Bulletin of the School of Oriental and African Studies*, XXIV (1961), p. 66.
3 A *tiyūl* was an assignment of land made to officials in lieu of salary; in the case of military governors, the grantee had the obligation to provide a contingent of troops when required to do so by the shah.
4 The site of Ismā'īl's great victory over the Āq Quyūnlū ruler Alvand in 1501.
5 See Savory, "Principal Offices", p. 68.
6 Sir John Chardin, *Voyages du Chevalier Chardin en Perse, et autres lieux de l'Orient*, 10 vols. (Amsterdam 1711), vol. VI, p. 18.
7 There was a nice convention that "men of the pen" were not, in general, executed for their crimes.
8 The word *qūrchī* is derived from the Mongolian and means "archer".

9 C. Thornton Forster and F. H. Blackburne Daniell, *The Life and Letters of Ogier Ghiselin de Busbecq* (London 1881), vol. I, p. 300.
10 Anon, *A Chronicle of the Carmelites in Persia*, 2 vols. (London 1939), vol. I, pp. 47–8.
11 Tūrān: the land of the Turkish peoples, as opposed to Iran, the land of the Aryan peoples.
12 Sharaf al-Din Bitlīsī, *Sharafnāma*, ed. V. Véliaminof-Zernof, 2 vols. (St Petersburg 1860–2), vol. II, pp. 251–2.
13 *Shah 'Abbas*, vol. I, p. 131.
14 See *Shah 'Abbas*, vol. I, pp. 139–40.
15 Full details of Humāyūn's visit to Iran are contained in Riazul Islam, *Indo-Persian Relations* (Tehran 1970), pp. 22–47.
16 Riazul Islam, appendix C, p. 197.
17 *Shah 'Abbas*, vol. I, p. 370 (transliteration adapted).

4 Safavid empire under Shāh 'Abbās the Great

1 R. M. Savory, "The Office of *Khalīfat al-Khulafā* under the Safavids", in *Journal of the American Oriental Society*, LXXXV (1965), p. 449.
2 This and the following quotation from *Shah 'Abbas*, vol. II, p. 554.
3 *Shah 'Abbas*, vol. II, p. 757.
4 The *tumān* in 1622 was worth approximately £3.6.8 (see *Carmelites*, vol. II, p. 775).
5 The *Dīvān*, or "Collected Poems" of Ḥāfiẓ, is commonly used for this purpose. The "'Irāq" referred to in the poem is 'Irāq-i 'Ajam, the ancient Media, not Mesopotamia. Baghdād was recaptured by Shāh 'Abbās in a subsequent campaign in 1623.
6 *Shah 'Abbas*, vol. II, p. 1226.
7 The legendary hero of the Iranian national epic, the *Shāhnāma*. I am indebted to my colleague, Dr Glyn Meredith-Owens, for the translation of the Ottoman letter. See *Shah 'Abbas*, vol. II, pp. 1275 ff.
8 Nicolas Sanson, *The Present State of Persia* (Paris 1695), p. 128.
9 Jean de Thévenot, *Travels of M. de Thévenot in the Levant*, newly done out of the French [by A. Lovell], part II: *Persia* (London 1687), p. 78.
10 Sir John Malcolm, *History of Persia*, 2 vols. (London 1815), vol. I, p. 550.
11 Malcolm, p. 565.
12 Lt.-Col. P. M. Sykes, *A History of Persia*, 2 vols. (London 1915), vol. II, p. 268.

5 Relations with West during Safavid period

1 Sir Arnold Wilson, *The Persian Gulf* (Oxford 1928), p. 121.
2 *A Chronicle of the Carmelites in Persia*, 2 vols. (London 1939), vol. I, p. 29, gives the figures of 20 cannon and 10,000 men. The latter figure in particular is not credible.
3 *Carmelites*, vol. I, pp. 84–7.
4 *Carmelites*, vol. I, pp. 90–1.

5 See R. M. Savory, "The Sherley Myth", in *Iran*, v (1967), pp. 76–7.
6 For the full story, see *Don Juan of Persia: a Shi'ah Catholic 1560–1604*, ed. G. Le Strange (London 1926).
7 The Safavid shahs were commonly termed by Western writers "Sophie", "Sophy", "Sophi" or "Soffi". All these terms were probably corruptions of Ṣafī, the name of the founder of the Safavid Order, rather than of Ṣūfī, as the Safavid supporters called themselves.
8 Anthony Jenkinson, *Early Voyages and Travels to Russia and Persia*, Hakluyt Society, 1st series, nos. LXXII and LXXIII, 2 vols. (London 1886), vol. I, p. 147.
9 *A Short Account of the Journey from Poland to Constantinople and from there to Astrakhan*, by Master Andrew Taranowsku, chamberlain to His Majesty the King.
10 An imperial decree, which may be issued only by the shah.
11 Samuel Purchas, *Hakluytus Posthumus or, Purchas his Pilgrims*, 20 vols. (Glasgow 1905–71), vol. IV, p. 279.
12 Fortune did not smile on the unfortunate Gouveia. On his way back to Spain, he was captured by Algerian corsairs and held to ransom for two years. On finally reaching Portugal, he decided to spend the rest of his life in a monastery!
13 Quoted by C. R. Boxer in his introduction to the *Commentaries of Ruy Freyre of Andrada* (London 1930), p. xxii.
14 George N. Curzon, *Persia and the Persian Question*, 2 vols. (1892; repr. London 1966), vol. II, p. 411, n. 1, quoting *Purchas his Pilgrims*.
15 *Shah 'Abbas*, vol. II, p. 1204.
16 *Some Yeares' Travel*, quoted in Curzon, vol. I, p. 36, n. 3.
17 For additional details, see Laurence Lockhart, "Marie Petit and her Persian Adventure", in *The Asiatic Review*, XLII, no. 149 (1946), pp. 273–7.
18 See Laurence Lockhart, *The Fall of the Ṣafavī Dynasty and the Afghān Occupation of Persia* (Cambridge 1958), pp. 463–4.
19 Curzon, vol. II, p. 464.
20 For this quotation from *Persia and the Persian Gulf Records*, vol. XIV, in the India Office Library, and for other material in this chapter, I am indebted to my friend Laurence Lockhart, who generously placed it at my disposal shortly before his death.

6 Flowering of the arts under the Safavids

1 R. M. Savory, "Land of the Lion and the Sun", in *The World of Islam*, ed. Bernard Lewis (London 1976), p. 251.
2 Anthony Welch, *Shāh 'Abbas and the Arts of Isfahan* (The Asia Society Inc. 1973), p. 13.
3 Laurence Binyon, J. V. S. Wilkinson and Basil Gray, *Persian Miniature Painting* (New York 1971), pp. 106–7.
4 Binyon *et al.*, p. 109.
5 Binyon *et al.*, pp. 109–10.
6 Welch, *Arts*, p. 13.
7 Stuart Cary Welch (ed.), Metropolitan Museum of Art (New York 1972).

8 *Book of Kings*, p. 15.
9 *Book of Kings*, p. 25.
10 *Book of Kings*, p. 24.
11 A. Upham Pope, *An Introduction to Persian Art since the Seventh Century A.D.* (London 1930), p. 109.
12 Anthony Welch, "Painting and Patronage under Shah 'Abbas I", in *Iranian Studies*, vol. VII (1974): *Studies on Isfahan Part II*, p. 458.
13 *Calligraphers and Painters, A Treatise by Qāḍī Aḥmad, son of Mīr-Munshī (circa A.H. 1015/A.D. 1606)*, translated by V. Minorsky (Washington 1959), p. 192. The translator notes that subsequent copyists of this manuscript, considering this action by the Shāh unbelievable, changed the words to "involuntarily expressed a thousand approvals and praises".
14 Welch, "'Abbas I", p. 484.
15 Welch, "'Abbas I", p. 481.
16 Anthony Welch, *Artists for the Shah* (New Haven 1976), pp. 186–7.
17 Welch, "'Abbas I", p. 485.
18 Welch, "'Abbas I", p. 486.
19 Welch, "'Abbas I", p. 487.
20 Welch, "'Abbas I", pp. 490–1.
21 Binyon *et al.*, p. 161.
22 Welch, *Arts*, p. 21.
23 Richard Ettinghausen, "Stylistic Tendencies at the Time of Shah 'Abbas", in *Iranian Studies*, VII (1974): *Studies on Isfahan Part II*, p. 610.
24 Ettinghausen, pp. 600–1.
25 Ettinghausen, pp. 602–3.
26 Ettinghausen, p. 602.
27 Arthur Upham Pope (ed.), *A Survey of Persian Art*, 6 vols. (Oxford 1938–58; repr. 1964–8), vol. IV, p. 1647.
28 *Nisba*: that part of a Muslim name which indicates a person's place of birth.
29 Pope, *Survey*, vol. VI, p. 2296.
30 *Ibid.*
31 Pope, *Survey*, vol. VI, p. 2297. Note 1 on this page gives a complete list of the animals, birds and fish which have been identified in the Milan carpet.
32 Pope, *Survey*, vol. VI, p. 2298.
33 Pope, *Survey*, vol. VI, p. 2433.
34 Pope, *Survey*, vol. VI, pp. 2434–5. The carpets are now housed in the Residenz Museum at Munich.
35 R. M. Savory, "Safavid Persia", in *Cambridge History of Islam*, 2 vols. (Cambridge 1970), vol. I, p. 421.
36 Quoted in Pope, *Survey*, vol. VI, p. 2431.
37 Pope, *Survey*, vol. VI, p. 2432.
38 Pope, *Introduction*, p. 165. Preceding quotation is also from this source.
39 Pope, *Introduction*, p. 160.
40 Pope, *Introduction*, pp. 160–1.
41 Pope, *Introduction*, p. 161.
42 Pope, *Introduction*, pp. 93–4.
43 *Ibid.*
44 Pope, *Survey*, vol. VI, p. 1647.

45 Margaret Medley, "Islam, Chinese Porcelain and Ardabil", in *Iran*, XIII (1975), p. 36.
46 Pope, *Introduction*, p. 95.
47 See J. A. Pope, *Chinese Porcelains from the Ardabil Shrine* (Washington, D.C., 1956).
48 Pope, *Survey*, vol. IV, p. 1649.
49 Pope, *Survey*, vol. IV, p. 1650.
50 Pope, *Survey*, vol. IV, pp. 1650–1.
51 Arthur Lane, *Later Islamic Pottery*, 2nd edn (London 1971), pp. 97–8.
52 Pope, *Survey*, vol. IV, pp. 1651–5.
53 Pope, *Survey*, vol. IV, pp. 1659–63.
54 Farajollah Bazl, in Pope, *Survey*, vol. IV, pp. 1705–6.
55 A. S. Melikian-Shirvani, "Safavid Metalwork: A Study in Continuity", in *Iranian Studies*, VII (1974): *Studies on Isfahan Part II*, p. 543.
56 Shirvani, pp. 543–4.
57 Shirvani, p. 544.
58 Robert Hillenbrand, "Art in the Persian Gulf", in *The Persian Gulf States*, ed. A. Cottrell *et al.* (Baltimore 1980) (at press).
59 I.e., the Prophet Muḥammad, his daughter Fāṭima, and the Twelve Imāms of the Ithnā 'Asharī Shī'īs.
60 Shirvani, p. 558.
61 Shirvani, p. 560.
62 Quoted in Pope, *Survey*, vol. VI, p. 2574.
63 H. Russell Robinson, *Oriental Armour* (New York 1967), p. 38.
64 Russell Robinson, *Oriental Armour*, p. 46.

7 "Iṣfahān is half the world"

1 Laurence Lockhart, *Famous Cities of Iran* (Brentford 1939), p. 14.
2 *The Travels of Ibn Battuta*, vol. II, ed. Sir Hamilton Gibb, Hakluyt Society, 2nd series, no. CXVII (Cambridge 1962), p. 295.
3 Wilfrid Blunt and Wim Swaan, *Isfahan: Pearl of Persia* (London and Toronto 1966), p. 13.
4 A. Upham Pope (ed.), *A Survey of Persian Art*, 6 vols. (Oxford 1938–58; repr. 1964–8), vol. III, p. 1180.
5 *Ibid.*
6 *Shah 'Abbas*, vol. II, p. 90.
7 Donald Wilber, "Aspects of the Safavid Ensemble at Isfahan", in *Iranian Studies*, VII (1974): *Studies on Isfahan Part II*, p. 408.
8 Sir Roger Stevens, *The Land of the Great Sophy* (London 1962), p. 172.
9 Thomas Herbert, *A Relation of Some Yeares Travaile into Afrique, Asia, Indies* (London 1634), p. 86.
10 *Shah 'Abbas*, vol. II, p. 1037.
11 Bagher Shirazi, "Isfahan the old; Isfahan the new", in *Iranian Studies*, VII (1974): *Studies on Isfahan Part II*, p. 588.
12 Anthony Welch, *Shah 'Abbas and the Arts of Isfahan* (The Asia Society Inc. 1973), p. 18.
13 Stevens, p. 183.

14 Pope, *Survey*, vol. III, p. 1185.
15 Pope, *Survey*, vol. III, p. 1186.
16 Quoted in Wilber, p. 407.
17 Wilber, p. 407.
18 Robert Byron, *The Road to Oxiana* (London 1950), pp. 177–8.
19 Blunt and Swaan, p. 71.
20 Byron, p. 135.
21 The above description of the bazaar is based on 'Ali Bakhtiar's excellent article, "The Royal Bazaar of Isfahan", in *Iranian Studies*, VII (1974): *Studies on Isfahan Part I*, pp. 320–47.
22 Quoted in Wilfred Blunt, *Pietro's Pilgrimage* (London 1953), p. 127.
23 Stevens, p. 184.
24 George N. Curzon, *Persia and the Persian Question*, 2 vols. (1892; repr. London 1966), vol. II, p. 34.
25 John Fryer, *A New Account of East India and Persia*, vol. III, Hakluyt Society 2nd series, no. XXXIX (London 1915), p. 16. Fryer is referring to the houses of the nobility.
26 Wilber, p. 409.
27 Sir John Chardin, *Voyages du Chevalier Chardin en Perse, et autres lieux de l'Orient*, ed. L. Langlès, 10 vols. (Paris 1811), vol. VIII, p. 43, quoted in Curzon, vol. II, p. 37.
28 Curzon, vol. II, p. 38.
29 Curzon, vol. II, pp. 38–9.
30 Quoted in Curzon, vol. II, p. 39.
31 Curzon, vol. II, p. 45.
32 Blunt and Swaan, p. 147.
33 The name means "a thousand *jarīb*". A *jarīb* equals 10,000 square metres, but the name should not be taken as indicating the size of the gardens in any literal sense, since the word *hazār*, "one thousand", is used vaguely in Persian to denote any large number.
34 Curzon, vol. II, p. 47.
35 Jean Baptiste Tavernier, *Les six voyages de Jean Baptiste Tavernier en Turquie, en Perse et aux Indes*, 2 vols. (Paris 1677), vol. I, p. 410.
36 Herbert, p. 87.
37 Tavernier, p. 418.
38 The term *gabr* (anglicised as "guebre") is a pejorative term used by Muslims to denote adherents of the pre-Islamic religion of Iran, Zoroastrianism.
39 Herbert, p. 37.
40 Voluntary self-immolation of a Hindu widow.
41 Stevens, p. 174.
42 Curzon, vol. II, p. 26, n. 1.
43 Quoted by Sir Roger Stevens, " European Visitors to the Safavid Court", in *Iranian Studies*, VII (1974): *Studies on Isfahan Part II*, p. 429.

8 Social and economic structure

1 *History of Persia*, 2 vols. (London 1815), vol. II, p. 482.
2 Malcolm, vol. II, p. 491.

3 Jean de Thévenot, *Travels of M. de Thévenot into the Levant*, newly done out of the French [by A. Lovell], part II: *Persia* (London 1687), p. 99.
4 Malcolm, vol. II, pp. 434–5.
5 Jean Baptiste Tavernier, *Les six voyages de Jean Baptiste Tavernier en Turquie, en Perse et aux Indes*, 2 vols. (Paris 1677), vol. I, pp. 530–1.
6 Malcolm, vol. II, pp. 456–7.
7 Malcolm, vol. II, p. 456.
8 Tavernier, vol. II, p. 613.
9 See Adam Olearius, *Voyages très-curieux et très-renommez faits en Muscovie, Tartarie et Perse, etc., traduits de l'original et augmentez par le sr. de Wicquefort*, 2 vols. in 1 (Amsterdam 1727), vol. I, p. 684.
10 Sir E. Denison Ross (ed.), *Sir Anthony Sherley and his Persian Adventure* (London 1933), pp. 219–20.
11 Tavernier, vol. I, pp. 98–9.
12 For a description of this office, see *Tadhkirat al-Mulūk*, translated and explained by V. Minorsky (London 1943), p. 58; hereinafter referred to as *TM*.
13 Tavernier, vol. I, pp. 554–8.
14 Amin Banani, "The Social and Economic Structure of the Persian Empire in its Heyday", a paper submitted to the Harvard Colloquium on Tradition and Change in the Middle East, December 1967, p. 18.
15 *Shah 'Abbas*, vol. II, p. 955.
16 Banani, p. 19.
17 *TM*, p. 27.
18 A. K. S. Lambton, *Landlord and Peasant in Persia* (Oxford 1953), p. 106.
19 Lambton, pp. 127–8.
20 John Emerson, "Ex Occidente Lux: Some European Sources on the Economic Structure of Persia between about 1630 and 1690", unpublished University of Cambridge Ph.D. thesis (1969), p. 244. This dissertation was made available to me by the kindness of Dr Emerson.
21 Emerson, p. 245.
22 Thévenot, p. 100.
23 Banani, p. 22.
24 *TM*, p. 30.
25 *TM*, p. 29.
26 *TM*, p. 30.
27 *TM*, p. 21. For more details on the *jīra*, see *TM*, 153.
28 *TM*, p. 21 (both of above quotations).
29 *Sir Anthony Sherley*, p. 209.
30 Emerson, pp. 224–5.
31 Tavernier, vol. I, p. 107.
32 Emerson, p. 222.
33 Emerson, pp. 214–15.
34 Emerson, p. 215.
35 Emerson, p. 218.
36 Emerson, pp. 220–1.
37 George N. Curzon, *Persia and the Persian Question*, 2 vols. (1892; repr. London 1966), vol. II, p. 398.

38 Niels Steensgaard, *The Asian Trade Revolution of the Seventeenth Century* (Chicago 1973), p. 377.
39 Steensgaard, p. 381.
40 Tavernier, vol. II, p. 604.
41 Thévenot, vol. II, p. 110.
42 The enforced settlement of some 13,000 Armenian families in the silk-growing Caspian provinces of Gīlān and Māzandarān ended in disaster, since the damp climate of those provinces caused the death of many of the Armenians.
43 R. W. Ferrier, "The Armenians and the East India Company in Persia in the Seventeenth and Early Eighteenth Century", in *Economic History Review*, 2nd series, XXVI (1973), p. 40.
44 Steensgaard, pp. 380–1.
45 Steensgaard, pp. 381–5.
46 Ferrier, p. 44.
47 Ferrier, p. 47.
48 Quoted by Steensgaard, p. 402.
49 Quoted by Steensgaard, p. 407.
50 Quoted by Ferrier, p. 50.
51 Quoted by Ferrier, p. 56.
52 Ferrier, p. 62.
53 *TM*, p. 19.
54 Banani, pp. 21–2.
55 Ferrier, p. 56.
56 Ferrier, p. 55.
57 Ferrier, p. 39.
58 Ferrier, p. 40.
59 Tavernier, vol. II, p. 611.

9 Intellectual life under the Safavids

1 E. G. Browne, *A Literary History of Persia*, 4 vols. (Cambridge 1925–8), vol. IV, pp. 24–9. Some scholars apply the term *sabk-i hindī* to the whole corpus of Indo-Persian poetry. For an excellent summary of the conflicting views on the subject, see Aziz Ahmad, "The formation of Sabk-i Hindī", in C. E. Bosworth (ed.), *Iran and Islam* (Edinburgh 1971), pp. 1–9.
2 Jan Rypka *et al.*, *History of Iranian Literature*, ed. Karl Jahn (Dordrecht 1968), p. 292.
3 Quoted in Aziz Ahmad, "Safawid Poets and India", in *Iran*, XIV (1976), p. 117.
4 Ehsan Yar-Shater, "Safavid Literature: Progress or Decline", in *Iranian Studies*, VII (1974): *Studies on Isfahan Part II*, pp. 223–5.
5 In *Iranian Studies*, VII (1974), pp. 217–70).
6 Yar-Shater, p. 220.
7 Quoted in Yar-Shater, p. 260.
8 Ahmad, p. 119.
9 A poem consisting of stanzas each containing seven lines.
10 *Shah 'Abbas*, vol. I, p. 275.

11 Yar-Shater, p. 250.
12 Ahmad, p. 120.
13 Ahmad, pp. 121; 124.
14 All quotations from Yar-Shater, pp. 221–5.
15 Yar-Shater, p. 222.
16 Yar-Shater, p. 224.
17 Yar-Shater, p. 220.
18 Yar-Shater, p. 225.
19 Yar-Shater, pp. 225–6.
20 Yar-Shater, p. 228.
21 Yar-Shater, p. 237.
22 Yar-Shater, pp. 240–1.
23 Browne, vol. IV, p. 251.
24 Browne, vol. IV, p. 165.
25 Yar-Shater, p. 240.
26 Browne, vol. IV, p. 252.
27 Browne, vol. IV, p. 251.
28 Browne, vol. IV, p. 229.
29 Quoted in Browne, vol. IV, p. 242.
30 Yar-Shater, p. 244.
31 Yar-Shater, pp. 244–5.
32 H. A. R. Gibb, "Ta'rīkh", reprinted in *Studies in the Civilization of Islam* (Boston 1962), p. 134.
33 Browne, vol. IV, p. 107.
34 Chicago 1974, vol. III, p. 42.
35 "Persian Biographical Literature", in *Historians of the Middle East*, eds. B. Lewis and P. M. Holt (Oxford 1962), p. 147–8.
36 "The Historiography of Ottoman–Safavid Relations in the 16th and 17th Centuries", in *Historians of the Middle East*, eds. Lewis and Holt, p. 200, n. 8).
37 See, for example, T. J. de Boer, *The History of Philosophy in Islam* (1903; repr. New York, 1967).
38 Quoted in Browne, vol. IV, p. 425.
39 Seyyed Hossein Nasr, *Three Muslim Sages* (Cambridge, Mass., 1964), pp. 55–6.
40 Nasr, *Sages*, pp. 58–9.
41 Nasr, *Sages*, p. 64.
42 Particularly A. von Kremer; see Nasr, *Sages*, p. 154, n. 44.
43 Nasr, *Sages*, p. 80.
44 Browne, vol. IV, p. 429.
45 Seyyed Hossein Nasr, "Religion in Safavid Persia", in *Iranian Studies*, VII (1974): *Studies on Isfahan Part I*, p. 278.
46 Seyyed Hossein Nasr, "Sadr al-Din Shirazi, his Life, Doctrines and Significance", in *Indo-Iranica*, XIV (1961), p. 8.
47 Nasr, "Sadr", p. 6.
48 Nasr, "Sadr", p. 9.
49 Nasr, "Sadr", p. 9.
50 Nasr, "Sadr", p. 10.
51 Nasr, "Sadr", p. 14. For fuller details of Mullā Ṣadrā's doctrines, the reader

is referred to the works of Seyyed Hossein Nasr and Henri Corbin.

52 Nasr, "Sadr", pp. 15–16.

53 See Cyril Elgood, "Persian Science", in *Legacy of Persia*, ed. A. J. Arberry (Oxford 1953), p. 293.

54 Elgood, "Science", p. 300.

55 Max Meyerhof, "Science and Medicine", in *The Legacy of Islam*, eds. T. W. Arnold and Alfred Guillaume (London, Toronto and New York 1931), p. 325.

56 Meyerhof, p. 323.

57 Meyerhof, pp. 329–30.

58 Cyril Elgood, *Safavid Medical Practice* (London 1970), p. 18.

59 Jean de Thévenot, *Travels of M. de Thévenot into the Levant*, newly done out of the French [by A. Lovell], part II: *Persia* (London 1687), p. 88.

60 Elgood, *Medical Practice*, p. 154.

61 Elgood, "Science", p. 317.

62 Elgood, *Medical Practice*, p. 30.

63 Elgood, *Medical Practice*, p. 285.

64 *Shah 'Abbas*, vol. II, p. 1038.

65 Thévenot, p. 105.

66 O. Wright, "Music" in *The Legacy of Islam*, new edn, eds. Joseph Schacht with C. E. Bosworth (Oxford 1974), p. 489.

10 Decline and Fall of the Safavids

1 See E. G. Browne, *A Literary History of Persia*, 4 vols. (Cambridge 1925–8), vol. IV, pp. 111–12.

2 *A Chronicle of the Carmelites in Persia*, 2 vols. (London 1939), vol. I, pp. 350–1.

3 Sir John Malcolm, *History of Persia*, 2 vols. (London 1815), vol. I, p. 382.

4 *Carmelites*, vol. I, p. 405, quoting a contemporary description by Père Sanson.

5 Mīr Muḥammad Bāqir Dāmād, d. 1631/2. Eminent theologian and philosopher.

6 Shaykh Bahā al-Dīn 'Āmilī, *shaykh al-islām* of Iṣfahān, d. 1622. Author of the *Jāmi'-i 'Abbāsī*, a popular manual of Shī'ī law (see Browne, vol. IV, p. 407).

7 Malcolm, vol. I, pp. 371–2.

8 "Tradition" is used here in the technical sense of *ḥadīth*, a saying attributed to the Prophet or one of the Imāms and authenticated by a chain of reliable transmitters.

9 Browne, IV, p. 368.

10 R. M. Savory, "The Office of *Khalīfat al-Khulafā* under the Safawids", in *Journal of the American Oriental Society*, LXXXV (1965), p. 502.

11 Naṣr Allāh Falsafī, *Zindigānī-yi Shāh 'Abbās-i avval*, vol. I (Tehran 1955), p. 183.

12 Falsafī, p. 186.

13 Browne, vol. IV, p. 404.

14 *Z̠ikr-i khafī*: "the *z̤ikr* which is uttered silently in the heart". *Z̠ikr-i jalī*: "the *z̤ikr* which is uttered audibly".
15 Browne, vol. IV, p. 369.
16 Amin Banani, "The Social and Economic Structure of the Safavid Empire in its Heyday", a paper submitted to the Harvard Colloquium on Tradition and Change in the Middle East, December 1967, p. 6.
17 Sir John Chardin, *Voyages du Chevalier Chardin en Perse, et autres lieux de l'Orient*, 10 vols. (Amsterdam 1711), vol. VI, p. 26 (my translation).
18 Chardin, vol. VI, p. 30 (my translation).
19 *Carmelites*, vol. I, p. 421.
20 *Dīvānbegī*: in later Safavid times, the highest legal authority in the state. His court was the highest court of appeal.
21 Laurence Lockhart, *The Fall of the Ṣafavī Dynasty and the Afghān Occupation of Persia* (Cambridge 1958), p. 99, quoting the contemporary Safavid historian, Muḥammad Muḥsin.
22 Lockhart, p. 104.
23 Lockhart, p. 107.
24 Lockhart, p. 108.
25 Lockhart, p. 111. The account of the Afghān invasion and occupation which follows is based in the main on Lockhart.
26 *Mullābāshī*: during the reign of Shāh Sulṭān Ḥusayn, we find an official by this title as head of the religious classes. His powers clearly exceeded those of the *ṣadr*.
27 Lockhart, p. 125.
28 I am indebted to my friend, Dr E. Llewellyn-Thomas, for this diagnosis.
29 For the text of this Treaty, see J. C. Hurewitz, *Diplomacy in the Near and Middle East*, 2 vols. (Princeton 1956), vol. I, pp. 42–5.
30 Lt.-Col. P. M. Sykes, *A History of Persia*, 2 vols. (London 1915), vol. II, p. 330.
31 For full details of the Safavid pretenders who appeared after the deposition of Shāh Sulṭān Ḥusayn, see J. R. Perry, "The Last Safavids (1772–1773)", in *Iran*, IX (1971), pp. 59–69.
32 Perry, p. 68.

Index

Printed in the United States
100680LV00005B/24/A

9 780521 042512